# Complex Governance Networks

What are the roles of governments and other actors in solving, or alleviating, collective action problems in today's world? The traditional conceptual frameworks of public administration and public policy studies have become less relevant in answering this question. This book critically assesses traditional conceptual frameworks and proposes an alternative: a complex governance networks (CGN) framework.

Advocating that complexity theory should be systematically integrated with foundational concepts of public administration and public policy, Göktuğ Morçöl begins by clarifying the component concepts of CGN and then addresses the implications of CGN for key issues in public administration and policy studies: effectiveness, accountability, and democracy. He illustrates the applicability of the CGN concepts with examples from the COVID-19 pandemic and metropolitan governance, particularly the roles of business improvement districts in governance processes. Morçöl concludes by discussing the implications of CGN for the convergence of public administration and public policy education and offering suggestions for future studies using the CGN conceptualization.

*Complex Governance Networks* is essential reading for both scholars and advanced students of public policy, public administration, public affairs, and related areas.

**Göktuğ Morçöl** is Professor of Public Policy and Administration at The Pennsylvania State University in Harrisburg. His research interests are complexity theory, metropolitan governance, business improvement districts, and research methodology. He teaches courses in research methods, program evaluation, and policy analysis.

# Routledge Research in Public Administration and Public Policy

**A Guidebook for City and County Managers**
Meeting Today's Challenges
*James M. Bourey*

**Modern Weights and Measures Regulation in the United States**
A Brief History
*Craig A. Leisy*

**COVID-19 Pandemic, Public Policy and Institutions in India**
Issues of Labour, Income, and Human Development
*Edited by Indranil De, Soumyadip Chattopadhyay,*
*Hippu Salk Kristle Nathan, and Kingshuk Sarkar*

**Governance in the 21st Century**
An Expanded View
*Morris Bosin*

**Behavioural Public Policy in Australia**
How an Idea Became Practice
*Sarah Ball*

**Service-Learning for Disaster Resilience**
Partnerships for Social Good
*Edited by Lucia Velotti, Rebecca M. Brenner & Elizabeth A. Dunn*

**Complex Governance Networks**
Foundational Concepts and Practical Implications
*Göktuğ Morçöl*

For more information about this series, please visit: www.routledge.com/
Routledge-Research-in-Public-Administration-and-Public-Policy/book-
series/RRPAPP

# Complex Governance Networks
Foundational Concepts and Practical Implications

Göktuğ Morçöl

NEW YORK AND LONDON

First published 2023
by Routledge
605 Third Avenue, New York, NY 10158

and by Routledge
4 Park Square, Milton Park, Abingdon, Oxon, OX14 4RN

*Routledge is an imprint of the Taylor & Francis Group, an informa business*

© 2023 Taylor & Francis

The right of Göktuğ Morçöl to be identified as author of this work has been
asserted in accordance with sections 77 and 78 of the Copyright, Designs and
Patents Act 1988.

All rights reserved. No part of this book may be reprinted or reproduced or utilised
in any form or by any electronic, mechanical, or other means, now known or
hereafter invented, including photocopying and recording, or in any information
storage or retrieval system, without permission in writing from the publishers.

*Trademark notice*: Product or corporate names may be trademarks or registered trademarks,
and are used only for identification and explanation without intent to infringe.

ISBN: 978-0-367-51328-3 (hbk)
ISBN: 978-0-367-51332-0 (pbk)
ISBN: 978-1-003-05339-2 (ebk)

DOI: 10.4324/9781003053392

Typeset in Times New Roman
by Newgen Publishing UK

# Contents

| | |
|---|---|
| *List of Figures* | ix |
| *Preface* | xi |
| *Acknowledgments* | xiv |

| | | |
|---|---|---|
| 1 | Introduction | 1 |
| | *An Overview of the Literatures  4* | |
| | *COVID-19  12* | |

**PART I**

| | |
|---|---|
| **Concepts** | 15 |

| | | |
|---|---|---|
| 2 | Governance | 17 |
| | *A Brief History of Governance  18* | |
| | *Conceptualizations of Governance  19* | |
| | *Polycentrism  23* | |
| | *COVID-19 and Governance  25* | |
| | *Summary  27* | |

| | | |
|---|---|---|
| 3 | Governance Networks | 29 |
| | *A Brief History of Network Thinking and Science  30* | |
| | *Governance Networks  33* | |
| | An Ideal Type of Governance Networks and Typologies  34 | |
| | *COVID and Governance Networks  38* | |
| | *Summary  39* | |

| | | |
|---|---|---|
| 4 | Complexity | 41 |
| | *A Definition of Complexity  42* | |
| | *Systems  43* | |
| | Systemness  45 | |
| | Systems and Networks  48 | |
| | *Multiplicity, Variations, and Nonlinearity  49* | |

vi   *Contents*

*Self-Organization 51*
  A Historical Background 51
  Complexity Theory and Self-Organization 52
  Self-Organization in Governance Networks 53
*Emergence 56*
*Coevolution 57*
*Complexity and COVID-19 60*
  Coevolution: A Macro View of the Pandemic 60
  Defining Systems 63
  Nonlinearity 65
  Self-organization 67
*Summary 68*

**PART II**
**A Complex Governance Networks Conceptualization**          73

5   Introduction of the Conceptualization          75
  *The Micro–Macro Problem and Collective Problems of*
    *Human Societies 76*
  *A Brief Background of the Micro–Macro Problem 79*
  *Why the Micro–Macro Problem is Important for Understanding*
    *Social Systems 81*
  *The Micro–Macro Problem and Policy Process Theories 82*
  *Micro, Macro, and Other Levels 83*
  *Summary 83*

6   Micro Units          85
  *Rationality of Actors/Agents 86*
  *Criticisms of the Rationality Assumption 87*
  *(Bounded) Rationality in Policy Process Theories 90*
  *Complexity Theory and Rational Actor 91*
  *Summary 92*

7   Micro to Macro          94
  *Aggregation or Emergence? 99*
  *Irreducibility 102*
  *Mechanisms of Emergence 104*
  *Modeling the Micro to Macro Processes 107*
  *Summary 109*

*Contents* vii

8 Macro to Micro: Background and Conceptualizations
of Downward Causation   112
*Structuration 116*
*Summary 121*

**PART III**
**Implications of the Complex Governance Networks
Conceptualization for Key Issues in Governance**   123

9 Wicked Problems and Effectiveness   125
*Wicked Problems 125*
   What Are Wicked Problems? 127
   The Uses of the Term Wicked Problems in the Literature and
     Its Criticisms 130
*Effectiveness 132*
   Effectiveness in Public Policy and Administration 133
   Effectiveness of Governance Networks 134
*Summary 138*

10 Accountability   139
*Definitions and Conceptualizations of Accountability 139*
   An Overview of the Conceptualizations of Accountability 140
   Multidimensional Accountability Models 143
*Governance Networks and Accountability 148*
*Accountability in Complex Systems 150*
*Accountability in Metropolitan Governance 154*
   Business Improvement Districts and Accountability 157
*Summary 162*

11 Democracy   165
*Conceptual Clarifications 166*
*Self-Organization, the State, and Democracy 167*
*Ideal Types of Democracy 170*
   Liberal Democracy 170
   Deliberative/Discursive Democracy 174
   Practice-Based Democracy 174
   Configurations of the Three Ideal Types 176
*Democracy in the Public Administration and Governance*
   *Networks Literatures 178*
   Public Administration and Democracy 178
   Governance Networks and Democracy 180
   Role of the State: Meta-governance 181
*Summary 182*

viii  *Contents*

## Conclusions: A Summary of the Book's Contents  185
*The Complex Governance Networks Conceptualization 187*
*General Conclusions 188*
  A Non-Dichotomous, Configurational View of Governance
    Processes 188
  Convergence of the Fields of Study? 191
  Self-Organization and Adaptive Governance 192
  So What? 194

*References*  196
*Index*  216

# Figures

| | | |
|---|---|---:|
| 1.1 | Publications in the Web of Science (Aggregates and Public Administration) | 5 |
| 1.2 | Trends in Public Administration and related fields by decade | 6 |
| 1.3 | Two-mode network maps of the public administration literature in three decades | 10 |
| 3.1 | The Könisberg bridge problem superimposed on today's map of Kaliningrad | 31 |
| 3.2 | Two-mode network map of the public administration literature in the 2000s | 32 |
| 9.1 | Publications on "wicked problems" in the Web of Science | 126 |
| 10.1 | Total number of journal publications on governance, networks, and complexity in urban and regional studies between 1990 and 2019 | 156 |

# Preface

The topic of book has occupied my mind since I finished writing my previous book: *A Complexity Theory for Public Policy* (2012a). In *A Complexity Theory* my goal was to present the implications of complexity theory for public policy studies. The complexity of public policy processes was recognized by almost everybody who practiced policy analysis or policymaking or who studies policy processes. Then the question was, did complexity theory bring anything new to our understanding of policy analysis and policymaking processes? I hope my book provided some answers to this question.

As I gathered information and synthesized it when I was writing *A Complexity Theory,* I began to think that public policy was not the best framework to conceptualize how complex systems that we call societies are governed or how they govern themselves. The nascent literature on "governance processes" in general and "governance networks" in particular began to seep into my cognitive space. As I show in Chapter 1 of this book, this literature had emerged in the 1990s and it was taking shape in the first decade of the 2000s. Governance was about both public policy making and implementation (public administration, public management). It was more than that. Governance was not only about governments making policies and implementing them, but many other actors participating in these processes.

This was not a new discovery in the public policy or public administration literatures. For example, as early as in the 1970s, Vincent Ostrom and Elinor Ostrom had studied polycentric governance systems in metropolitan areas, where multiple governmental and non-governmental actors participated in solving their collective problems. What was new in the 1990s and early 2000s was that other scholars began recognizing the multiplicity of actors in policymaking and administration processes and called thus phenomenon. I was familiar with the Ostrom's and their colleagues' works, but this recognition by the broader community of scholars helped me rethink my conceptualization. What I covered in *A Complexity Theory* was not only public policy processes anyway; "governance" was a better conceptualization.

After this realization, it took me quite a while to get to writing this book, partly because of personal reasons, but mostly because the world

xii  *Preface*

was changing drastically in this period. It took me a while to absorb the developments in the literature and synthesize them into a coherent conceptualization. There was an exponential increase in the number of publications on governance, governance networks, and complex systems (see Chapter 1). Several other authors published highly valuable books on these topics. They all contributed to my learning and thinking as this book was shaping up in my mind. I cite them in appropriate places in this book. My goal was to write a book that would contribute to the existing literature on, particularly by synthesizing the insights of complexity theory with those of the governance networks literature, hence the title of the book: *Complex Governance Networks*.

I drafted the conceptualization I present in this book in a few earlier journal publications and book chapters. As I began to write it, a major development forced me to revise my outline for the book: the COVID-19 pandemic. When I finished writing the book, the pandemic was ongoing. So, it is difficult to judge its impacts on the governance processes in human societies. It may cause major economic disruptions, exacerbate social inequalities, and instigate social upheavals in the coming years, possibly decades.[1] Although we do not know all the repercussions of COVID-19, it is clear that the pandemic has already impacted all humanity profoundly. We cannot ignore its implications for human collective problem solving and governing. So, COVID-19 pandemic has become part of the storyline in this book. I draw examples from the experiences of human societies in the pandemic era and cite academic studies on COVID-19, when they are relevant, in the following chapters.

The reader will notice that there are both public administration and public policy literatures cited in this book. That is not accidental. I have my intellectual grounding in both and, as many others observed before, there are large overlaps between the subject matters of these two fields of study. Despite the efforts by the founders of these two fields to carve out their own separate domains of study, they are interwoven in practice and difficult to separate in theory.

In today's world, the conceptual separation between public policy analysis (knowledge of policymaking) and public administration (knowledge of policy implementation) is even less tenable. The governance literature, which I cited above and will discuss in Chapter 1, explicitly or implicitly shows that policymaking and administration are closely related. The complex governance networks conceptualization I propose in this book is grounded in this general understanding.

Another point I want to make here is that complex governance networks is not a theory or framework, but a conceptualization. In the book, I use terms concept, conceptualization, notion, theory, and framework, following Merriam Webster's definitions and my understanding of the uses of these terms in the social scientific literatures. Merriam Webster's defines *concept* as "something conceived in the mind" and "an abstract or generic idea generalized from particular instances." *Notion* represents a looser understanding. According to Merriam-Webster's, it means "an individual's conception or impression of something known, experienced, or imagined" or "a personal inclination, whim." In Merriam Webster's definition of the term, *conceptualization* is action oriented; it means "to form a concept of; especially: to interpret conceptually." I use this term to mean an intentional act of drawing a conceptual picture of a segment of reality; so, it is more than a single concept. *Framework* is "a basic conceptional structure (as of ideas)" according to Merriam Webster's. In that sense, a framework is a more articulate version of conceptualization. Merriam Webster's defines *theory* as "a plausible or scientifically acceptable general principle or body of principles offered to explain phenomena."

What I propose in the book is not a tightly articulated theory, at least not yet. It may not be even considered a framework, when compared to the sophisticated frameworks like Elinor Ostrom's (1990, 2005) institutional analysis and development framework. So, what I propose in this book is a conceptualization in its current form. With conceptual refinements and empirical testing, this conceptualization can become a framework in the future.

In the book, I make the case for a complex governance networks framework by articulating a group of concepts into a coherent whole and giving real-life examples, particularly from the COVID-19 pandemic and urban/ metropolitan governance. COVID-19 is of course a new topic, and we all are learning about the complex dynamics the pandemic has unleashed in our societies. I draw lessons and examples from the burgeoning, but still limited, literature on the pandemic. If empirical studies are available on the topic, I summarize or quote them. These summaries are not exhaustive of the available literature. I have selected the ones I think are most relevant to my conceptualization. The literature on urban/metropolitan governance has a longer history, and there are more refined conceptualizations and empirical studies in this area. I cite relevant sources and examples from this literature throughout the book.

A final note: I have developed the ideas and concepts presented in this book over time and they have been published before. (See the acknowledgments.) In this book, I use some selected material that have been published. I cite their sources in the coming chapters.

## Note

1 There are various assessments of the long-term impacts of the pandemic. Here is a sample. United Nations, Everyone Included: Social Impact of COVID-19: www.un.org/development/desa/dspd/everyone-included-covid-19.html

World Health Organization, Impact of COVID-19 on People's Livelihoods, Their Health and Our Food Systems: www.who.int/news/item/13-10-2020-imp act-of-covid-19-on-people's-livelihoods-their-health-and-our-food-systems

Coronavirus Will Change the World Permanently. Here's How. www.polit ico.com/news/magazine/2020/03/19/coronavirus-effect-economy-life-society-analysis-covid-135579

# Acknowledgments

No book is the product solely of its author's mind, needless to say. Many others take part in the writing of a book, some more directly than others. Some provide intellectual nourishment to the author through their own works and/or their direct contributions to the book with their insights, comments, and criticisms. Others provide emotional and social support and comfort.

I owe debts of gratitude to many scholars and researchers who have stimulated and guided my thinking with their writings. I am sincerely thankful to the authors of all the sources I cite in this book. Each and every one of them made contributions to my learning and thinking. There are two scholars I want to mention specifically. They are scholars in the best sense of the word: learned persons whose works influence others' thinking and research deeply over long periods of time.

The first scholar I want to single out is Professor Charles True Goodsell, a teacher, colleague, and friend. He influenced my thinking and writing in many and profound ways over decades. What I present in this book may not look or sound like what he articulated or argued in his voluminous writings—he may even disagree with some of what I say in the book. He has influenced me at a deeper level, however, with his boundless intellectual curiosity and personal and intellectual integrity. He is one of very few scholars who asked questions that others in the public administration community neglected or did not find important. (In his latest book, he confesses that he has been a free spirit in his own intellectual pursuits and that he "followed the unpredictable calls of [his] own curiosity," Goodsell, 2022, Preface).

In doing so, Charles Goodsell expanded the intellectual horizons of public administration researchers on many fronts. He made the "case for bureaucracy," when the term "bureaucracy" was, arguably still is, closely associated with rigidity and incompetence in the delivery of public services. He explored the social meanings in the architectural designs of public buildings, particularly the state capitols, in the United States. He uncovered the "mission mystiques" in a range of federal and state agencies. He used innovative research tools (text and images) to highlight the good works done daily by public servants.

He also explored the meaning of "publicness," which is the foundational concept of public administration and public policy studies. He brought together the literatures in architecture, urban planning, political philosophy, and public administration to show that public (collective) action happens in multiple social realms—individuals' acts in public spaces, architectural designs of buildings, and the functioning of institutions. He also demonstrated that public services can be delivered and public values can be created, not only by public agencies, but also by many other individuals and organizations that are guided by altruistic motives. His questioning of the traditional ways of thinking about public administration and public service delivery has been deeply influential in my thinking, as the reader may notice on the following pages.

The second scholar I want to single out is William Newlin Dunn, whom we lost in May 2022. He was a professor at the University of Pittsburgh and I was a Ph.D. student at Virginia Tech when I first encountered his works and him in person. He was one of those intellectuals who opened doors into new ways of thinking in public policy analysis. He showed us that policy analysis is not about crunching numbers and running algorithms only. These activities take place in political and socially constructed environments, which make policy analysis processes highly complex. Many others also pointed out the political and socially constructed nature of analytical processes and their complexity. William Dunn demonstrated how complex social and political factors can be systematically integrated into a rigorous analytical process in his various writings, most notably in his monumental textbook *Public Policy Analysis: An Integrated Approach* (2017).

He demonstrated particularly that the way a policy problem is structured/defined (i.e., constructed in a single mind and in social relations) influences the ways it can be solved. This insight was the inspiration for my dissertation research on problem structuring processes. His key insight led me over time to explore how human minds construct and process information. The appreciation I developed for the complexity of cognitive construction and information processing processes motivated me to better understand the complexities of public policy processes, which was the topic of my previous book *A Complexity Theory for Public Policy* (2012), and the complexities of the broader governance processes, which is the topic of this book.

I am also thankful to all the students at the institutions I have taught: Middle East Technical University, Virginia Tech, Kennesaw State University, and Pennsylvania State University. I have learned from them while I was teaching them. Of these students, I want to single out my Ph.D. students at Penn State, particularly Saahir Shafi, Aravind Menon, and Tiangeng Lu, who will be my colleagues soon. I coauthored one of the chapters of this book with Saahir and Aravind. They joined me in an intellectual journey to rethink what democracy means, particularly in a period when the resilience of liberal democracies has been questioned and challenged even in the United States, the oldest liberal democracy and one of the most institutionalized liberal democracies in the world. With her

xvi *Acknowledgments*

high intelligence and deep analytical skills, Tiangeng contributed to the literature search and analyses that I present in the first chapter of the book.

I want to thank the anonymous reviewers of my book proposal to Routledge and the reviewers of the finished version of the book. Their insights and criticisms forced me rethink what I had written and helped me improve the book manuscript.

Natalja Mortensen, senior acquisitions editor at Routledge, deserves my special thanks. She worked patiently with me in this book project from the beginning, as well as in my previous book project.

I also want to acknowledge the permissions granted by the following publishers of my earlier publications, parts of which I used in this book:

> Routledge, for allowing me to use extracts from my previous book *A Complexity Theory for Public Policy* (2012);
>
> Lasse Gerrits, coeditor-in-chief of the journal *Complexity, Governance & Networks*, for allowing me to use extracts from an article I published in this journal (Morçöl, 2014); and
>
> Oxford University Press, for allowing me to use large parts of an article my colleagues and I published in the journal *Perspectives on Public Management and Governance* (Morçöl, Shafi, & Menon, 2022).

Last, but certainly not least, I want to express my gratitude for my wife Tülin and my son Taylan. Without them being in my life, it would be neither possible nor meaningful to write this book.

# 1 Introduction

How do human societies try to solve their collective problems? How do individual behaviors lead to collective outcomes? How do collective (institutional and cultural) structures affect individual behaviors? I propose a complex governance networks conceptualization to help answer these questions in the context of the early 21st century.

Needless to say, these questions are asked for the first time in this book. Many others before me asked the questions and contemplated philosophical and empirical answers to them. I do not pretend to know all the answers to the questions, but I do think that they are important to ask, particularly at these critical times in human history. This is a time when what we think we know about technology, society, and economy are being challenged. It is particularly important for public administration and public policy scholars (I am one of them) to ask the questions to better understand their own fields of study from a broader perspective, particularly at the present time.

Very few people, if any, would disagree with the proposition that human societies are undergoing major transformations. We may not be able to understand these transformations completely, but we can begin to make a few observations. Take the example of the politics of today. The traditional definitions of the right and the left are difficult to recognize. Think of Donald Trump's presidency. Was he a small-government "conservative" in the context of American political traditions? Also, take the public policy and public administration processes of our times. There is more direct involvement in them by non-governmental actors (see Chapter 2) and the imaginary lines between the public and private realms have been blurred. Technological transformations, particularly the ones in information technology (artificial intelligence, social media) and biotechnology (e.g., immunotherapy and m-RNA vaccines), are driving these changes.

Some conceptualizations (tentative theories) can help us to make sense of the transformations. The following are a few examples in which the authors grapple with questions about collective problem solving in human history and particularly the role of the state in it. The state is considered the biggest and most important actor in collective problem solving in both social theory and popular understanding of the social world. The

DOI: 10.4324/9781003053392-1

## 2   Introduction

"nation-state" is most recognized form in recent history. So, let's begin with a question about its place in today's world.

Are we experiencing the "demise of the nation state" (Dasgupta, 2018)? If the answer is yes, then this has major implications in the fields of public administration, public policy, and political science, particularly for our understanding of "the state" (which I will come back to in Chapter 11) and the practices of liberal democracy and accountability (see Chapter 10). Dasgupta argues that the nation-state was a good fit to solving societies' problems in the 20th century, but that no longer is the case in the 21st century. He notes that the concept of nation-state includes first and foremost the principle of "territorial sovereignty," which has as relatively short history and that this notion is a European invention whose origins can be found in the Treaty of Westphalia in 1648. The roughly 400 years of the nation-state is less than 0.3% of the 150,000 years of human history. Even the history of "the state," which is a more general category, is not much longer than 3,000 years (Fukuyama, 2011; Graeber & Wengrow, 2021).

Dasgupta points out that the political authority of the state over a defined territory is being challenged in the Western societies, as a result of the fragmentation of governmental structures and the increased reach of big tech companies. He gives the example of the European Union, in which the sovereignty of the state is diffused. Another example would be Facebook, with its almost 3 billion users around the world as of August 2021.[1] More important, its global reach defies any national borders and claims to sovereignty. Dasgupta also reminds us that the nation-state has never been a complete force in most of the developing world; in many countries quasi-states have been developed at best. Several states in the Middle East (e.g., Syria and Iraq) were artificially created after the collapse of the Ottoman empire, whose multilayered and dynamic governmental and political-economic structures evolved over six centuries (Yerasimos, 1974).

If Dasgupta's generalizations sound too broad and speculative, I can point to the more specific works of and arguments by several others in the public administration and public policy literatures, which I will discuss in the following chapters. As early as in the 1970s, Vincent Ostrom (1974, 1999a, 1999b) and others observed that public policies were made and implemented by multiple actors in polycentric systems and public services were delivered in collaborations between bureaucratic governmental organizations and others (nonprofits, private businesses). These observations began to crystallize and scholars made more systematic conceptualizations in the 1990s and 2000s. Elinor Ostrom (1990, 2005) refined Vincent Ostrom's conceptualizations in her institutional analysis and development framework.

Other authors made similar observations. Feiock (2013), Kettl (2002,2015), Koliba, Meek, and Zia (2011), Kooiman (1993), Rhodes (1997), Torfing, Peters, Pierre, and Sørensen (2012) all agree that the policymaking and administration capabilities of central nation-states have diminished and the political and policymaking processes have become multi-centered in the late 20th and early 21st centuries. Similar observations and arguments are made in the broader literatures of political and social theory. Bevir (2010) and Jessop (1990, 2016) even question whether the state has ever been a unified entity, let alone being a central problem solver for societies. Castells (2000) observes that in the late 20th-century societies have become so multi-centered and networked that we must rethink the nature and role of the state in them.

The observation that societies are (or have become) multicentric (or polycentric) is the common denominator of governance conceptualizations (Chapter 2 in this book). These conceptualizations were more refined in the governance networks literature (Chapter 3). Meanwhile, a separate literature on the applications of complexity theory in public administration and public policy was taking shape (Chapter 4). Very few scholars integrated complexity theory in their conceptualizations of governance networks (e.g., Koliba et al., 2011). Complexity theory remained separate from the studies on governance networks.

My goal in this book is to integrate these three streams of literature more systematically—governance, (governance) networks, and complexity theory—in a conceptualization. The conceptual/theoretical developments and supporting empirical works conducted in the literatures constitute the bases of this conceptualization.

I begin with a systematic analysis of the literature in the next section. It is followed by a background information about the COVID-19 pandemic, which is a running example throughout the book. The impacts of the pandemic on human lives are undeniable. It has implications for complex governance networks, and I discuss those implications in relevant chapters of the book.

In the following chapters, I first summarize the contributions of the governance, (governance) networks, and complexity theories separately (Chapters 2–4, respectively). In Part II, I present the complex governance networks conceptualization. The concept that is at the core of this conceptualization is the "micro–macro problem." I introduce the problem in Chapter 5. In the chapters that follow, I discuss its three important components: the nature of micro units (Chapter 6), how micro (individual) behaviors lead to the emergence of macro structures (Chapter 7), and how macro structures affect micro behaviors (Chapter 8).

Part III is about the implications of the conceptualization in the two areas. Chapter 9 covers their implications for effectiveness (of public policies, administration, and more importantly governance networks). Part of the discussion in this chapter is about the so-called wicked problems. This oft-used, and in my view misused, concept should be part of the discussions to better understand the effectiveness issues in complex governance networks. Chapter 10 is about accountability. Chapter 11 is about democracy. Complex governance networks have significant implications for both. I conclude the book with a summary and implications of the conceptualization I propose.

4 *Introduction*

## An Overview of the Literatures

R. A. W. Rhodes's *Understanding Governance* (1997), Donald Kettl's *Transformation of Governance* (2002/2015), and Lester Salamon's *The Tools of Government* (2002) were the pioneers of governance and governance network studies. They were followed by Mark Bevir (*Democratic Governance*, 2010) and Jacob Torfing, Guy Peters, Jon Pierre, and Eva Sørensen (*Interactive Governance*, 2012). The governance conceptualizations were refined as "public management networks," "governance networks," or "governance regimes" by Robert Agranoff (*Managing within Networks*, 2007); Christopher Koliba, Jack Meek, and Asim Zia (*Governance Networks in Public Policy and Administration* 2011); Kirk Emerson and Tina Nabatchi (*Collaborative Governance Regimes*, 2015); Erik Hans Klijn and Joop Koppenjan (*Governance Networks in the Public Sector*, 2016); and Naim Kapucu and Qian Hu (*Network Governance*, 2020).

A related, but separate, stream of literature was taking shape in the 1990s and early 2000s: the literature on complexity theory applications in public administration and policy, to which I contributed. Douglas Kiel's *Managing Chaos and Complexity in Government* (1994) and Louise Comfort's *Shared Risk: Complex Systems in Seismic Response* (1999) can be cited as the early well-known contributions to this literature. The literature burgeoned in the 2000s with contributions by others, including but not limited to, Mary Lee Rhodes, Joanne Murphy, Jenny Muir, and John Murray (*Public Management and Complexity Theory,* 2011) and Lasse Gerrits (*Punching Clouds: An Introduction to the Complexity of Public Decision-Making,* 2012). It would be unfair not to mention that many others contributed to this literature in the last two decades, but it would also be impractical to list them all here. It is important to note that, as I show later in this chapter, the literature on complexity theory evolved separately from the literature on governance/governance networks in public administration and policy, until recently.

The complexity theory applications have been recognized in some publications on governance networks. Kettl (2002) recognizes the potential in networks studies and that complexity theory can complement governance network studies (pp. 110– 114). Koliba and his colleagues (2019) observe that governance networks are complex adaptive systems (pp. 211–250). Kapucu and Hu (2020) also recognize the complexity of network governance processes. Elinor Ostrom (1990, 2005) recognizes the importance of complexity theory concepts in understanding institutional structures and policy processes and specifically advances and refines our understanding of self-organization (see Chapter 4).

In addition to this very brief overview of the literature, a systemic analysis of the journal publications on these topics will help us better understand the trends in the literature. My colleagues and I collected journal articles from the Web of Science (WoS) using a comprehensive set of keywords: collaborative governance, collaborative network, complexity theory, complex network, complex governance, self-organization, self-organizing, self-governance, self-governing, governance network, network governance, collaborative public administration, collaborative public management, complex systems, complex adaptive systems, and complex governance. These keywords are inclusive of the concepts and topics of the complex governance networks conceptualization I propose in this book.

Initially, we did not set a period for our searches, but it became clear that there were very few publications before the 1990s, which matched our understanding of the timeline of the relevant literature. (See the dates of the book-length publications above.) That is why the following charts and tables include journal articles that were published in the 1990s, 2000s, and 2010s. We did not specify a particular field of study in our searches to be able to capture what is available in the literature in general. In our searches and analyses, we accepted the WoS's designations of fields of study. We analyzed the WoS data in aggregates first and then broke them down by decades and by the WoS field designations. Figure 1.1 shows both the aggregated results (inclusive of the journals listed in the Science Citation Index (SCI), Social Science Citation Index (SSCI), and Arts and Humanities Citation Index (AHCI) of the WoS) and the results for the field "public administration," which is designated as inclusive of both public administration and public policy by the WoS.

The trend lines in Figure 1.1 show that there were increases in the number of publications on the topics of complex governance networks in aggregate (combination of the publications in SCI, SSCI, and AHCI) and in public administration. The trend line for the aggregate number of

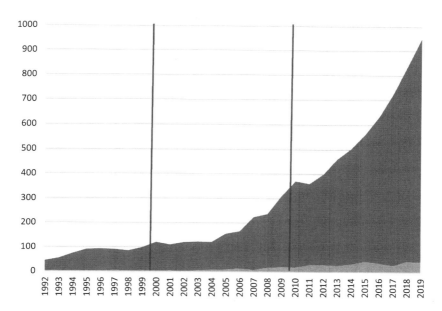

*Figure 1.1* Publications in the Web of Science (Aggregates and Public Administration).

publications indicates an exponential increase, while the increase in public administration is smoother. So, the interest in complexity, governance, and networks studies increased much faster in other fields, compared to the increase in public administration in these three decades.

The trend lines in Figure 1.2 provide us with more close-up view of the trends in public administration and related fields of study: business/management, political science and international relations, ecology/environment, regional and urban studies, economics, education, and health policy and administration. We can make two observations on this figure. First, the rate of increase accelerated in all fields, which is similar to the aggregate trend in Figure 1.1. Second, the fields of ecology/environment and business/management stand out with their higher numbers from the rest of the fields, including public administration. These two fields constituted a 30% of the total publications between 1990 and 2019, economics followed these two as a distant third, with 6% of total publications, political science and international relations had 5.5% of the publications and public administration had 5.2% (not shown in the figure).

Are there differences among the fields in their specific areas of interest (i.e., the keywords used in the publications in these fields)? Answers to this question can be found in Table 1.1. In this table, the keywords my colleagues and I used in our searches are combined into five categories: complexity

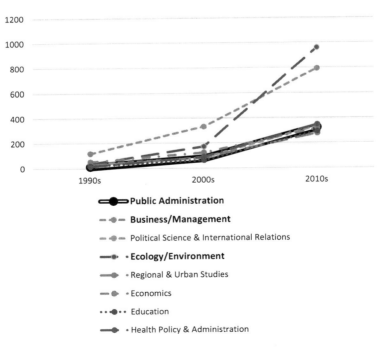

*Figure 1.2* Trends in Public Administration and related fields by decade.

*Table 1.1* Percentages of Publications in Selected Fields by Decade

| Field and Decade | Complexity | Self-organization | Self-governance | Governance Networks | Collaborative Governance | Total |
|---|---|---|---|---|---|---|
| Business/Management (1990s) | 53.7 | 38.1 | 4.5 | 1.5 | 2.2 | 100.0 |
| Business/Management (2000s) | 63.2 | 28.3 | 3.8 | 2.2 | 2.5 | 100.0 |
| Business/Management (2010s) | 61.8 | 19.5 | 3.4 | 6.4 | 8.9 | 100.0 |
| Business/Management (1990s–2010s) | 61.3 | 23.7 | 3.6 | 4.8 | 6.5 | 100.0 |
| Ecology/Environment (1990s) | 34.6 | 40.4 | 21.2 | 0.0 | 3.8 | 100.0 |
| Ecology/Environment (2000s) | 51.1 | 18.8 | 10.8 | 11.7 | 7.6 | 100.0 |
| Ecology/Environment (2010s) | 47.5 | 18.4 | 9.4 | 10.7 | 13.9 | 100.0 |
| Ecology/Environment (1990s–2010s) | 47.6 | 19.4 | 10.1 | 10.5 | 12.4 | 100.0 |
| Economics (1990s) | 44.6 | 37.5 | 16.1 | 1.8 | 0.0 | 100.0 |
| Economics (2000s) | 58.1 | 19.9 | 16.9 | 2.9 | 2.2 | 100.0 |
| Economics (2010s) | 56.7 | 17.9 | 17.0 | 4.8 | 3.6 | 100.0 |
| Economics (1990s–2010s) | 55.7 | 20.5 | 16.9 | 4.0 | 2.9 | 100.0 |
| Pol. Sci. & Int. Rel. (1990s) | 30.3 | 18.2 | 48.5 | 3.0 | 0.0 | 100.0 |
| Pol. Sci. & Int. Rel. (2000s) | 25.0 | 13.6 | 25.0 | 33.0 | 3.4 | 100.0 |
| Pol. Sci. & Int. Rel. (2010s) | 30.8 | 9.2 | 21.4 | 22.8 | 15.8 | 100.0 |
| Pol. Sci. & Int. Rel. (1990s–2010s) | 29.7 | 10.6 | 23.9 | 23.3 | 12.5 | 100.0 |
| Public Administration (1990s) | 33.3 | 50.0 | 8.3 | 0.0 | 8.3 | 100.0 |
| Public Administration (2000s) | 34.1 | 10.6 | 14.1 | 30.6 | 10.6 | 100.0 |
| Public Administration (2010s) | 17.7 | 6.6 | 8.3 | 29.3 | 38.2 | 100.0 |
| Public Administration (1990s–2010s) | 21.2 | 8.5 | 9.4 | 28.8 | 32.1 | 100.0 |
| SSCI Total (1990s) | 42.1 | 45.5 | 10.8 | 0.6 | 1.0 | 100.0 |
| SSCI Total (2000s) | 52.3 | 29.4 | 10.5 | 4.4 | 3.3 | 100.0 |
| SSCI Total (2010s) | 54.5 | 20.2 | 10.0 | 6.5 | 8.7 | 100.0 |
| SSCI Total (1990s–2010s) | 53.1 | 24.2 | 10.2 | 5.6 | 7.0 | 100.0 |

8   *Introduction*

(complexity theory, complex adaptive systems, and complex networks), self-organization (one of the key concepts in complexity theory, see Chapter 4), self-governance (a concept related to self-organization, but has specific usages particularly in political science), governance networks (inclusive of "networks governance"), and collaborative governance (a concept closely related governance networks, but used separately by some in the literature). (A quick note: Self-organization is a concept of complexity theory, but it is used by some scholars who are not complexity theorists or researchers themselves, such as Elinor Ostrom (1990, 2005).) To ensure brevity (and leave out unnecessary details), Table 1.1 includes only business/management, ecology/environment, economics, political science and international relations, and public administration and excludes regional and urban studies, education, and health policy and administration. The latter group of fields had smaller numbers if publications in the period studied.

There are noteworthy patterns in the table. The keywords that are associated with complexity (complexity theory, complex adaptive systems, complex networks) are the most frequent ones in the business/management, ecology/environment, and economics literatures in all three decades. The frequencies of their usages in these three fields increased over time, particularly in business/management and ecology/environment. The concepts and methods of complexity theory were used in more than 50% of the publications in these three fields, with the exceptions of ecology/environment and economics in the 1990s, and their uses increased over time. If the percentages of complexity theory can be combined with those of self-organization, the dominance of complexity theory in these fields become even more apparent. (As I noted earlier, self-organization is a concept of complexity theory; so, its uses in the literature can be considered as applications of complexity theory.) We can conclude from the findings in the figure and table that complexity theory is highly and increasingly popular in these fields. Table 1.1 shows that the patterns in these three fields are parallel to the overall patterns in the SSCI: Complexity theory is a major area of interest among scholars and that the interest increased over time.

Table 1.1 presents a different picture for political science and international relations and public administration. Complexity theory was not as popular in these two fields. The keywords were more evenly distributed among the publications in these fields in the three decades (1990s, 2000s, and 2010s). But there were increases in the keywords of governance networks and collaborative governance over time, particularly in public administration.

The findings in Table 1.1 point to a divide between the two groups of fields. Complexity theory was a primary area of interest for business/management, ecology/environment, and economics scholars. Among public administration scholars (including public policy scholars) and political scientists (including international relations scholars), that was not the case; instead, these two groups of scholars were interested primarily in governance networks and collaborative governance.

*Introduction* 9

Then should we say that this is the way it is and that public administration, public policy, political science, and international relations scholars do not need to be interested in complexity theory? (Remember that in this book my goal is to make the case for *complex* governance networks and show how complexity concepts can be useful particularly for public administration and public policy.) Before we reach such a conclusion, let's review the more nuanced pictures displayed in Figure 1.3. This figure displays two-mode network maps of the public administration literature in the 1990s, 2000s, and 2010s. The network[2] maps show the specific keywords used in the same literature searches from which I generated Figures 1.1 and 1.2 and Table 1.1. A major difference between the categories used in Table 1.1 and Figure 1.3 is that in the latter the original keywords are displayed (they are combined into the categories displayed in Table 1.1).

(a)  1990s
(b)  2000s
(c)  2010s

We can make a few observations on these maps. They get more crowded as the time passes, which is partly a result of the increase in the number of publications over time. But, more importantly, it is because the segments of the literature (i.e., the journal articles that used the different keywords included in the searches) got integrated more over time.

A little bit of background on two-mode maps would help explain this integration process. Two-mode networks maps are products of two-mode social network analyses. In the analysis whose results are displayed in Figure 1.3, each journal article was linked to others through the keywords they commonly used. For example, if two articles commonly used "self-governance," they are linked in the map. If a group of articles used the same keyword, they form a cluster. An example is the "self-governance" cluster in the lower-left corner of the 1990s' map. Six journal articles are linked to each other in that cluster through the "self-governance" keyword in the middle.

With this description of two-mode maps in mind, we can observe that in the 1990s, in addition to the "self-governance" cluster, there were two other and minor clusters: "complex network" and "self-organization" clusters, with two articles attached to each. Each of the keywords "governance network" and "collaborative network" were used in one article. None of the other keywords was used in the public administration journal articles listed in the Web of Science database in this period. We can call the 1990s formative years of the complex governance networks literature: There were only few publications and, other than the self-governance studies, they were not integrated in any meaningful clusters.

We can also see that the picture of the literature changed in important ways in the 2000s and 2010s. In the 2000s, "governance networks" formed as an independent cluster (not linked to any other keywords). More

10  *Introduction*

**(a) 1990s**

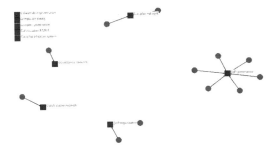

**(b) 2000s**

**(c) 2010s**

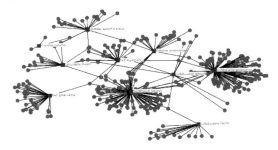

*Figure 1.3* Two-mode network maps of the public administration literature in three decades: (a) PADM Network 1990s, (b) PADM Network 2000s, and (c) PADM Network 2010s.

interesting, not only that "complexity theory" and "complex adaptive systems" entered picture in this decade, but they were linked to each other quite strongly (through four articles), as one would expect, but also to "self-organization," which is not surprising, given that self-organization is a concept used in complexity theory. "Self-organization," in turn, was linked to "self-governance," which is a more specific form of the former. One can also observe that the other keywords formed minor clusters, except for "collaborative network." In the 2010s, all the keyword clusters were linked to each other, except for the lone cluster of "complex network." Particularly important for the purposes of this book is that the "complexity theory," "complex adaptive system, and "complex governance" clusters were linked to the others.

Figure 1.3 is a picture of an increasingly integrated literature, in which the researchers linked more concepts together in their studies. Particularly important for the purposes of this book is that the studies that included complexity theory concepts (complex adaptive systems, complex governance, and self-organization) are linked increasingly to those that used governance networks and collaborative governance concepts over time. So, the complex governance networks conceptualization I propose has a basis in this evolving literature.

A few more observations about the evolution of the literature would help me make my case better. As the books I cited above and the 1990s map show that the literature was just beginning to form in that period. The 2000s were more important. In this period, the governance networks literature was partly theoretical, with discussions of the nature governance and governance networks (Andresani, 2006; Bevir & Richards, 2009; and Catlaw, 2009), but there were also important conceptual refinements, for example about the types of governance networks (Provan & Kennis, 2007). The role of governments in governance processes and networks became a focus of the conceptualizations in this period. Sorensen and Sorensen and Torfing (2006, 2009) and others offered the concept of "meta-governance" to define the role of governments.

In the 2000s, the articles in the complexity cluster were about introducing the main concepts of complexity theory and some initial applications. Most of the applications were about the policy areas of environment, urban areas, and homeland security, rather than the traditional issues of public administration (effectiveness, accountability/democracy). The articles on self-organization were related to complexity theory. Some of the authors specifically mentioned complexity. Self-governance papers were related to political science problems (the state, institutions, etc.). This group of papers were more international in their coverages (Philippines, New Zealand, Sri Lanka, Estonia, etc.).

In the 2010s, the studies on governance networks seemed to have matured. In most of the studies, the researchers used more refined concepts and focused on specific issues in governance networks, such as network effectiveness/performance; network nanagement, boundary spanning; democracy, accountability, and participation; and the role of governments (e.g., meta-governance). The largest numbers of studies in this cluster were about the United States and Europe, but there were studies on other countries, such as China, as well. The articles in the collaborative governance

12 *Introduction*

cluster also seemed to be maturing. The most frequently cited article of this period, Emerson, Nabatchi and Balogh (2012), offered a conceptual framework for collaborative governance studies. The articles in this cluster also focus on performance/effectiveness issues and democracy/participation issues. There were several articles that studied the trust issues in networks. There were studies on multiple countries in this cluster.

The complexity cluster of the articles published in this decade seem to be less mature, compared to the ones in governance networks and collaborative governance clusters. There was no common conceptualization or methodology in these articles. Some identifiable themes in this cluster were systemic resilience/robustness, feedbacks, decision making/planning, and socio-technical or ecological systems. Primarily European scholars were interested in complexity studies and *Public Management Review* was the primary venue for their publications.

The articles in the self-organization cluster were not highly connected to the complexity clusters. There were only three articles with common keywords to complexity, all published in *Public Management Review* (Castelvono & Sorrentino, 2018; Eppel, 2012; Meek & Marshall, 2018). The articles in this cluster were more connected to governance and network studies and political economy (polycentricity).

## COVID-19

This is a very brief overview of the COVID-19 pandemic. I will follow up on this example in the coming chapters and make more detailed points.

By the time I completed writing this book (winter of 2021–2022), the COVID-19 pandemic was still raging. The Sars-Cov-2 virus and its variants had killed more than five million people around the world, more than 800,000 in the United States alone.[3] The pandemic also disrupted the daily lives of millions of people, with frequent lockdowns, mask mandates, and other restrictions. Consequently, particularly children and young people faced mental health problems.[4] The worldwide economic growth slowed. The pandemic disrupted the supply chains of various industrial products around the world, which fueled the high inflation rates in many countries.[5] The stresses of the pandemic and the public health measures taken to slow and control it created social and cultural reactions and political divisions in many countries.[6]

COVID-19 was once-in-a-century pandemic. It was not the first pandemic (outbreak in viral infections on a global scale) though. Viruses and bacteria have existed for millions of years, long before humans appeared on the world scene. The ancestors of humans must have had encountered viruses hundreds of thousands of years ago and probably many of them died from viral infections, but some survived and a specific type of viruses, retroviruses, entered their genes. It is possible that the first (worldwide, or large-scale) pandemic broke out 20,000 years ago, as human societies began to interact more with each other (Soulmi et al., 2021). A quite well-known,

*Introduction* 13

and more recent, historical example is the Antonine Plague that occurred in the Roman Empire between 165 and 180 AD (Harper, 2021). At its peak, the Antonine Plague killed 2,000 Romans per day and its death toll was between 7 and 10 million people, in an empire of 70 million.

SARS-CoV-2 (severe acute respiratory syndrome) coronavirus, which caused the COVID-19 pandemic, appeared first in late 2019. At the time of this writing (winter of 2021), its multiple variants had emerged. The World Health Organization named these variants with the letters of the Greek alphabet (Alpha, Beta, Gamma, Delta, Mu, and Omicron).[7] Some of the new variants were more transmissible (e.g., Delta and Omicron), compared to the previous ones. Others were not (e.g., Gamma).

A major public health tool used against viruses are vaccines. COVID-19 vaccines were developed at a rapid pace and made available to the public in the late 2020. The invention, manufacturing, and administration/delivery processes of COVID-19 vaccines involved multiple actors: scientists, biotechnology companies, vaccine manufacturers, governments, national and international public health organizations (such as the US National Institutes of Health and the World Health Organization), medical doctors, local pharmacies, and others. These processes also involved hundreds of millions of individuals, particularly in the administration/delivery phase of the process, some of whom were informed and eager to be vaccinated and others who were misinformed and hesitant, or outright resistant, to getting vaccinated. The vaccine invention, manufacturing, and administration/delivery processes involved many actors (including governments, private companies, and others) interacting in multiple complex governance networks. I elaborate on these networks in the following chapters.

## Notes

1 Number of monthly Facebook users: www.statista.com/statistics/264810/number-of-monthly-active-facebook-users-worldwide/
2 Two-mode network maps is one of the tools used in social network analysis. I will discuss social network analysis briefly in Chapter 3, but not specifically two-mode network analysis or the maps generated using this kind of analysis. The description of the maps in Figure 1.3 can help explain the basics of these tools.
3 Coronavirus in the United States: Latest Map and Case Count, *New York Times*, www.nytimes.com/interactive/2021/us/covid-cases.html
4 Tami Benton, COVID 19 and Children's Mental Health. www.ssa.gov/ndf/documents/T%20Benton%20-%20NDF%2004-15-21%20-%20FINAL.pdf
5 How the Supply Chain Broke, and Why It Won't Be Fixed Anytime Soon, *New York Times*. https://nyti.ms/3nm13Lc
    Alberto Cavallo, Inflation Dynamics during COVID-19. www.nber.org/reporter/2021number3/inflation-dynamics-during-covid-19
6 American Individualism is an Obstacle to Wider Mask Wearing in the US. www.brookings.edu/blog/up-front/2020/08/31/american-individualism-is-an-obstacle-to-wider-mask-wearing-in-the-us/?utm_campaign=Brookings%20Brief&utm_medium=email&utm_content=94314931&utm_source=hs_email

14 *Introduction*

Is It Still a Mandate If We Don't Enforce It? The Politics of COVID-related Mask Mandates in Conservative States. https://journals-sagepub-com.ezacc ess.libraries.psu.edu/doi/full/10.1177/0160323X211035677?utm_source=sum mon&utm_medium=discovery-provider

7 Wikipedia Entry "Variants of SARS-CoV-2." https://en.wikipedia.org/wiki/ Variants_of_SARS-CoV-2

# Part I
# Concepts

# 2 Governance

In the introductory chapter, I did not differentiate between governance and networks. In the literature, these terms are usually combined as "governance networks" or "network governance." In this chapter, I focus on governance only. Governance networks will be the topic of the next chapter.

The term governance has its roots in and implications for political economy, public policy, and public administration. The conceptualizations of governance predate those of governance networks. Also, the terms "governance" and "governance networks" used in the literature refer to different, but related aspects of the same phenomenon. Governance refers to the process of collective problem-solving in human societies. Governance networks refer to the structural relations among the participants of this process.

Governance is typically associated with governing, which in turn is associated with government (the state). And it is a common understanding in at least today's liberal democratic societies that the state is the primary agent in solving collective (public) problems and delivering public services (safety and security, education, healthcare, etc.). This understanding has come under scrutiny by governance theorists who argued, and demonstrated with empirical evidence, that the processes of solving collective action problems involve multiple participants (not just governments) and the roles of governments in governance processes have been altered, if not diminished, in these processes.

Pierre and Peters's (2005) dichotomous typology of governance models helps us conceptually locate the different perspectives on governance. They observe that there are "state-centric governance models" (the "étatiste models"), in which the state plays a central role, and "governance without government" models, in which the state has no role, or a weak role to play (pp. 2–48). This dichotomy is useful to begin a discussion on the role of governments in governance, but we should recognize that the perspectives in the literature on this topic are not dichotomous. I will not summarize and discuss the entire spectrum of perspectives on this topic here—it would take another volume to cover them. Instead, I provide brief synopses here and in the next section. More specific discussions on the roles of governments in larger governance processes, particularly in relation to the

DOI: 10.4324/9781003053392-3

18  *Concepts*

effectiveness of efforts to solve social problems, accountability of collective actions, and democratic participation, can be found in Part II.

Goodsell (2016), who is among the most ardent defenders of public administration in general and public bureaucracies in particular (see Goodsell, 2015), makes the case that it would be a mistake to attribute the full responsibility to represent and care for a population to governments. He points out that in American society there is a range of (nongovernmental) institutions that are built with altruistic motivations and they contribute to the efforts to solve public problems. A group of critical theorists also acknowledge the limited roles of governments in governance processes (e.g., Bevir, 2014; Jessop, 2016; and Ishakhan & Slaughter, 2014). They hold a variety of views on this topic, which I will come back to in sections of Part II, but they agree that that the roles of the state (governments) vary and that these roles should be defined in broader social contexts. Coming from a very different theoretical perspective (rational choice, public choice), Vincent Ostrom (1974), Elinor Ostrom (1990, 2005), and their colleagues posit that collective action processes are polycentric. They do not use the term "government" specifically though. I summarize their contributions in a separate section in this chapter and discuss more specific implications in Part II.

In the next section, I summarize why the governance conceptualizations emerged. This summary will help provide background for the following discussions of the models of governance. In the following section, I turn to polycentrism, which is less state-centric; because of its different theoretical roots, it is more appropriate to cover it in a separate section. The COVID-19 pandemic is a good case to illustrate the implications of governance conceptualizations.

## A Brief History of Governance

In the previous chapter, we saw that the keywords "self-governance" and "governance networks" began to emerge in the literature that was included in the Web of Science in the 1990s and these concepts began to mature in the 2000s. The history of thinking on "governance" is longer than what the Web of Science database suggests.

Kettl (2002) notes that the term "governance" has been used by the French since the 14th century (p. 119) and that indirect governmental tools, such as governments relying on contractors—tools we recognize as tools of governance today—existed for millennia. The Roman legions relied on their defense contractors, for example. The scope and scale of government contracting increased in the American government toward the end of the 20th century, he observes. Meanwhile, similar developments were taking place in Europe, particularly Britain (Rhodes, 1997).

These developments motivated some American and European public administration scholars to rethink their understandings of how public administration works. Peters and Pierre (1998) observe that the participation of multiple actors in governance processes was already happening in the second half of the 20th century, and the US and European scholars were merely catching up to this reality in the last couple of decades of the century.[1] There were even earlier conceptualizations of governance, such as Harlan Cleveland's (1972). He argued that multiple horizontally related organizations always play roles in multilateral public decision-making and problem-solving.

The increased interest in governance in the academic literature is a result of a series of observations social theorists and public policy and administration researchers make: that societies have become multicentered in the later 20th century (Castells, 1996; Jessop, 1990) and that in today's world no governmental or private actor has the capacity to solve the increasingly complex and dynamic problems of societies (Goldsmith & Eggers, 2004; Kooiman, 1993).

According to Nye (2002), the electronic technology revolution of the late 20th century changed the way human societies organize to solve their problems. Centralized and bureaucratic organizational forms—particularly, the hierarchically ordered nation-state—were suitable for the problems of the earlier industrial revolutions, because industrial production required central control. The new technologies made central control more difficult and unnecessary. Consequently, the nation-state has become a mismatch to today's problems: It is too big for some problems and too small for others. That is why state and local governments and local businesses have gained importance at subnational levels and supra-governmental entities, like the United Nations, World Bank, and the European Union, have become more important in dealing with larger and global problems. In this new world, distance is less of a problem and globalization is the norm. Others concur with Nye and observe that the roles of governments in solving collective problems by themselves have diminished or at least changed, as the policy-making capabilities of nation-states have diminished and the political and policymaking processes have become de-centered or multicentered (Kettl, 2002; Koliba, Meek, & Zia, 2011; Kooiman, 1993; Rhodes, 1997; Torfing, Peters, Pierre, and Sørensen, 2012).

## Conceptualizations of Governance

Provan and Kenis (2007) observe that in the public administration literature, governance refers narrowly to the funding and oversight roles of government agencies, especially regarding the activities of private organizations that have been contracted to provide public services (p. 230). The conceptualizations by Frederickson (2002), Salamon (2002), and Kettl (2002) corroborate this observation, but there are some openings to broader views of governance in them.

Frederickson's (2002) "mismatch problem" for American public administration in the early 21st century is illustrative of the reasoning behind the narrow conceptualizations of governance. Her argues that there is a

## 20  Concepts

mismatch between the social problems and opportunities on one hand and the "capacities of the governmental jurisdictions" on the other (p. 11). To cope with the mismatch, public administrators representing different jurisdictions form "formal and informal horizontal and vertical linkages and patterns of cooperation," which Frederickson calls "administrative conjunction" (p. 11). The best examples of administrative conjunction can be found in American metropolitan areas, where professional public administrators who work for local governments, councils of government, regional special districts, and others cooperate with each other. This description of governance is an extension of the "intergovernmental relations" studies, which have a long tradition in American political science and public administration.

Salamon (2002) proposes a broader view of governance: Not only multiple governmental organizations work in conjunction, but also nonprofits and private corporations work with them in solving problems and delivering public services. He argues that in the second half of the 20th century the scope of government actions expanded and their forms had changed in the United States and other countries. Instead of delivering public services directly, governments began employing an array of "indirect tools": loans, loan guarantees, grants, contracts, social regulation, economic regulation, insurance, tax expenditures, vouchers, and others. In doing so, they relied on third parties, nonprofits, and private corporations (banks, private hospitals, social service agencies, industrial corporations, universities, and others). As an example of these developments, he notes that in the fiscal year 1999, only 28.1% of the US federal government's public service delivery was through "direct government" (activities such as delivery of goods and services, income support, interests, and direct loans); the remainder of the activities were indirect. This "third-party government" has created a "complex collaborative system," in which governments share their "public authority" with nonprofits and private actors (p. 2).

Salamon argues that the "traditional public administration paradigm," whose main concern is the internal operations of public agencies (human resources, budgeting, and task accomplishment), no longer help us understand this new world of public actions. To capture the new realities, he proposes a new perspective: the "new public governance paradigm." In this paradigm, the unit of analysis in policy analysis and public administration is shifted "from the public agency or the individual public program to the distinctive tools or instruments through which public purposes are pursued" (p. 9).

Kettl's (1988a, 1988b, 2002) observations echo those of Frederickson and Salamon. Kettl (1988a, 1988b) observes that governments always relied on private organizations in the production and delivery of some public services and names this phenomenon "government by proxy." He notes that there was an increase in government by proxy since the Second World War, particularly in the 1970s and early 1980s, mainly because of the budgetary constraints for governments in this period, but also because of the rising influence of public choice theory in governmental affairs. The federal government and other governments relied more heavily on contracting out, grants, loans, and text incentives in this period. Government by proxy makes it more difficult to control public service delivery mechanisms, manage information among governmental and other actors, and hold actors democratically accountable, he argues.

Kettl (2002) discusses these trends and the problems they generate in a more conceptual and historical manner. He points out that there is a mismatch between the traditional public administration conceptualizations and the social problems of the late 20th century. In this period, the traditional "Wilsonian principles" of public administration, which are "built on the foundation of a theory of hierarchy and authority," do not fit the actual work of public administration, which has become less hierarchical and more indirect (through contracts, etc.) (p. ix). He observes that toward the end of the 20th century, the task of delivering public services became increasingly shared among governments, nonprofits, and private corporations (p. 118). He uses the term governance in this context: It is "a way of describing the links between government and its broader environment" (p. 119).

A commonality among Frederickson's, Salamon's, and Kettl's conceptualizations is their state-centeredness. Although they acknowledge the roles of nongovernmental actors, the state still, or should be, at the center of public service delivery in their view. There are also those whose conceptualizations are less state-centered. According to Rhodes (1997), governance is a description of "self-organizing, interorganizational networks characterized by interdependence, resource exchange, rules of the game and significant autonomy from the state" (p. 15). According to Goldsmith Eggers (2004), a broad shift in governance is occurring around the globe, which they call "governing by network." The characteristics of this shift are heavy reliance on partnerships, philosophy of leveraging nongovernmental organizations to enhance public value, and varied and innovative business relationships (p. 6).

Ansell and Gash's (2008) now classic definition of "collaborative governance" is also less state-centered: It is

> a governing arrangement where one of more public agencies directly engage nonstate stakeholders in a *collective decision-making process* that is formal, consensus oriented, and deliberative and that aims to make or *implement public policy or manage public programs* or assets. [italics added].

> (p. 544)

Emerson and Nabatchi's (2015) definition of public governance is similar: It includes the "processes and institutions for *public decision-making and*

## 22 *Concepts*

*action* that include actors from both government and other sectors" [italics added] (p. 15).

The public policy literature does not directly deal with the concept of governance, but there are similar conceptualizations in it. The traditional definitions of public policy are state-centered. For example, in the traditional textbooks of public policy processes (e.g., Dye, 2013; Simon, 2007), public policy is defined as actions by unified governmental actors, what these actors choose to do or not to do. In her history of policy analysis, Radin (2013) demonstrates that these simplistic definitions do not capture the actual practices of policy analysis or policymaking. As policy analysis practices spread globally, the boundaries of public policies and programs and the distinctions between "domestic" and "international" and those between the "private" and "public" realms became blurred, she notes. In the 1990s, more interest groups formed their policy "think tanks" and policy-analytical practices became decentered. Government agencies were no longer the centers of knowledge production in policy-making. In the early 21st century, policy analysis and public decision-making became even more complex, as they involved collaborations between and networks of multiple governmental and nongovernmental actors, Radin observes.

Heinelt (2010) argues that we should use the concept "governance" to better understand and describe these multicentered policy processes. He further argues that "democratic political systems have to be considered as a complex and broad web of various forms of interest articulation and intermediation as well as decision-making" (p. 2). Social theorist Jessop (2016) offers an even more expansive view of governance. He observes that governance processes take place not only in local service delivery but at all levels of collective action. As he puts it: "[g]overnance practices range from the expansion of international and supranational regimes through national and regional public-private partnerships to more localized networks of power and decision-making" (p. 166).

In all the definitions of governance cited above, a common element is that multiple actors—not only the state, or a governmental organization, but also "private actors"—are involved in the making of "public" policies and administering them. Some authors also stress that these actors are both autonomous and interdependent (Torfing et al., 2012, p. 16; Klijn & Koppenjan, 2016, p. 21; Jessop, 2016, p. 166). The involvement of these interdependent "public" and "private" actors in governance processes has led to the blurring of the lines between the public and private realms, between the state and civil society, in the late 20th and early 21st centuries (Kettl, 2002; Ishakhan & Slaughter, 2014), which have profound implications for collective problem-solving in human societies in general and public policy and public administration studies in particular. I addressed these implications elsewhere (Morçöl, 2016), but more conceptual and empirical works are needed on this topic.

## Polycentrism

The governance conceptualizations of the late 20th and early 21st centuries had their precedents in the theories of polycentrism, whose roots were in the 1950s. That is when a group scholars formulated theories that have become to be known as rational choice, public choice, or polycentricity. The differences among these terms are not central to the discussions in this section. So, I refer only to polycentrism.

It is important to stress that early polycentrism theorists addressed similar issues as the issues governance theorists concerned about today, such as multiple actors interacting in public service delivery. Polycentrism theorists advanced strong and cogent conceptualizations that can help shed light on the theoretical discussions today.

In the early conceptualizations of polycentrism, the main argument was that public service delivery does not have to be organized centrally and hierarchically; instead, it can be done more efficiently by multiple and competing local governments and private organizations. Tiebout (1956) advanced the argument that when there are multiple and competing local governments that make public services such as education and refuse collection available, people can "vote by their feet" to obtain them at the lowest level of taxes. When there are multiple jurisdictions to choose from, Tiebout argued, people will make rational choices and an efficient equilibrium between public goods and tax prices will emerge.

McGinnis (1999) notes that Tiebout's work was the starting point for the later theories of polycentricity. Polycentrism theorists generalized his hypothesis and argued that the availability of multiple service providers to choose from was the prerequisite of self-governance: "the ability of groups of individuals to work out problems for themselves" (p. 3). In their jointly written essay, Vincent Ostrom, Charles Tiebout, and Robert Warren (1961) formulated the concept of "polycentric order" and argued that complex systems of overlapping jurisdictions can deliver services more efficiently than centralized governments.

Polycentrism theorists also dealt with a key conceptual and empirical problem: Is there link between the rational choices and actions of individuals and collective (public) outcomes? In other words, how would we know that the choices they make yield beneficial results for the community or larger society? Do we not need a coercive intervention by a higher (an external) authority (e.g., the state) to ensure that the outcomes of these choices and actions are beneficial to society? These questions were at the core of Garret Hardin's (1968) "tragedy of commons" conjecture, in which the actions of selfish individuals lead to the destruction of common resources. He argued that the problem could be solved by the intervention of an external force, the state.[2] I will come back to the problem of the links between individual actions and collective outcomes in Chapter 7 and Hardin's conjecture in various parts of this book.

## 24   *Concepts*

Olson (1965) argued that the actions of rational and selfish individuals can lead to beneficial collective outcomes, but only if they are in a small group. He stressed that large groups of individuals who act spontaneously cannot generate good collective outcomes: "The larger a group is, the farther it will fall short of obtaining an optimal supply of any collective good, and the less likely that it will act to obtain even a minimal amount of such a good" (p. 35).

We can infer from Olson's argument that Hardin's "tragedy of commons" is more likely to happen in larger groups and that larger groups, communities, and societies need to be governed by external actors (e.g., the state). It is an open question whether this is correct. Graeber and Wengrow (2021) point out that there is no historical evidence for a direct relationship between the size of a society and whether it needs be governed by a state. There were ancient societies that were large and without any states (they self-governed), and there were others of similar size that did have states. I will come back to the issues of self-organization and self-governance in Chapters 4 and 11.

Vincent Ostrom's (1974) conceptualization concurs with what Graeber and Wengrow tell us about human history. Ostrom acknowledges the possibility that beneficial collective outcomes may be generated in groups of all sizes. The key issue, according to Ostrom, is the *configuration of institutional arrangement* in which individuals act. He notes: "No single form of organization is presumed to be good for all circumstances. Rather any type of organizational arrangement can generate a limited range of preferred effects" (p. 55). Ostrom stresses that institutional arrangements mediate the relationship between individual motivations and action on the one hand and (good and bad) collective outcomes on the other.

To better understand Ostrom's (1974) position on institutional arrangements, one should look into his criticism of the "traditional model of public administration," which had been developed by Woodrow Wilson, Frank Goodnow, and others earlier in the 20th century. He argues that public administration was in an intellectual crisis (in the 1970s) and the traditional model was the source of this crisis. In the traditional model, the assumption is that to generate socially desirable outcomes, there should be a center of power in any system of government, that administration should be separated from politics, and that the former should be organized bureaucratically (hierarchically and in clear lines of authority) in order it to be effective and efficient (p. 24).

Ostrom challenges the traditional model's assumption is that all forms of administration must be hierarchical and bureaucratic. Infinite configurations of institutional arrangements are possible and socially desirable outcomes can emerge under different institutional arrangements. Self-interested and rational individuals may act within these institutional arrangements to generate public goods.

The concept of "configuration of institutional arrangements" is central in Vincent Ostrom's conceptualization of polycentrism. Later, Elinor

Ostrom (1990, 2005) refined it in her "institutional analysis and development framework" and more recent "social-ecological systems framework." She won the Nobel prize in economics in 2009 for her theoretical advancements and the empirical verifications provided by her and her colleagues.

There are obvious parallels between governance theorists' notion that multiple actors are involved in governance processes and Vincent Ostrom's and Elinor Ostrom's conceptualization that multiple institutional configurations are possible in collective problem solving. There is also an implication of these recognitions of multiplicity of actors and institutional configurations: that they generate complexity. Governance theorists and polycentrism theorists acknowledge that governance processes and "polycentric orders," respectively, are inherently complex (Kettl, 2002; McGinnis, 1999, p. 5). Vincent Ostrom (1974) specifically argues that a polycentric system is necessarily complicated (p. 106), that the appearance of disorder ("anarchy") in democratic administration does not mean that there is a disorder (p. 94), and that a "system of democratic administration depends upon an ordered complexity in social relationships" (p. 132). Complexity is the topic of Chapter 4 in this book.

## COVID-19 and Governance

The insight of governance theorists that multiple actors are involved in governance processes can be observed in the case of COVID-19 pandemic, particularly in the invention, manufacturing, and administration/delivery processes of COVID-19 vaccines. It would not be possible to describe the full process of and all the actors involved in vaccine development here (that would likely to take several other books), but a brief overview could help make the case that the vaccine development was a complex process in which multiple actors played roles. There were scientists, biotechnology companies, vaccine manufacturers, governments, national and international public health organizations (such as the US National Institutes of Health and the World Health Organization), parcel shipping companies (FedEx and UPS), medical doctors, local pharmacies, and others; they all played various roles in the vaccine development and delivery processes.

The US federal government, particularly its agency National Institutes of Health (NIH), played significant roles in the development of messenger RNA (mRNA) vaccines. The NIH scientists had been working on prototype coronavirus vaccines for years.

Once the DNA sequence of SARS-CoV-2 virus was published by the Chinese scientists in February 2020, more than 120 teams of academic scientists and commercial manufacturers around the world began collaborating with each other through information exchanges and sharing resources to develop vaccines (Pagliusi et al., 2020). Among them were the NIH scientists who collaborated with Moderna, a small vaccine research and development company, to produce one of the first mRNA vaccines.[3]

## 26  Concepts

The federal government financed Moderna's research and development and manufacturing of the vaccines partly, and other parts came from Emory University, Vanderbilt University Medical Center, and the Dolly Parton COVID-19 Research Fund.[4] In the meantime, two biotechnology companies Pfizer and BioNTech were collaborating to develop their vaccine based on the mRNA platform technology BioNTech scientists had been working for years.[5] Behind these stories were thousands of scientists who discovered mRNA in the 1960s, developed its delivery methods in the 1970s, and tested the first mRNA flu vaccine in mice in the 1990s.[6] The COVID-19 pandemic accelerated this decades of work and brought them to the successful development and worldwide application of the mRNA vaccines.

The vaccine delivery and administration process also involved many organizations and individuals: vaccine manufacturers, governments, parcel shipping companies (FedEx and UPS), medical doctors, local pharmacies, and individuals who accepted or rejected to be vaccinated. It took major logistical operations by the US government agencies and parcel shipment companies to deliver the vaccines to local hospitals, pharmacies, and medical doctors' offices.

Once the vaccines were approved, the governments of richer countries (e.g., the United States, the United Kingdom, members of the European Union, and Israel) purchased them in large quantities. Then they were shipped to distribution centers through elaborate logistical systems using technologies like "cold chain" (super cold deep freezers) to protect their molecular integrity.[7] The US federal government and state governments employed information technology specialists to develop and run special algorithms in distributing vaccines among the state and among the localities within the states.[8] In some occasions, state governments in the United States collaborated with private companies for the logistics of vaccine distributions (e.g., Washington State Governor's reliance on Starbucks's expertise for vaccine delivery[9]). The World Health Organization's Covax program (an international collaboration that involved multiple countries) was involved in the delivery of vaccines to countries in Africa and others.[10] Then the contents of each vaccine vile was administered to individuals by medical professionals and pharmacists.[11]

Some individuals were eager to get vaccinated, and the first doses were delivered in December 2020.[12] But many others were "hesitant," even "resistant," to accepting the vaccines (a long and complex story, which would require at least another book to cover). As a result, even after the COVID vaccines became widely available (at least in the United States and other economically developed countries), large segments of populations remained unvaccinated. The choices and behaviors of these individuals were influenced by the information they obtained from media, social media, and their direct relationships with their families, friends, and acquittances.[13] As of late December 2021, only 62% of the American people were vaccinated.[14]

The vaccine invention, manufacturing, and administration/delivery processes involved not one, but multiple complex systems (and governance networks) interacting with each other. I will come back to the COVID-19 and vaccine topics in the following chapters.

## Summary

This chapter is about one of the three components of complex governance networks. Governance is a term used in various contexts and differently by different authors. The most common understanding of the term is that there are multiple actors involved in collective problem-solving processes. After providing a brief history of the uses of this term, I discussed the various conceptualizations of governance, from more state-centric conceptualizations to those that recognize the multi-centeredness of governance processes. The most well-developed version of the latter group of conceptualizations are polycentrism theories, which are covered in a separate section. The chapter ended with illustrations of multiple actors' involvements in the development, delivery, and administration of COVID-19 vaccines. The next chapter is about how these actors are connected in network relations.

## Notes

1 In this discussion, I will skip the developments such as the New Public Management movement and literature. As Klijn and Koppenjan (2016) note, although governance is occasionally conflated with New Public Management, the two are actually not related (p. 7). The New Public Management aims to improve the effectiveness and efficiency of public bureaucracies, whereas governance is about multiple actors in collective action problem solving.
2 Hardin was not the first to formulate this commons problem. English economist William F. Lloyd did that in a pamphlet in 1883 (https://en.wikipedia.org/wiki/Tragedy_of_the_commons#Lloyd's_pamphlet).
3 COVID-19 Vaccine Development: Behind the Scenes: https://covid19.nih.gov/news-and-stories/vaccine-development
4 US News & World Report, Fact check—Moderna Vaccine Funded by Government Spending, with Notable Private Donation: www.usatoday.com/story/news/factcheck/2020/11/24/fact-check-donations-research-grants-helped-fund-moderna-vaccine/6398486002/.
5 Shot of a Lifetime: How Pfizer and BioNTech Developed and Manufactured a COVID-19 Vaccine in Record Time: www.pfizer.com/news/hot-topics/shot_of_a_lifetime_how_pfizer_and_biontech_developed_and_manufactured_a_covid_19_vaccine_in_record_time
   BioNTech's Covid-19 Portal: https://biontech.de/covid-19
6 The Long History of mRNA Vaccines: https://publichealth.jhu.edu/2021/the-long-history-of-mrna-vaccines
7 The Pfizer–BioNTech COVID-19 Vaccine Requires to Be Kept at Temperatures Below -70 Centigrade.

## 28   *Concepts*

8  Where Do Vaccine Doses Go, and Who Gets Them? The Algorithms Decide, *New York Times*, https://nyti.ms/3rtbu04

9  Washington State Taps Starbucks for Help with Covid Vaccine Rollout, NBC News.. www.nbcnews.com/news/us-news/washington-state-taps-starbucks-help-covid-vaccine-rollout-n1254607

10  Covax. www.who.int/initiatives/act-accelerator/covax
    Covid: WHO Scheme Covax Delivers First Vaccines:- www.bbc.co.uk/news/world-africa-56180161

11  How the Vaccine Will Reach Your Arm: BBC News
    www.bbc.co.uk/news/resources/idt-66c2dc60-855d-4307-9174-e21f65e9702d

12  First Covid Vaccine is Administered in the US: www.bbc.com/news/av/world-us-canada-55307642

13  The Game is Not Yet Over, and Vaccines Still Matter: Lessons from a Study on Israel's COVID-19 Vaccination
    www.brookings.edu/blog/up-front/2021/09/13/the-game-is-not-yet-over-and-vaccines-still-matter-lessons-from-a-study-on-israels-covid-19-vaccination/?utm_campaign=Brookings%20Brief&utm_medium=email&utm_content=159977144&utm_source=hs_email

14  *New York Times* Vaccination Statistics: www.nytimes.com/interactive/2020/us/covid-19-vaccine-doses.html?

# 3 Governance Networks

The term governance is increasingly used together with the term networks, either as "governance networks" or "network governance." In these usages, "governance" refers to the process of collective problem solving in human societies, and "governance networks" refers to the structural relations among the participants of this process.

We can observe various networks in our daily experiences. Think about electrical power grids, which connect powers stations to relay stations and to the users of electricity; water distributions networks, which connect pumping stations, reservoirs, and homes; transportation networks, which connect bus and train stations, and airports through roads, which are used by personal cars and taxis; and the citations networks among scholarly publications (Latora et al., 2017, p. xiv). Think also about social relationships: friendship networks, underground crime networks, professional networks, and business networks such as supply chains.

The social media platforms like Facebook, Twitter, and LinkedIn are very large networks. They link individuals to each other as "friends" and "followers" in a variety of ways. They allow network participants to "like" each other's posts or "retweet" them. These personal links, likes, and retweets can be analyzed to find patterns in relationships using powerful algorithms. Then these patterns can be used to "suggest" new friends to network participants. The patterns can also be used to "target" specific individuals and groups to market products they are likely to purchase. The products may be merchandises, like dishwashers, and services, like vacation rentals. The products may also be political, ideological, or cultural messages, including conspiracy theories, like Q Anon.

The "Internet of Things" is the largest network of them all. IBM's blog defines it as follows.

> In a nutshell, the Internet of Things [IoT] is the concept of connecting any device (so long as it has an on/off switch) to the Internet and to other connected devices. The IoT is a giant network of connected things and people—all of which collect and share data about the way they are used and about the environment around them.

DOI: 10.4324/9781003053392-4

30  *Concepts*

That includes an *extraordinary number of objects of all shapes and sizes*—from smart *microwaves*, which automatically cook your food for the right length of time, to *self-driving cars*, whose complex sensors detect objects in their path, to *wearable fitness devices* that measure your heart rate and the number of steps you've taken that day, then use that information to suggest exercise plans tailored to you. There are even *connected footballs* that can track how far and fast they are thrown and record those statistics via an app for future training purposes. [Italics added] [1]

Once we begin thinking in terms of networks, everything around us will look like a network, or part of a network. And that would be a fairly accurate description of our realities. People and "things" around us are connected with each other and those connections form networks. So, the "network" is a useful abstraction. This abstraction can help us understand various kinds of relationships in nature and in societies, and the connections between natural and social entities (individuals, groups, institutions).

"Governance networks" should be viewed as a form of these networks and there is a growing literature on them. Before providing a brief overview of this literature, a historical background of network thinking will help us understand its background.

## A Brief History of Network Thinking and Science

Mark Newman, Albert-László Barabási, and Duncan Watts (2006), all major contributors to "network science" (or the study of "complex networks"),[2] trace its history to 1763. That was when mathematician Leonard Euler studied a bridge problem in the city of Königsberg in Prussia (today's Kaliningrad, an enclave of the Russian Federation on the Baltic Sea).[3]

A Google map of the central city of Kaliningrad is shown in Figure 3.1. The approximate positions of the seven bridges Euler studied when it was Königsberg are superimposed on the map to illustrate the mathematical problem Euler faced. Five of these bridges have been replaced by more recent structures, which are shown in the map. Two of the seven bridges do not exist today; they are the middle bridges connecting the island to the shores in Figure 3.1.

Euler's problem was how to find a path that crossed the seven bridges that existed then, *exactly once each*. As the story goes, the people of Königsberg had tried to find such a path for a long time and failed. Euler proved mathematically that such a path did not exist. One might ask, what was the point in such a trivial finding? Newman, Barabási, and Watts (2006) remind us that Euler's mathematical solution to the problem was the beginning of what is known today as the "graph theory." A graph is a mathematical (abstract) object that consists of points (called "nodes" or "vertices") and lines (called "ties," "links," or "edges"). Graph theory is the

Governance Networks 31

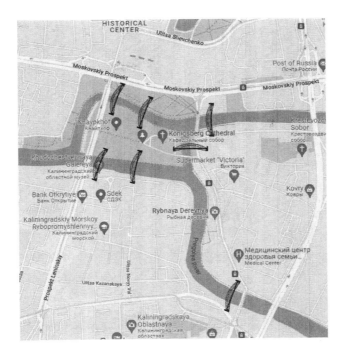

*Figure 3.1* The Könisberg bridge problem superimposed on today's map of Kaliningrad.
(*Source*: Generated by the author using Google Maps: www.google.com/maps/ @54.7060336,20.511029,15z)

mathematical basis of "social network analysis," which is a set of conceptual and mathematical tools that are used in analyzing and finding patterns in social networks (Wasserman & Faust, 1994, pp. 92–94), such as governance networks.

To illustrate the concepts used in the above paragraph, let's go back to a network map I introduced in Chapter 1: Figure 1.3b (reproduced here as Figure 3.1). Because it is the map of a special kind of network (two-mode network), there are two kinds of nodes (vertices) in it: circles and squares. The circles represent journal publications and the squares represent keywords. The lines connecting them are ties (edges). So, the map is an illustration of which journal articles are linked to which keywords (i.e., which journal publications used which keywords). In this network map, we can see how the keywords are grouped.

In Chapter 1, I interpreted these groupings as clusters in the literature and traced the evolution of the literature by interpreting the clusters and their connections in three decades: the 1990s, 2000s, and 2010s. This was a very simple version of social network analysis. Social network analysis has many tools that can be applied to study further the structures of networks

## 32  Concepts

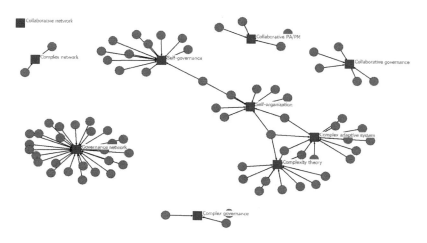

*Figure 3.2* Two-mode network map of the public administration literature in the 2000s.

like these. One can analyze the centralities of the nodes (which nodes are more central in a network), personal networks of individual nodes (how many connections each node has, how dense these connections, etc.), whether a particular network is structurally similar to another one, and so on. For the purposes of this book, I will skip the details of these analytical tools and others. For more information, I refer the reader to the books on this topic written by Borgatti et al. (2018), Latore et al. (2017), and Wasserman and Faust (1994).

Now, let's return to the history of network science. Since Euler's mathematical description of networks as graphs, network science evolved through multiple paths: natural sciences, mathematics, sociology, information sciences, and others. This evolution did not take a linear path. Instead, it jumped between scientific disciplines. The graph theory was applied in chemistry, at the molecular and atomic levels, in the late 19th century (Sylvester, 1878). Hungarian mathematician Dénes Kőnig's *Theory of Finite and Infinite Graphs* (1936/1990) was the first book published on this subject. Graph theory found most of its applications in sociology (Newman, Barabási, & Watts, 2006). Jacob Moreno developed "sociograms" (graphical representations of social links) in the 1930s, which became the basis of the applications in sociology, which in turn became known as social network analysis (Wasserman & Faust, 1994, pp. 9–17). Since the 1930s, social network analysis methods have become much more detailed and sophisticated, thanks to the developments in graph theory, statistical and probability theory, and algebraic models in them (Wasserman & Faust).

Latora and his colleagues (2017, p. xv) point to two major developments in the 1990s as the turning points in the evolution of network science: Duncan

Watts and Steven Strogatz's (1998) mathematical demonstration of the existence of "small-world networks" and Albert-László Barabási and Reka Albert's (1999) demonstration of the existence of "scale-free networks." Watts and Strogatz showed that several natural, mechanical, and social networks have common characteristics. They analyzed particularly the neural network of the worm *Caenorhabditis elegans*, the power grid of the western United States, and the graph of collaborations among film actors. All these networks were highly clustered, and they had short path lengths. Watts and Strogatz called these the characteristics "small-world networks."

Barabási and Albert showed that the links between the nodes of large networks, like genetic networks and the World Wide Web, follow a scale-free "power law" distribution. These distributions are lopsided: A small number of nodes are connected to large number of other nodes, and the rest of the nodes are connected to smaller numbers of nodes.

Barabási and Albert also identified a generic mechanism that created such power law distributions: *preferential attachment*. As the networks expand by the addition of new nodes, these new nodes attach preferentially to nodes that are already well connected. They showed that this mechanism is the basis of self-organization in networks and that it is quite universal among large networks. I will return to preferential attachment in Chapter 7, where I discuss micro to macro relations in social networks.

Latora and his colleagues (2017) draw two lessons from Watts and Strogatz's (1998) and Barabási and Albert's (1999) works. First, networks are not mere mathematical abstractions; they exist in real life and their structures can be identified mathematically. Second, some of the structural properties of networks are universal. These lessons are important for studies on governance networks as well. There are few direct applications of "small-world networks" or "scale-free networks" in governance studies.[4] Still a general lesson can be drawn from Watts and Strogatz's and Barabási and Albert's works: Governance networks can have some generalizable properties as well. Indeed, some researchers aimed to generalize, beginning with developing a typology of these networks, which I discuss in the next section.

## Governance Networks

As the literature review in Chapter 1 shows, there were very few studies on governance networks in the 1990s, and the number of publications began to increase exponentially in the 2000s. The applications of governance networks in public administration practice predate the literature. Isett and her colleagues (2011) note that networks were being used in public service delivery as early as in the 1970s; their applications expanded in the 1980s, during Reagan's presidency; and they became more widespread in the 1990s, when the Clinton administration tried to shrink the size of the federal government and launched the "reinventing government" initiative.

34    *Concepts*

Although the literature on governance networks has decades of history, there is no common conceptualization developed and used by the researchers. In their comprehensive review of the literature, Provan, Fish, and Sydow (2007) could not find an overarching conceptualization that would guide empirical studies of governance networks at that point. More than a decade after their review of the literature, no commonly accepted conceptualization, let alone a tightly formulated theory, of governance networks has emerged yet. The concept of "governance networks" is used usually in conjunction with, or interchangeably with, the terms "policy networks" and "public management networks." Each of these three concepts has its conceptual history and there are differences, as well as similarities, among them. (For the different usages and meanings of the terms, see Compston, 2009, and Agranoff, 2007).

### *An Ideal Type of Governance Networks and Typologies*

Despite this lack of commonality in the conceptualizations, there are some threads in the literature that can be sewn together to define an "ideal type" (an abstract knowledge) of governance networks, applying Max Weber's (2010) conceptual analytical method. I propose an ideal type in this chapter. (There is another discussion of ideal types in Chapter 11.) Two clarifications are necessary here. First, the following ideal typical definition includes both governance conceptualizations (Chapter 2), and the additional network characterizations of governance processes. Second, I summarize the typologies of governance networks developed in the literature at two levels of analysis: micro and macro levels. This conceptualization of micro and macro levels is important. It is the fundamental conceptual tool of the complex governance networks conceptualization, which I present in Part II of this book (Chapters 5–8).

The following ideal typical definition of governance networks is based on the definitions and characterizations in the following: Agranoff (2007); Goldsmith Eggers (2004), Ishakhan and Slaughter (2014); Jessop (2016); Kettl (2002); Kickert, Klijn, and Koppenjan (1997); Klijn and Koppenjan (2016); Koliba, Meek, and Zia, and Mills (2019); Koppenjan and Klijn (2004); Meier and O'Toole (2006), Rhodes (1997); Sorensen and Torfing (2005); and Torfing et al. (2012). I cite specific sources where they are most directly relevant in the following definition and later discussions.

(1)  Governance is a broad process that involves both public policymaking and implementation (public administration).
(2)  Multiple actors play roles in the making and administering public policies. They may be governmental organizations, nonprofits, and private organizations and individuals in various roles (political leaders, community leaders, business leaders, etc.) (e.g., Torfing et al., 2012, p. 16; Klijn and Koppenjan, 2016, p. 21; Jessop, 2016, p. 166). Goldsmith Eggers (2004) characterize "governing by network" as

heavy reliance on partnerships, philosophy of leveraging nongovernmental organizations to enhance public value, and varied and innovative business relationships (p. 6).

(3) These actors are both autonomous from each other and interdependent (Meier & O'Toole, 2006; Rhodes, 1997; Torfing et al., 2012, p. 16; Klijn and Koppenjan, 2016, p. 21; Jessop, 2016, p. 166).

(4) They are not under the hierarchical and bureaucratic control of "the state" (Meier & O'Toole, 2006). In these networks, there is no hierarchical center. In that sense, as Rhodes (1997, p. xii) notes, the idea of network governance has close affinity with Luhmann's "centerless society." These centerless networks are self-governing (self-organizing) (Agranoff, 2007; Koliba et al., 2019).

(5) Governance networks blur conceptual and territorial lines. The involvement of interdependent "public" and "private" actors in governance networks has led to the blurring of the lines between the public and private realms, between the state and civil society, in the late 20th and early 21st centuries (Kettl, 2002; Ishakhan & Slaughter, 2014). Because governance networks involve actors in multiple predefined territories, they do not fit into the territorial delineations and they challenge the notion of "sovereign authority" (Rhodes, 1997). Koppenjan and Kline (2004, p. 4) cite "deterritorialization" created by globalization as an example. The lack of territorial definitions of governance networks has implications for democracy, which I will discuss in Chapter 11.

Networks, in general, and governance networks, in particular, can be studied at two levels: *micro and macro levels*. The term micro refers to the individuals and organizations or organizational units within a governance network and the term macro refers to the network as a whole. Provan, Fish, and Sydow (2007) reviewed the studies on governance networks at these two levels. They point out that the micro-level studies have helped answer questions like what are the impacts of network ties among individual actors on organizational performance, which positions in organizational networks are most influential, and how individuals in these positions within networks in respond to changes within and outside the network?

An example of the studies at the micro level is Scholz, Berardo, and Kile's (2008) study of the water governance issues in 22 estuaries in the United States. They observed that there were multiple organizations involved in the governance of these estuaries and this created a fragmented governance structure. One of the questions the researchers aimed to answer was how do network positions of the actors affect collaboration among them? The "nodes" (actors) in their analyses were the (governmental and nongovernmental) organizations involved in these networks. They measured the "network positions" of the organizations in terms of their "degree centralities" and "betwenness centralities," both of which are social network analysis measures that indicate how "central" a node is within a network. "Collaboration and agreement" among network actors are

36 *Concepts*

obviously important, as they can affect the effectiveness of the network. (Scholz and his colleagues did not specifically measure "network effectiveness" in this study.)

What they found was that an organization's degree and betweenness centralities were significant predictors of their tendencies to collaborate with the other organizations in networks and that between centrality was a better predictor between the two. A brief note on the social network analysis measures they used is necessary here: Degree centrality measures the number of connections a node has and betweenness centrality measures the extent to which the organization is "in-between" others. In other words, degree centrality is the measure of "how many friends a node (an individual or organization) has" and betweenness centrality is the measure of the "gatekeeping" role of the node. Gatekeepers can control the flow of information in a network. Scholz and his colleagues conclude that more connected and gatekeeping organizations are more likely to collaborate in a governance network.

Network researchers may also study the relations between the micro and macro levels in networks (i.e., the "micro–macro problem," a topic I will return to in Part II). Although Scholz and his colleagues did not specifically focus on the micro–macro relations in their study, that is implicit in it. Degree and betweenness centralities (both of which are micro-level measures) can be measured only in relation to the whole of the network (macro level). In other words, how central an actor in a network is depends on the size and structure of the network the actor is embedded. Scholz and his colleagues made this implicit assumption, but they did not specifically study more direct micro–macro relations (e.g., how micro processes can affect macro structures). I will discuss this issue and give examples in Part II.

In their literature review, Provan, Fish, and Sydow (2007) observe that there were very few whole network studies (macro-level studies) and these studies were primarily conceptual discussions or descriptive case studies. Since the publication of their literature review, the number of macro-level studies has increased, but Provan and his colleagues' point has some resonance today. Macro-level empirical studies are more difficult to conduct and many, if not most, studies at this level have remained conceptual. The most important contributions of these macro-level studies are the typologies the researchers developed. These typologies are important because they illustrate the efforts to find common patterns in governance networks and generalize about their structures. I provide a brief overview of these typologies here first. Then I will give an example of macro-level empirical studies.

The earlier typologies were quite broad and vague in their conceptualizations and categories. The typologists did not even use the term governance networks systematically; instead, they developed typologies about various networks used in public policymaking, problem solving, and service delivery.

Wilks and Wright's (1987) early typology (cited in Rhodes, 1997, pp. 40–42), is an example. They defined three types: policy universes, policy communities, and policy networks. A "policy universe" is a large population of actors who share a common interest in a policy area and contribute to the policy processes regularly. A "policy community" is a system of actors who not only share a common interest, but also share resources with each other and strive to optimize their relationships. A "policy network" links the outcomes of policy processes to the members of a specific policy community and/or it links multiple policy communities.

Marsh and Rhodes's (1992) typology (cited and revised in Rhodes, 1997, pp. 43–45) was a simplified version of Wilks and Wright's. They defined tightly integrated "policy communities" and loosely integrated "issue networks." Policy communities are characterized by common values among members and interactions among them, mostly exchange relationships. In issue networks, both the values and interactions are variable and transient.

The typologies that were developed in the 2000s were more specific and tightly conceptualized. Kapucu and Hu (2020, pp. 37–45) offer a typology of typologies, based on their review of the literature. In their review, they found that networks can be sorted into types on five dimensions.

The first dimension is "network purpose." The primary example is Agranoff's (2007) frequently cited typology of "public management networks."[5] Agranoff (2007) grouped them into the following categories: informational networks, developmental networks, outreach networks, and action networks. Informational networks and outreach networks are similar in that they do not directly engage in policymaking or service delivery; instead, they are preparatory for further action and problem solving (pp. 51–52). In informational networks, actors exchange information and learn from each other's experiences and knowledge. In developmental networks, actors not only exchange information but also develop capacities to solve public problems. Outreach and action networks are more action-oriented (p. 67). In outreach networks, actors plan, strategize, and mutually adjust and design programs to solve problems. In action networks, actors make formal agreements and engage in collaborative action.

The second dimension in Kapucu and Hu's framework is "network function." They cite information diffusion networks, resource exchange networks, capacity building networks, and service provision networks as the types on this dimension. The third dimension is "network formality." The two categories are formal and informal networks. The fourth dimension is "research foci." On this dimension, Kapucu and Hu make distinctions between public management/collaborative networks (networks that are designed for service delivery), policy networks (whose aim is to influence policy processes), and governance networks (which have broader foci and whose aim is to coordinate action to reach common goals). The fifth dimension in Kapucu and Hu's framework is "network application domain." They cite emergency management networks, economic development networks, and social service networks as examples.

38   *Concepts*

Provan and Kenis's (2007) is the most well-known typology in the literature.[6] They identify three types of governance networks based on their forms and structural properties: participant-governed networks, lead-organization governed networks, and networks with a network administrative organization. Participant-governed networks are, as the name suggests, governed by actors who are members of the network, without any external interference or guidance. The exchange and power relations among the participants may not be equal, but they are not heavily lopsided either. In lead-organization governed networks, the power and exchange relations are more lopsided. There is a lead organization that provides most of the resources for network activities and coordinates the activities. The leadership of this organization is not formal. In the type of networks with network administrative organization, the leadership role is formally designated.

This summary of typologies shows that there has been some progress in tightening the conceptualizations, but ambiguities remain. For example, there still is a tendency to separate public service delivery networks ("public management networks," or collaborative networks) from policy process networks (policy networks) and the term "governance networks" is used to refer to both, but it is defined as a separate category. Referring back to the discussions on small-world networks and scale-free networks earlier in this chapter, I can say that there is no such generality or mathematical precision in the typologies of governance networks. Whether that can be done in the future remains to be seen.

Provan, Fish, and Sydow (2007) argue that governance network studies should go beyond typologies and answer some key questions about the macro structures of networks. What are the conditions of the emergence of different network structural forms? Particularly, what is the role of governmental entities in shaping and constraining network structures? Another problematic area is how networks evolve. For example, does network evolution occur in predictable ways? Do networks change continually or reach points of stability? Another important area of study, which Provan, Fish, and Sydow (2007) does not mention specifically is network effectiveness. The question is, what kinds of network structures are more effective? I will come back to this question in Chapter 9.

Another important question Provan, Fish, and Sydow (2007) did not ask specifically is about the implications of governance networks for participation, democracy, and accountability in governance networks. There are some studies on these topics. I will summarize and discuss them in Chapters 10 and 11.

## COVID and Governance Networks

There are no specific applications of governance network conceptualizations, as of the writing of this book, to the best of my knowledge. There are no specific network analyses either. That is probably

Governance Networks 39

because the pandemic is ongoing and it is too early to conduct elaborate studies. Despite the lack of studies on the governance networks and COVID-19, some effects of network relations in the pandemic processes can be inferred from a couple of studies.

A study conducted by ETZ Zürich Center for Law and Economics shows that in the United States, the viewers of Fox news, which was closely aligned with Trump's political views, were less likely to get vaccinated, while the viewership of the other two major cable news networks did not make any difference in vaccination rates.[7] This is an example of what networks scientists call "homophily," the tendency of people to think and act like others who are like themselves. Why does it matter? Identifying homophily in watching certain television channels or being members of certain social media groups, certain ethnic groups, or families can yield insightful results that can help us understand public health problems like "vaccine hesitancy," which turned out to be a major problem during the COVID-19 pandemic.

Applying social network analysis methods, we can also study the impacts of the direct and indirect connections (interactions) among members of groups on vaccine hesitancy. A survey conducted in Israel in March and August of 2021 is a partial example of this. The survey results showed that the *source of information people received* was influential in their decisions to get vaccinated or not.[8] Among the sample of Israelis in the study, individuals were getting their information from experts (health care providers and scientific articles), family members, friends, acquaintances (neighbors, colleagues), media, and social media. The researcher found that people who were influenced by family members (direct interactions with close members of one's community) and the news in the mass media (indirect interactions with larger communities of experts and social leaders) were more likely to get vaccinated, while those who got their news from social media (a different kind of indirect interactions with larger communities of social media "friends") were less likely to get vaccinated.

An earlier study that was conducted on the resistance to measles vaccines in the United States in 2019, before the COVID-19 pandemic began, yielded similar findings. Those who received their information primarily from social media were more resistant to measles vaccines.[9]

## Summary

The previous chapter was about the multiplicity of actors in governance processes and the multi-centricity (or polycentricity) of such processes. The topic of this chapter was how to study the structures of governance processes. The primary conceptualization of these structures is "governance networks." Also, the concepts "policy networks," "public management networks," and the like are used interchangeably. In these conceptualizations, the insights of and advances in network sciences have been applied. These insights and advances and were, as well as a brief

40    *Concepts*

overview of social network analyses, were the topics of a section in this chapter.

Network scientists identified some universal network structures, like "scale-free networks" and "small-world networks." These or other conceptualizations have not been applied systematically in governance network studies. There is no common definition of governance networks either, but the scholars of this field developed their own conceptualizations and typologies, which are summarized in section of this chapter. There are no direct and elaborate applications of governance networks conceptualizations of or social network analyses in the COVID-19 pandemic case, but there are a few studies whose implications are relevant; these studies were summarized in the last section.

## Notes

1  What is the Internet of Things (IoT)? www.ibm.com/blogs/internet-of-things/what-is-the-iot/
2  Wikipedia Entry "Network Science". https://en.wikipedia.org/wiki/Network_science
3  Wikipedia Entry "Seven Bridges of Königsberg". https://en.wikipedia.org/wiki/Seven_Bridges_of_K%C3%B6nigsberg
4  My Google Scholar searches in June 2021 yielded very few studies of partial applications of small worlds in governance networks (e.g., Scheinert et al., 2015; Scholz et al. 2008; Zia et al., 2017). There were many more applications in business management (e.g., studies on the "small worlds" of corporate governance networks). There were even fewer applications of scale-free networks in governance networks.
5  His book was cited 1,125 times as of June 2021 (Google Scholar).
6  In Google Scholar, there were 4,005 citations of their work as of June 2021.
7  Cable News and COVID-19 Vaccine Compliance - Research Collection - ETH Z. https://www.research-collection.ethz.ch/handle/20.500.11850/496948. Center for Law & Economics Working Paper Series. Volume. 2021 (09). www.research-collection.ethz.chx
8  The Game is Not Yet Over, and Vaccines Still Matter: Lessons from a Study on Israel's COVID-19 Vaccination. www.brookings.edu/blog/up-front/2021/09/13/the-game-is-not-yet-over-and-vaccines-still-matter-lessons-from-a-study-on-israels-covid-19-vaccination/?utm_campaign=Brookings%20Brief&utm_medium=email&utm_content=159977144&utm_source=hs_email
9  Vaccine Misinformation and Social Media (ScienceDaily). www.sciencedaily.com/releases/2020/02/200217163004.htm

# 4 Complexity

Governance researchers observed that it is beyond the capacities of governments to solve collective problems in human societies and that multiple interdependent actors are involved in the processes of collective problem-solving. Social theorists of governance defined them as inclusive of both public policymaking and administration processes. Governance networks theorists and researchers developed typologies of these multiactor processes of policymaking and administration and studied the structured relations in them. Using social network analyses, they aimed to uncover the links between actors in governance networks and the structural properties of these networks. What is implicit, or sometimes explicit, in the conceptualizations of governance processes and governance networks is the understanding that these processes and structures are complex. That is because there are multiple and various kinds of interdependent actors (governmental organizations, nonprofits, and private organizations) involved in them and governance processes are self-organizing and dynamic (i.e., complex).

Just to clarify, self-organization and dynamics are key conceptual tools in complexity theory, but there are others (nonlinearity, emergence, and coevolution). I briefly discuss these complexity theory concepts in this chapter, particularly in the context of understanding governance networks. More elaborate discussions of complexity theory concepts can be found in my earlier book *A Complexity Theory for Public Policy* (2012a).

I should note here it is not only complexity theorists who recognize the complexity of relationships in nature and societies; many others do too. It is intuitively obvious that social processes are complex. By extension, it is not difficult to understand that governance processes are complex as well. Some public administration and public policy theorists explicitly state the complexity of their subject matters. A subset of them apply the concepts of complexity theory in their conceptualizations.

Kettl (2002, pp. 113–114) recognizes the complexity of non-bureaucratic forms of governance processes. Most policy theorists and practitioners understand that textbook definitions of public policy—such as Dye's (1992, p. 2) (it is "whatever governments do or not do") and Simon's (2007) ("what governments ought or ought not do, and does or does not

DOI: 10.4324/9781003053392-5

42  *Concepts*

do")—are oversimplifications of complex policy processes. Alternative theories to these simplifications have been developed.

For example, punctuated equilibrium theorists recognize that policy processes are complex in the sense that there are negative and positive feedback loops involved in them, which lead to punctuated (nonlinear) paths of change, from equilibria to nonequilibria (Baumgartner, Jones, & Mortensen, 2018, p. 56). Sabatier (2007) recognizes the complexity of policy processes and points out that they are composed of multiple actors (governmental agencies, legislatures, researchers, journalists, and judges), who have different values and priorities and act over time in various policy domains and on multiple levels of governmental institutions.

Elinor Ostrom (2005) articulated a more elaborate vision of the complexity of policy processes. She recognizes complexity as a general problem for policy theories (pp. 242–243). She defines the complexity first in terms of many variables that contribute to the workings of policy processes (p. 9). Second, she cites the multiple levels at which policies are made (federal, state, and local) (p. 13). Third, she recognizes that social/policy systems are in constant interactions with complex and dynamic ecological systems (p. 256). Fourth, and the most importantly, Ostrom proposes two frameworks to understand the complexity of policy processes and their interactions with other (e.g., ecological) systems: the institutional analysis and development framework and the social-ecological systems framework (E. Ostrom, 1990, 2005, 2009). In these frameworks, particularly in the former, she articulates a theory of the configurations of factors that enable or disable the processes of self-governing (self-organization) in common pool resources systems (pp. 244–245).

These theorists' recognitions of the complexity of policy processes are important, but each one conceptualizes complexity differently. Their conceptualizations do not add up to a coherent framework of understanding the complexity of public policy and administration processes. Elinor Ostrom's theory of self-organization in common pool resources and her framework of social-ecological systems are the most comprehensive ones. Even her frameworks do not include all potential contributions of complexity theory in a comprehensive understanding of governance processes.

It is my goal in this chapter to summarize complexity theory concepts and discuss their implications for governance processes. I begin with a definition of complexity and present a brief history of complex systems thinking. Then I define the key concepts of complexity theory (nonlinearity, self-organization, emergence, and coevolution). There is a separate section on the applications of these concepts in the case of COVID-19 pandemic.

## A Definition of Complexity

The concepts of complexity theory have long roots in human history, but only in recent decades they jelled into a relatively coherent system of ideas. Still, there is no completely articulated complexity theory yet, to the best

*Complexity* 43

of my knowledge. (For discussions of the lack of coherent theory, see Anderson, 1999; Dent, 1999; Guastello, 1995; Marion, 1999). There is no clear agreement on the definition of complexity and related concepts either (Mitchell, 2009, chapter 7). There is not even a clear agreement on what the name of the theory should be. A few related names have been used since the 1980s: "chaos theory," "study of dynamical systems," "nonlinear studies" (Gleick, 1987), the "science of complexity" (Prigogine & Stengers, 1984; Waldrop, 1992), "nonlinear paradigm" (Kiel, 1992), "the new sciences of complexity" (Kauffman, 1995), and "complex adaptive systems theory" (Anderson, 1999). More recently, the terms "complexity theory" and "complex adaptive systems" theory have gained more acceptance, as the increased uses of these terms in the Web of Science (see Table 1.1 in Chapter 1) indicate. Another concept that has gained traction is "complex networks" (see Table 1.1; also, Kickert et al., 1997; Latora et al., 2017).

I prefer to use the term "complexity theory," as I explained in my earlier book (Morçöl, 2012a). This term signifies not only the characterizations of complex systems but also an understanding of our knowledge of them. In other words, the term has ontological, epistemological, and methodological underpinnings and implications. These underpinnings and implications inform the conceptualizations I present in this book. I make occasional references to them, but I do not elaborate on them in this book, as much as I did in the previous book.

Among the conceptual tools used by complexity theory, systems, non-linearity, self-organization, emergence, and coevolution are the most applicable ones in studying governance networks. Just to give a brief preview, what makes a governance network (system) complex is not only in the large number of elements it is composed of, but also the differences among its components and particularly the nonlinearity in the relations among them. Think about the different kinds of actors involved in governance networks (public, nonprofit, private; individual, organizational, small, big) and the multiple dimensions on which they interact (legal, economical, personal/informal, etc.). There are self-organizational mechanisms in complex systems and their structural properties emerge through these mechanisms and their coevolution with other systems. Think of the spontaneous emergence of the governance network forms (see the previous chapter) from the interactions of these actors. I will get back to these concepts later in the chapter.

## Systems

Sawyer (2005) traces the history of complexity theory to systems theories. Capra (1996) notes that systems thinking emerged in several disciplines simultaneously in the 1920s. Particularly Ludwig von Bertalanffy's (1968) "general systems theory" of the mid-20th century is important to emphasize. His definition of systems is the most articulate basis of our current understanding of complex systems and their characteristics (nonlinearity, self-organization, emergence, and coevolution).

44 *Concepts*

In von Bertalanffy's definition, a system is composed of *interdependent parts* and together they constitute an *irreducible whole*. They cannot be assembled or disassembled mechanically. A system is also interrelated with other systems and it is part of a larger system.

To clarify what he meant by this definition, I should refer to his description two types of "complexes of elements" (pp. 54–57). In the first type of complexes, the elements can be isolated and their relations can be characterized in a summative manner. The elements of this type of complexes can be isolated in the sense that their properties (e.g., atomic weights and colors) and behaviors can be defined in isolation (independently of their contexts, relations with other elements). The characteristics of these complexes are summative in the sense that if we add up the numbers of their elements, we will always come up with the same total (regardless of their contexts, their relations with other elements). These complexes are not systems by von Bertalanffy's definition.

In his second type of complexes, the characteristics of the elements depend on their relations with other elements. They are "interdependent" and their relations are "strong" and "nonlinear" (p. 19). He calls this second type of complexes "systems." Because of the interdependencies among their elements, systems exhibit "emergent" (holistic, irreducible) properties. He points out that systems are holistic not only spatially (that the properties of a particular whole at a given time are irreducible to the properties of its elements at that time) but also temporally (i.e., the present behavior of the whole depends on its past behavior; pp. 56–57).

The spatial irreducibility is known today's complexity theory as "emergence." It is also concept used in sociology to refer to the macro-level (structural) properties of societies (such as culture and institutions), which can maintain their existence (semi-)independently of the properties and characteristics of their individual members. The dependence of present behavior of a particular societal whole on its past behavior is known as "path dependence" in complexity theory. I will get back to these concepts in the following sections and in Part II.

Von Bertalanffy does not differentiate between non-systems and systems in absolute terms. The differences are temporary and one type can turn into the other one. He uses two terms to signify these transitions: "progressive segregation" and "progressive centralization." Progressive segregation occurs when a system passes "from a state of wholeness to a state of independence of the elements. . . . [when] a unitary system splits up gradually into independent causal chains" (p. 68). Progressive centralization is the opposite: independent elements, whose relations are summative, become interdependent; a holistic complex of elements, a system, emerges. Biological organisms go through progressive centralization in natural evolution: certain organic molecules in a collection of molecules become more central, and this collection turns into an organism (p. 73).

From von Bertalanffy's definitions of concepts, we can draw the conclusions that (1) a system is a group of elements that are interdependent

*Complexity* 45

and that the properties of a system are not a mere sum of the properties of its elements, but they are holistic; (2) systemic relations are nonlinear; and (3) transitions between systems and non-systems can occur. These conceptualizations are the bases of the later conceptualizations of complex systems.

In the 1960s and 1970s, Jay Forrester and others applied systems conceptualizations in the social sciences. Forester applied them in his analyses of industrial dynamics (Forrester, 1961), urban dynamics (Forrester, 1969), and world dynamics (1971). In *Urban Dynamics*, he proposed that urban areas should be understood as complex systems that are composed of businesses, people, and houses, whose relations are facilitated by taxes, land-use density, and job availability. The dynamic interactions among these elements go through oscillating patterns and settle into equilibria in certain times. In this book, he specifically used the term "complex system" and defined it as "high-order, multiple-loop, nonlinear feedback structure" (p. 107). He noted that not only urban areas but also national governments, economies, and international trade as complex systems.

Applications of complex system concept and related analytical tools (such as systems dynamics modeling and agent-based modeling) proliferated in the following decades, particularly in urban studies. Several researchers studied urban evolution patterns using complexity theory concepts like "dissipative structures"[1] (Allen & Sanglier, 1981; Allen, 1982), "nonlinearity" (Allen, Sanglier, Engelen, & Boon, 1985; Allen, Engelen, & Sanglier, 1986), and "path dependency" (Engelen, 1988). Batty (2007) demonstrated how urban dynamics can be studied using the cellular automata and agent-based simulation, and fractal geometry models.[2]

The increased popularity of complexity concepts and methods since the 1990s can be observed also in the literature summary of "urban and regional studies" in Table 1.1 (Chapter 1). As the table shows, in public administration and policy studies, these applications are less frequent, but a few works should be cited here. Kiel's (1994) illustrations of chaos theory applications and Comfort's (1999) self-organizations in complex systems were the early examples. In the 2000s, more researchers and theorists applied various complexity concepts (see the journal article literature summary in Figure 1.3). The book-length applications include Gerrits (2008, 2012), Geyer and Rihani (2010), Morçöl (2012); Rhodes, Murphy, Muir, and Murray (2011), and Teisman, van Buuren, and Gerrits (2009).

### Systemness

Von Bertalanffy's (1968) characterization of general systems (that they are composed of elements) should be modified, or at least qualified, for social systems, like governance systems (networks). That is because the "elements" in social systems are human beings with individual cognitions that are shaped in cultural belief systems and values. Social systems are constituted by the shared cognitions and actions of these individuals.

46  *Concepts*

Giddens's (1984) conceptualizations of "system integration" and "systemness" capture these characteristics of social systems. In his formulation, these systems are comprised of "situated activities of human agents, reproduced across time and space" (p. 25). So, a key issue is how actors see themselves and others, and how they act based on these perceptions will determine whether there is a system or not and how it is shaped. Think of the members of an "advocacy coalition" (Sabatier & Jenkins-Smith, 1993). The coalition is a system to the extent that its members perceive each other as having similar values on the policy issue as their own and that they act together based on such perceptions.

A certain "complex of elements," to use von Bertalanffy's term, is a system only when it is situated within its environment, according to Giddens. Its behaviors depend on this situatedness, and the system should be understood in the context of its relations with its environment. This environment is defined both spatially (geographically) and temporally. Think of the policy positions and actions of the advocates and opponents of the mask and vaccination mandates during the COVID-19 pandemic They were situated within a cultural, political, economic, and institutional environments. The cultural environment in the United States affected not only the politics in this country but also the reactions to governmental policies like the mask and vaccine mandates. The "libertarian" worldviews affected some in the United States not only for their affiliation with a political party, Republican Party, but also their resistance to the mandates. These libertarian values are spatially (geographically) more concentrated in the South, Midwest, and West of the country and rural communities.[3] These geographical concentrations are not accidental. The belief systems that led to the anti-vaccine sentiments were maintained by generations of individuals and transmitted from one generation to the next.

But the reader may justifiably argue that these geographical and temporal definitions are oversimplifications. Not all rural Midwesterners were opponents of mask or vaccine mandates, for example. Indeed, that is why we cannot define them as an advocacy coalition (a system) whose boundaries are fixed. That is why systems cannot be defined in categorical terms, as both von Bertalanffy (1968) and Giddens (1984) recognize.

Giddens's use of the term *systemness*, rather than *system*, is important in this sense. In his view, a system should not be defined in dichotomous terms: either there is a system or not. (Remember that von Bertalanffy also defined systems in degrees.) Giddens argues that to the extent that the activities of human actors are situated in an environment and to the degree that these activities are reproduced across time and space, we can say that they constitute a social system. Therefore, a collection of relationships among a group of human actors may be *more or less systemic*. Then how do we determine to what extent they are systemic? To what extent is there a system?

Giddens's two other concepts, *social integration* and *system integration*, help researchers discern the degree of reproduction of actors' activities in a

*Complexity* 47

given situation. He defines social integration as "reciprocity between *actors in contexts of co-presence*" and system integration as "reciprocity between actors *or collectivities across extended time-space*" [emphases added] (p. 28). In his definition, social integration signifies the co-presence of actors in the form of face-to-face relations (p. 28). Family relations and kinship relations are typical examples of social integration. (Think of how family members affected each other's view on the efficacy of COVID-19 vaccines.) System integration differs from this in the sense that it does not require face-to-face presence of actors, but it still does require sustained interdependency relations over time, whether these relations are direct or indirect. National economies and societies are examples of this. Also think of the effects of social media, particularly the spread of disinformation and misinformation about vaccines, in shaping the views of individuals and communities and their resistance to the vaccines or acceptance of them.[4]

The concepts of social integration and system integration are tools we can use to observe the degree of systemness in a given situation. To the extent that the relations of actors in a given situation are interdependent and to the extent that they are sustained, we can say that they are integrated and that there is a system. System integration is typical for governance networks: Actors may be in different locations and yet they are in interdependent relationships—most typically interdependent on each other's resources (Compston, 2009, pp. 18–19). To the extent that the activities of individual actors and organizations are integrated (i.e., reciprocated and reproduced across time and space), they constitute a governance system or governance network. Did the COVID-19 vaccine hesitance (or resistance) constitute a system? The answer is not categorical. To the extent that these actors were either socially or systemically integrated (they were in sustained face-to-face interactions or in interactions through social media) they constituted systems.

Some concepts and tools of social network analysis can be used to determine the level of systemness in a governance process. Social network analysts define networks in relational terms: The unit of analysis is not an individual actor, but the relations among actors. They look for patterns that emerge from such relationships using tools like centralization, density, fragmentation, and clustering coefficient (Wasserman & Faust, 1994; Knoke & Yang, 2008). These are tools of measuring levels of integration, or cohesion, in networks.

To what extent should the reciprocal activities of individual and collective actors be integrated to be considered a governance system? Gerrits's (2008) conceptualization of "policy action systems" helps answer this question. He proposes to define "policy action systems" in two broad categories based on the degree of their integration: "singular" and "composite" policy action systems. These are two different responses to the uncertainties policy actors face, according to Gerrits. In the case of a singular policy action system, multiple policy actors coalesce around common and few goals and engage in coherent patterns of action. In the case of a

48   *Concepts*

composite policy action system, actors are not united in their goals and the scope of their activities is open (pp. 209–214). Singular systems are highly integrated, or they have higher degrees of systemness, and composite systems are less integrated, or they have lower degrees of systemness.

Composite policy action systems are more common, and singular systems are rare in increasingly networked societies of our times, but on some occasions, actors can coalesce around single goals. For example, when there are strong challenges to the collective well-being of a pluralistic society (e.g., a war and unique challenges like the September 11, 2001, attacks in the United States), singular policy systems emerge. To what extent a particular policy action system is composite or singular an empirical question.

### Systems and Networks

Before I move on to next important concept of complexity theory, I want to clarify my use of the terms systems and networks interchangeably. To underscores why this is an issue, let us remember Figure 1.3 (Chapter 1). The figure shows that the keywords "governance networks" and "complex adaptive systems" were used in two separate literatures and they began to connect only in the 2010s. Table 1.1 shows that public administration and political science literatures separated themselves from complex systems studies that were prevalent in other fields. So, are the terms "network" and "system" really different?

Colander and Kupers (2014) note: "Many complex systems can be modeled as networks or graphs" (p. 125). This suggests that networks are models of systems, which is a fair observation, but it does not mean that these two are categorically different concepts. The commonality between the two concepts rests on the implicit or explicit references of both systems theorists and network scientists (including social network analysts) to complexity.

Barabási (2002), a prominent network theorist, views networks as "skeletons of complexity" (p. 222). Governance network theorists emphasize that complexity is the major characteristic of networks. Public service delivery networks are structurally complex, according to Klijn (1997). He points out that institutional or policy network theories, whose roots are in Allison's, Lindblom's, Cohen's, Kingdon's, and March and Olsen's process models of policymaking, recognize the complexity of policy processes. Bresser and O'Toole (1998) argue that networks may be relatively more or less complex and the degree of complexity of a network is determined by the degree of cohesion and degree of interconnectedness among its elements.

Both network and complexity theorists recognize that there are interdependency relations among the actors of a social network and the elements of a system. O'Toole (1997), for example, defines networks as "structures of interdependence involving multiple organizations or parts thereof, where one unit is not merely the formal subordinate of the others in some larger hierarchical arrangement" (p. 45). Bresser and O'Toole point out that interconnectedness refers to (a) the contacts between actors within the relevant policy formation process and (b) the relationships between them outside the policy process.

In summary, there are subtle and technical differences between the uses of the terms system and networks in the literature, but they can be used interchangeably without losing much conceptual clarity or analytical power. In this book, I use these terms and related concepts, such as system elements and network actors or agents, interchangeably, unless there are context-specific differences in their meanings.

## Multiplicity, Variations, and Nonlinearity

It makes intuitive sense that all systems system (an entity, group of individuals, a set of relationships) are complex, particularly when we observe that there are many elements (parts, individual human beings, etc.) in them. But only many elements do not make the system complex. Instead, the variations in the characteristics of its elements and their interrelationships make it simple or complex. For example, if there are thousands of identical boxes of identical size and identical contents, together they are not a complex system. It is not a complex job of moving them from one location to another, for example. That would be a tedious, repetitive, and time-consuming task, but not complex. The mover would not have to think about various contingencies and combinations of factors in the process. If the sizes and contents of the boxes are different, then their relationships with each other would not be uniform. The mover may not be able to stack them up neatly; instead, they will have to think about various combinations of methods to retrieve, transport, and deliver the boxes.

Compare this example to governance networks. The definitions and descriptions of governance and governance networks in the previous chapters make it clear that not only are there large number of actors in them, but also, they are not uniform in their sizes, capacities, and how they work. Various governmental organizations (e.g., federal, state, and local governments), nonprofits, and private organizations that constitute governance networks have various characteristics, and their relationships are not uniform. For example, they are not organized in clear and uniform hierarchical relationships. There may be some hierarchies (due to power differentials among them), as well as more lateral and interdependent (networked) relationships in them. These multitude of forms of relationships make them complex systems.

An important aspect of the relationships in complex policy networks is that their actors have various and dynamic perceptions of each other and their environments and various and dynamic preferences (Klijn, 1997, pp. 16–17). I will come back to the issue of actor perceptions and preferences in Chapter 6, where I discuss different kinds of actors (or agents): reactive and cognitive actors. For now, it is important to stress that

50  *Concepts*

these perceptions and preferences make the relationships among the actors in human systems (e.g., governance networks) even more complex.

Complexity theorists use a conceptual tool to describe the relationships among the actors in complex systems: *nonlinearity*. The simplest way to think about nonlinearity is to compare it to proportionality and linearity. Think about a straight line that represents a proportionate relationship between two variables. For example, let's assume that increasing the number of police officers in a neighborhood by one will drop the number of crimes by two. The mathematical equation for this relationship is as follows.

*Number of crimes = –2 × Number of police officers*

Can we expect this kind of proportionality in public policies? Intuitively, we can say that many other factors can mitigate the relationship between the number of officers and the number of criminal acts. A study by Princeton University researchers found, for example, that after increasing the number of officers beyond a certain level, the number of crimes may not drop anymore.[5] So, the relationship between the two is not linear.

Nonlinear relations can go both ways. Complexity researchers use the concept *feedback loops* to describe these bidirectional relationships. Meadows (2008) defines negative feedback as a "balancing feedback loop" in the sense that it dampens (checks, balances) the trends that disrupt the typical patterns (i.e., "aberrant behavior"). Positive feedbacks are "reinforcing feedback loops"; they amplify the trends that disrupt patterns and perpetuate aberrant behaviors (p. 31). Meadows illustrates the effects of positive feedback with the example of growth in bank savings at different interest rates: a small incremental change the interest rate can cause exponentially higher growth in the savings in the long term (p. 32). In other words, positive feedback loops generate disproportional (nonlinear) consequences in systemic relations. Because of these nonlinearities, positive feedback loops can cause runaway growth in systems. In an economic system, income growth stimulates higher inflation, which in turn stimulates income growth; for a while and to an extent, this may be healthy and desirable, but at one point this positive feedback loop can cause the behavior of the economic system to run out of control and the system may crash.

An example of the applications of feedback loops in public policy theory is Baumgartner and Jones's *punctuated equilibrium theory* (True, Jones, & Baumgartner, 2007, p. 157). In this theory, American policy processes are depicted as complex interactive systems. In these processes, fragmented and overlapping institutions and policy actors play roles. These complex systems are mostly static (they are in equilibria), but occasionally they undergo large-scale, drastic changes, which theorists characterize as "punctuations" in an equilibrium. Negative feedback loops stabilize the system, whereas positive feedback loops generate the punctuations.

Baumgartner and Jones (2002) cite two positive feedback mechanisms in the American policy processes: attention shifting and mimicking. People have limited attention spans and therefore they can focus on certain policy issues at a time and use information shortcuts in decision-making. Their attentions and or informational shortcuts may shift at those times when salient policy issues change due to triggering events. Policy venues and policy images change during those times. Because people also tend to mimic others' behaviors, this can have an amplifying effect during the times when attentions are shifted. Mimicking can lead to fads, "feeding frenzy," and "bandwagon effects."

Forester (1969) observed that both forms of feedback loops are non-linear in particularly the urban systems he studied. He points out that because of the multiple loop alignments in them, complex systems are highly insensitive to external efforts to change their behaviors (p. 108). This insensitivity to external efforts is an important element in understanding *self-organization*, another key concept of complexity theory and the topic of the next section.

## Self-Organization

### *A Historical Background*

If a system is insensitive to external interventions, as Forester (1969) observes, does this mean that it can organize its internal affairs, without an intervention by an external force or actor? This is the problem of self-organization, which in its most abstract and generic form can be formulated as: Do systems behave/move because of external events or internal mechanisms? More specifically, think about the actors in governance networks: Can they self-organize (and self-govern), or is an external authority is needed to organize them? Philosophers and scientists tried to answer these questions for millennia, philosophically and with scientific evidence, particularly in the areas of thermodynamics, biological evolution, and collective problem-solving in human societies. In this section, I briefly summarize these developments and conclude the section with a discussion of the most sophisticated and cogent refinement of the concept of self-organization: Elinor Ostrom's institutional analysis and development framework.

Complexity theorists did not invent the concept of self-organization. They are not only ones who use the concept either. The dichotomous notions of external (or central) direction versus spontaneity (self-organization) are as old as philosophical thinking. These notions coevolved over millennia and many schools of thought contributed to their coevolution. Complexity theorists refined the notion of self-organization and applied it in a wide range of areas of study, from physics to evolutionary biology and collective problem-solving in human societies.

The roots of the philosophical debates on the question "do systems behave/move because of external events or internal mechanisms" can be traced back to the ancient Greek philosophy. Aristotle's notion of "purposive finality of nature" is the earliest example of the "internal mechanism"

52   *Concepts*

theories (Knodt, 1995). In the 18th century, Immanuel Kant reformulated this notion as "inner teleology" or "internal purposes" (Taylor, 2001, pp. 84–93). The notions of purposive finality and inner teleology lost their primacy in philosophical thinking, in the 18th, 19th, and 20th centuries, as Newtonian science and logical positivism prevailed in this period (Morçöl, 2002, chap. 2).

### Complexity Theory and Self-Organization

The concepts of "self-organization" and "spontaneous emergence" regained popularity in the mid-20th century, as a result of the advances in cybernetics, general systems theory, and neural networks (Capra, 1996, p. 22). Complexity theorists contributed to these formulations by refining the general characteristics and mechanisms of self-organization in systems' evolutions. A key question they aimed to answer was this: Do systems self-organize toward more and higher-level order, or does self-organizational processes lead to system disintegration (Morçöl, 2012a, pp. 100–101)?

Anderson (1999) describes self-organization as a movement toward orderliness: "[C]omplex systems exhibit 'self-organizing' behavior: starting in a random state, they usually evolve toward order instead of disorder" (p. 218). Similarly, evolutionary biologist Stuart Kauffman (1993, 1995) argues that natural evolution is not an accidental process; because of the inner self-organizing mechanisms in natural systems, more complex orderliness emerges over time. He states: "[M]atter's incessant attempts to organize itself into ever more complex structures, even in the face of the incessant forces of dissolution described by the second law of thermodynamics" (Kauffman's interview quoted in Waldrop, 1992, p. 102).

Physicist Ilya Prigogine has a different take on the self-organizational processes in nature. He observes that thermodynamical systems exhibit self-organizational properties, but self-organizational processes in them do not always generate orderliness. In fact, these systems spontaneously evolve toward "far from equilibrium" conditions, under which either systemic properties break down (Prigogine uses the term "dissipation" for this) or new systemic properties emerge (Prigogine & Stengers, 1984; Nicolis & Prigogine, 1989; Prigogine, 1997).

Meadows (2008) identifies negative (balancing) and positive (reinforcing) feedback loops as the engines of self-organization and system dynamics. Through these loops, a system can "cause" its own behavior (p. 34). If negative feedback loops are predominant in a system, it will be more stable. If positive feedback loops are predominant, the exponential growth or decline in a system can cause crashing systemic relations and transforming one set of systemic relations to another set of relations. So, negative feedback is the source of orderly self-organization and positive feedback is the source of what Prigogine calls "dissipation" of a system and the emergence of a new system.

*Complexity* 53

In this summary of the complexity theory literature, we can observe the key contributions of complexity theorists to the general scientific understanding of self-organization. First, it is natural, not exceptional: Natural systems do not need external drives to organize; they can organize themselves. Second, self-organizational processes can lead to the breakdown of a system, or they can move it to a new organizational form. Third, negative and positive feedback loops in systems instigate two different kinds of self-organization: The former leads to a stable system, whereas the latter creates the dynamics of systemic change (dissipation or the emergence of a new order). The general observations are applicable to social systems in general, and governance networks in particular, which I discuss next.

### Self-Organization in Governance Networks

There are applications of the concepts of self-organization and feedback loops in the literatures on public policy and governance networks. The general theme in these applications is that self-organization is normal (not exceptional) in governance systems (networks). The discussions in this section are about the literature that are related to this theme. Forrester (1969) demonstrated the roles of feedback loops in self-organizing urban systems, as I noted earlier. There are a few passing references to the concept of dissipative structures in the literatures on public administration and economics (e.g., Kiel, 1994; Rosser, 2000), but there are no elaborate conceptualizations of dissipative structures in social systems in general and governance networks in particular.

Some authors applied the concept of self-organization in understanding governance processes in general and pointed to the limited roles of governmental actors in them. Salzano (2008) argues that the outcomes of public policies are not easily predictable or controllable because of the self-organizational and nonlinear relations among the actors in policy systems. That is why the policy actions by governmental actors should not be conceptualized as the causes of policy outcomes. Instead, we should recognize that these actors can at best "nudge" policy/governance systems toward "socially desirable states" (Zia et al., 2014). The aim of a government's policy intervention should not be to reach a pre-determined goal, but to enable the "target system to enhance…its capacity for self-steering" (Stewart & Ayres, 2001, p. 87). The success of a policy intervention should be determined in terms of how much it enhances the self-organizing capability of a social system.

These conceptualizations are insightful, but they should be refined and operationalized to be useful. Elinor Ostrom's (1990, 2005) institutional analysis and development (IAD) framework is the best example of how that can be done. Hers is the most comprehensive and articulate example of the applications of self-organization (or self-governance) in collective

## 54  Concepts

problem-solving.[6] Her primary contribution to our understanding of self-organization is to show that self-organization is not uniform concept, but it is conditional. She formulated the conditions and forms of self-organization in real-life collective problem-solving.

She shares complexity theorists' understanding that self-organization is normal, not exceptional. She aims to show that groups of individuals are capable of organizing themselves, particularly in their use of commonly shared resources, without an interference by external authorities (e.g., the state). Her studies on self-organization were inspired by her early skepticism of Garret Hardin's (1968) "Tragedy of Commons" conjecture.[7] As I noted in Chapter 2, in this conjecture, the actions of selfish individuals (herders) lead to the destruction of common resources (pasture). The inference one can make, then, is that the problem could be solved by the intervention of an external force, the government. Ostrom's objection to Hardin's conjecture is that it is an abstract conjecture, which is not related to real-life individuals or their relationships. Hardin describes an imaginary wide-open pasture where unnamed abstract herders, with no social histories or connections to each other, let their cattle graze as much as they could consume. These imaginary individuals are purely selfish and helpless and they would need an external authority (government) to come in to regulate their affairs.

To Ostrom, Hardin's "parable" is an example of the simplified thinking that permeates most classical economics and public administration theories. These oversimplifications are understandable to some degree, she thinks, because social scientists want to formulate simplified and abstract representations of reality to be able to understand and solve social problems. These oversimplified models may work sometimes, but not in most other times, because social problems are always complex.

People are not the abstract herders as they are described in Hardin's conjecture. Real human beings are cognitive individuals with personalities and cultural values, which lead them to connect with each other, understand each other, sometimes fight each other, and other times cooperate with each other. Usually, the oversimplified abstractions about individual human behaviors (that they are selfish and incapable of their collective affairs) are coupled with the assumption that governments are capable of objectively analyzing social problems, producing desired outcomes, and managing social resources for people (Ostrom, 2005, p. 220).

Public choice theorists such as Tullock (1979) dispute this assumption. They do not view governments as singular actors that could analyze and solve problems. Instead, governments are composed of individuals who are self-seeking actors, just like all other individuals. A government, therefore, cannot be the sole protector of the public interest. Tullock argues that public interest is the aggregated outcome of the actions of all self-seeking actors—governmental and nongovernmental (p. 31).

Ostrom follows this line of thinking in general, but she goes beyond the simplifications of the public choice theory, as I discussed elsewhere (Morçöl,

2014). She agrees that public interest can arise from the interactions of self-seeking individuals, but these governmental and nongovernmental actors are not necessarily fully rational in their preferences and actions. They can solve their collective problems, without an external interference or central planning, but they can do so under certain conditions. She and her colleagues demonstrated with their empirical studies that there are conditions that determine whether, and to what extent, individual actors can self-organize.

Ostrom identified and codified the conditions of self-organization in collective action processes, particularly in the management of common pool resources (CPRs). She defines a CPR as a "natural or man-made resource system that is sufficiently large as to make costly (but not impossible) to exclude potential beneficiaries from obtaining benefits from its use" (Ostrom, 1990, p. 30). Examples of CPRs are inland fisheries, meadows, forests, other common lands, and irrigation systems in agricultural areas (pp. 19–20, 61–88). She studied CPR situations particularly because, she notes, the processes of self-organization and self-governance are easier to observe in them compared to many others (p. 29). She later generalized her findings about CPRs to other collective action problems (Ostrom, 2005).

Ostrom (1990) poses this question: How come some individuals choose to work together and govern themselves, rather than each individual trying to maximize their own interest individually and ignoring others'? For example, how come the herders in a pasture work together, without external guidance or coercion? Are there conditions that enable them to do so?

She identifies two sets of conditions that determine whether individuals will participate in self-organizational collective problem-solving processes. The first set are the conditions that enable for individuals to form self-organizing institutions (enduring organizational forms). The second set are the conditions that enable them to maintain such institutions.

In the first set, there are two subsets of conditions: the attributes of resources available to appropriators (individual participants) and the attributes of the appropriators (individual participants) (Ostrom, 2005, pp. 244–245). The conditions in the first subset (*attributes of resources*) are: There are sufficiently *large resources* and a good *chance to improve them;* there are *reliable and valid indicators* of the conditions of resources available to the participants at a relatively *low cost*; and the resource system is sufficiently small so that the participants can develop accurate knowledge of the boundaries of the system (pp. 247–248). The conditions of the second subset (*attributes of appropriators*) are: The CPR system is *salient enough for their livelihood or their achievement of important social or religious values* so that they will be motivated to self-organize; they have sufficiently *common understanding* of the CPR system and how their actions will affect the system; appropriators have *"sufficiently low discount rate"* in relation to their future benefits and costs for participating in a self-governing system; *they trust each other* for keeping promises and reciprocating their actions; appropriators have enough *autonomy to carry out*

## 56  *Concepts*

*their actions* vis-a-vis "external authorities" (governmental authorities); and they should have *organizational experience and leadership skills* gained from earlier experiences (pp. 248–251). Combinations of the availability of the conditions in these two subsets will determine to what extent a self-organizing system can be established.

Once a self-governing system is established, it should be maintained. Ostrom formulated the conditions for self-governing CPR institutions to endure for a long period of time (1990, pp. 90–102), what she later called the "design principles for long-enduring institutions for governing sustainable resources" (2005, p. 259). She points to "trust and reciprocity levels among the participants" as important factors that will determine whether they will comply with the rules of the self-organized institutions and thus whether the institutions can be maintained. Ostrom observes that those systems in which participants select their own monitors of compliance—rather than external forces, such as governments, doing that—are more likely to survive for long periods of time (p. 265), as well as those in which "graduated sanctions" applied to rule breakers and those that have mechanisms of conflict resolution (pp. 265–268).

Elinor Ostrom's elaborate conceptualization of the conditions of self-organization led to many empirical studies and studies on conceptual refinements. Just to gain an understanding of the degree of interest in her IAD framework in general, I counted 99 publications between 1990 and 2000, 1,080 between 2001 and 2010, and 4,240 between 2011 and 2020 on this topic in Google Scholar.

Feiock and his colleagues' studies are illustrative of the applications of Ostrom's framework. They aimed to expand Ostrom's framework and identify the conditions of, barriers to, self-organization among organizational actors (not individual actors), particularly in metropolitan governance processes. In his study of the emergence, evolution, and performance of regional self-governance institutions, Feiock (2009) identified the limitations of self-organizing mechanisms in this context. Feiock, Steinacker, & Park (2009), investigated why some local governments engage in cooperative agreements while others do not, with a focus on transaction obstacles, such as bargaining, information, agency, enforcement, and division problems. In a more elaborate study, Feiock (2013) conceptualized collaborative mechanisms (e.g., informal networks, contracts, mandated agreements, councils of governments) and their configurations in different contexts.

## Emergence

Emergence is another concept that is relevant to conceptualizing governance networks. This concept is deeply ingrained in systems thinking in general and complexity theory in particular. The reader will remember from an earlier section that von Bertalanffy (1968) conceptualized systems as "complexes" that are composed of interdependent elements and that these complexes exhibit "emergent" (holistic, irreducible) properties. So, emergence is an essential part of the definition of a system. It is also a very concept in complexity theory. Despite its importance in systems thinking and complexity theory, this section on emergence is short. I discuss emergence comprehensively in Part II, particularly Chapters 7 and 8, where its relevancy and significance is more obvious.

For now, it will be sufficient to stress that emergence is interwoven with three concepts of complexity theory I have covered so far. (All three are covered in Part II.) The first one is the holism of systems. Systems have holistic properties that relate to the properties of its constituents but still different from them. In Capra's (1996) words, a system is an "integrated whole whose essential properties emerge from the relationships between its parts"; these properties are not reducible to the properties of the parts of the system (p. 30).

The second concept emergence is related to is self-organization. The holistic properties of a system emerge through self-organizational mechanisms. Those mechanisms, such as negative and positive feedback loops, have nonlinear effects. The micro–macro problem, which I present as the core problems of the complex governance networks conceptualization in Chapter 5, is about how emergence works in social systems, in general, and complex governance networks, in particular.

## Coevolution

The last concept of complexity theory that is directly relevant to conceptualizing complex governance networks is coevolution. Self-organizing systems that have emergent properties are not isolated from their environments, which consist of other self-organizing systems that have emergent properties. All these systems coevolve. Then an important question is, what are the mechanisms of, or patterns in, this coevolution?

Evolutionary biologists Paul Ehrlich and Peter Raven (1964) coined the term "coevolution" to refer to their observation that biological evolution does not happen only through species adapting to their environments by random mutations. Instead, species coevolve in reciprocal relationships with each other.

Another evolutionary biologist Stuart Kauffman (1995, pp. 207–208) proposes a similar conceptualization: It is not only a species that evolves to adapt to its environment but the environment evolves as well. That is because the environment of a species is composed of other species. "Each organism lives in the niche created by other organisms, each seeking its own living blindly creates the modes of living for the others" (p. 207). Kauffman posits that these complex coevolutionary processes also lead to changes in the mechanisms and patterns of coevolution. In other words, the "rules of the coevolutionary game" change as well.

He proposed the concept of "fitness landscapes," to describe coevolutionary processes. The species must fit the landscapes around them.

## 58 Concepts

Over the billions of years of the coevolutionary processes of the complex organisms on our planet, species kept "climbing up fitness landscapes toward peaks of high fitness" (p. 161), but those landscapes themselves also changed. So, fitness landscapes coevolved with species and, in the long run, the way a particular landscape and the species interacted (mechanisms of coevolution) changed. "The very process of coevolution itself evolves" (p. 208).

An example Kauffman (1995) cites is "complementary economies" (e.g., cars and gasoline as consumption complementarities).

> Goods and services in an economy live in the niches afforded by other goods and services.... [We] make a living by creating and selling goods and services that make economic sense in the niches afforded by other goods and services.
>
> (p. 240)

As goods and services coevolve, so do the patterns of their interactions. Technologies coevolve too. The developments in the hardware technology of desktop personal computers enabled the Internet to evolve from a limited network of communications into a worldwide web. In turn, the capabilities of the Internet (electronic mail and particularly electronic commerce) provided the niche for the hardware of personal computers to evolve into hybrids like the wireless telephones and handheld devices (and now a hybrid of telephones and telephones) (pp. 279–284).

Kauffman (1995) points out that coevolution is a self-organizational process; it does not need an external choreographer (p. 246) and that this self-organizational coevolutionary process happens at the "edge of chaos" (p. 302).[8] Biological systems have the tendency to evolve to the edge of chaos, at which point they undergo phase transitions into more complex states.

He also makes the point that coevolutionary processes do not always mutually support each other (they may not be harmonious); coevolving species may harm or even destroy each other. Kauffman gives the example of viruses. Viruses can make their hosts sick and even kill them, not intentionally though. They do not intend, because they are not even organisms in the strict sense of the word. They are nothing more than single-stranded RNA molecules. These simple and mindless molecules coevolved through being transmitted from one host (e.g., individual human being) to another. As they are transmitted, viruses may become more contagious and lethal. In their interactions with humans and other host organisms, they evolve (through mutations) and force the immune systems of their hosts to adapt (to survive). Over time, both the virus "species" and the host species (e.g., humans) become different (they coevolve) in some respects as a result of their interactions. This is a description of the SARS-CoV-2 virus, which caused the COVID-19 pandemic as well, obviously. I will come back to the issue of viruses in the context of the COVID-19 pandemic in the next section.

Some complexity theorists developed specific models of the mechanisms of coevolutionary processes. One of those mechanisms is feedback loops between coevolving systems. Through feedback loops systems modify their behaviors and reorganize (Gell-Mann as cited in Taylor, 2001, pp. 166–168). Another, and more specific, model is Kauffman's (1995) "NK model," which describes how different degrees of "ruggedness of landscapes" emerge. The ruggedness is a function of the number of parts constituting the evolving organism ($N$) and the amount of interconnectedness among the parts ($K$). When $K=N-1$ the landscape is very jagged. As $K$ increases from 0 to $N-1$, ruggedness increases (pp. 301–302).

These models have been applied only partly in the policy/governance networks literature, primarily by a group of Dutch scholars (Gerrits, 2008, 2010; Gerrits, Marks, & Van Buuren, 2009; Van Buuren, Gerrits, & Marks, 2009). The most important insight in these applications is that natural systems cannot be controlled by goal-oriented and intentionally designed policy systems. Policy analysts and policymakers may think that they can control natural forces by their policies and intentional acts, but Gerrits (2008) shows that this control-oriented approach to natural systems can backfire.

In his case studies of the estuaries in Germany, Netherlands, and Belgium, in the late 1990s and early 2000s, he demonstrates that the interactions between the policy systems (policymakers' decisions and actions) and the natural systems in these cases were coevolutionary. As the policymakers deepened the estuaries to allow larger ships access to the ports around them, the natural systems around them responded by increasing sediment accumulation and oxygen depletion in their basins (pp. 103–107). Gerrits (2008) demonstrates how the feedback loops between the determined the path of their coevolutionary processes. In the Unterelbe case, the efforts to deepen the estuary triggered a positive feedback loop. These efforts shifted the tidal regime in the harbor basin. The increased upstream transportation of the sediments resulted in increased sedimentation; consequently, it became necessary to increase dredging to maintain the harbor basin at the desired depth (p. 108).

In the section on systemness, earlier in this chapter, I mentioned in Gerrits's conceptualizations of two kinds of policy systems—singular and composite. They lead to two different kinds of consequences in coevolutionary processes. Singular policy action systems are closed to information coming from their environments. They are "self-referential" in the sense that they keep reinforcing their beliefs about the way things work in their environments and they set their policy goals by communicating only with those actors who support their own views and goals. Because of their self-referentiality, these systems are less likely to be successful, because they do not "fit" their environments. Composite policy action systems are

## 60    Concepts

more open to alternative views, including the views of their opponents. Consequently, they can gain a better understanding of their environments and their coevolutions with natural and other systems around them are more successful.

An example of the self-referentiality of policy systems is illustrated in a *New York Times* story.[9] In the US Congress, the representatives and senators who were inclined to downplay the connections between carbon dioxide emissions by human beings and global warming kept inviting global warming skeptics, who were a small minority in the scientific community, to Congressional hearings. They ignored most scientists, who thought that global warming was real, it was caused by the carbon dioxide emissions by humans, and it would have dire consequences. This singular policy system self-referentially reproduced itself and did not allow the US federal government to make major policy changes in this area.

## Complexity and COVID-19

In this section, I discuss the COVID-19 pandemic to illustrate the concepts of complexity theory covered in the previous sections. I do not follow the order of the previous sections here. I begin with coevolution, that last topic, because it is the most intuitively relevant one. It is followed by sections on defining systems, nonlinearity, and self-organization.

### *Coevolution: A Macro View of the Pandemic*

Humans and viruses have coevolved for a long period of time. Let us remember Kauffman's (1995) description of the coevolution of viruses with humans in the previous section. As these single-stranded RNA molecules are transmitted from one human to another, they may become more contagious and lethal. We have seen in this in the case of the SARS-CoV-2 coronavirus. It evolved in many variants, which were labeled with the letters of the Greek alphabet (Alpha, Beta, Gamma, Delta, Mu, and Omicron) Among these variants, some were more contagious and lethal (e.g., Delta) and one was more contagious but not more lethal (Omicron). As of this writing, the pandemic was ongoing, so it was not clear when and how the immune systems of humans would adapt to "live with" this coronavirus. These immune systems had adapted to live with other viruses, like many coronaviruses that cause common cold and others that cause various forms of influenza. There were some scientific estimates that humans would develop "herd immunity" to SARS-CoV-2, at which point COVID-19 would become an endemic, rather than pandemic, in 2022 or 2023.[10] That was when the two systems would continue their coevolution without the coronavirus killing its hosts as much as it did in the pandemic phase.

Another important part of this coevolutionary story is that viruses can mutate as they "jump" from one species to another (i.e., zoonotic transmission).[11] The coronavirus that caused the COVID-19 pandemic likely

*Complexity* 61

jumped from a bat, a pangolin, or other animal to humans at the Wuhan "wet market," where such "exotic animals" are sold routinely.[12] So, there are multiple complex biological systems (including human biological system) that interact, and conceivably coevolve, with each other and with complex human social systems.

There is another way humans and viruses coevolve. The ancestors of humans encountered viruses hundreds of millions of years ago and many of them died from viral infections, but some survived and a specific type of viruses, retroviruses, entered their genes. Soulmi and his colleagues' (2021) study shows that as early as 20,000 years ago a coronavirus that appeared in East Asia entered human bodies and left its fragments in the human genome. This way viruses have become parts of humans; the biological systems of humans and viruses coevolved for hundreds of thousands of years.[13]

Pandemics are more specific type of interactions between humans and viruses, or bacteria. During pandemics, not only humans and these pathogens interact biologically but also the social systems of humans interact with the pathogens. How do the concepts of complexity theory help us understand these systemic interactions?

To answer this question, let's begin with a definition of pandemics. They are viral and bacterial infections that are not contained in certain geographical locations; they spread beyond the borders of communities, countries, and continents. Why did viruses, which have existed at least for hundreds of millions of years, and interacted with humans for tens (or hundreds) of thousands of years, began to spread at pandemic levels among human societies and killed large numbers in short periods of time only in the last two millennia?

Harper's (2021a, 2021b) explanation is that viruses got the opportunity to spread at pandemic levels because of the opportunities presented to them as human societies became more interconnected and their interactions with animal species increased. In other words, the evolutions of social systems enabled pandemics. For example, the Roman Empire had become a governing system whose territory stretched from Britain to Egypt during the Antonine Plague (165–180 AD). Before that period, the empire had built and secured trade routes that extended within its territory around the Mediterranean Sea (Middle East and Northern Africa) and connected them to far-away lands, like China. The trade across the vast territories created opportunities for the virus that caused the Antonine Plague, which was likely to be an early ancestor of the smallpox virus, to spread quickly and infect and kill humans at large numbers.

We can conclude that human social evolution enabled the smallpox virus to replicate itself at much faster rates than that was possible before. The coevolution of these two systems (one social and one biological) does not depend only on the speed of the spread. As viruses spread from one organism (e.g., a human) to another, they can also mutate (evolve) and become more infectious, as its more lethal variants appear. In other words,

## 62 Concepts

the evolution of social systems can enable the evolution of the biological systems of viruses.

Some of the new variants of SARS-Cov-2 were more transmissible (e.g., Delta and Omicron) than others not (e.g., Alpha and Gamma), as I mentioned earlier. The differences in the transmissibility rates were not intentional or purposeful. When mutations happened in its "spike proteins" (specialized molecules that enable the viruses to enter human cells), some of them were better "fits" with their "environments" (human bodies), better in the sense that they could enter human cells more easily because of their shapes and thus they could replicate more quickly and easily. Because the immune systems of the human hosts of the original SARS-CoV-2 and its variants were not familiar with its spike proteins (that is why it was called a "novel coronavirus" in the beginning of the pandemic), their bodies could not fight to destroy the viruses.

As SARS-CoV-2 evolved, so did the immune systems of human bodies (coevolution of biological systems). In response to the pandemic, human societies evolved as well. COVID-19 affected the migration patterns around the world and accelerated the internal migration in the United States, particularly from densely populated big cities to suburbs and small towns.[14] The economies of the United States and others have been impacted in major ways too. The pandemic affected restaurants and retail sales at malls negatively, while online sales increased exponentially.[15] Governments imposed lockdowns on societies to restrict human interactions to stem the transmission rates. They also mobilized their scientific and economic resources and organizational capabilities to develop vaccines to help boost the immune systems of human bodies and antiviral drugs to counter the effects of the virus in human bodies.

A question is yet to be answered is, are these demographic shifts, economic trends, and governmental interventions going to endure after the pandemic ends? In other words, will societies go back to their ways, or will they coevolve with COVID-19? These questions can be answered retrospectively in the next few decades, but there already are some assessments and informed predictions. Florida (2020) predicts that the pandemic will contribute to the trends of families moving to suburbs while young people moving to cities. Acemoglu (2020) observes that due to the pandemic, governments began to play expanded roles in societies. He predicts that the continuation of this expansion is likely in the post-pandemic era, but it can take on different shades and colors in different societies.

The above narrative illustrates how the concept coevolution can help us understand the COVID-19 pandemic at the most macro level (biological and social system interactions). Other complexity concepts systems, nonlinearity, and self-organizations can help us conceptualize particularly the processes and interactions within social systems, such as the social systems in which COVID-19 vaccines were developed, distributed, and administered.

### Defining Systems

As I noted in Chapter 2, the invention, manufacturing, and administration/delivery processes of COVID-19 vaccines involved multiple actors: scientists, biotechnology companies, vaccine manufacturers, governments, national and international public health organizations (such as the US National Institutes of Health and the World Health Organization), medical doctors, local pharmacies, and others. These processes also involved hundreds of millions of individuals, particularly in the administration/delivery phase of the process, some of whom were informed and eager to be vaccinated and others who were misinformed and hesitant, or outright resistant, to getting vaccinated. The vaccine invention, manufacturing, and administration/delivery processes involved not one, but multiple complex systems (and governance networks) interacting with each other. I am not aware of any studies that described and/or analyzed all these complex systems and their interactions. But there are some that focused on some aspects of these systems, which I discuss in the next four chapters. The following is a brief overview.

As noted in Chapter 2, after the Chinese scientists sequenced the genome of Sars-Cov-2 virus in January 2020, more than 120 teams of academic scientists and commercial manufacturers around the world began collaborating with each other through information exchanges and by sharing resources to develop vaccines (Pagliusi et al., 2020). Because of their information and resource interdependencies, these individual and organizational actors can be considered a system. There were more integrated (more closely related) subgroups (those that are in more systemic relations) among them, for example the Developing Countries Vaccine Manufacturers Network, which was composed of organizations in China, India, Korea, Taiwan, and others (Pagliusi et al. 2020). The partnerships between the biotechnology and drug companies like BioNTech and Pfizer in the development of one of the mRNA vaccines, between Oxford University and Astra-Zeneca in the development of another vaccine were also examples of higher degrees of integration.[16]

Governmental organizations, like the US Federal Drug Administration, and international organizations, like the World Health Organization, reviewed the results of the vaccine trials conducted by the manufacturers for their efficacy and safety. Once the vaccines were approved, they were shipped to distribution centers through elaborate logistical systems. In these systems, the federal and state governments in the United States collaborated with private companies for vaccine distributions.

Once the vaccines were ready and the logistical challenges were overcome, the complexity of social behaviors made it difficult for them to be delivered to individuals' arms. In the United States, after the initial high demand for vaccines in the early months of 2021 (about 3 million doses daily in March and April of 2021), it declined significantly (to around

64  *Concepts*

400,000 doses daily in June 2021).[17] By December 2021, only 62% of the US population were fully vaccinated,[18] even though there were sufficient among of vaccines to inoculate all the eligible population (those who were 5 years and older at the time) in the country. The pent-up demand among those who were willing to get vaccinated had been satisfied at that point. The remaining population were those who were uninformed about vaccine availability, those who did not have the time or means to get to vaccination centers, the "vaccine hesitants," and the "vaccine resisters" ("anti-vaxxers").

The universe of those who were uninformed, unable, hesitant, and/or resistant constitutes a complex social system. I am not aware of any comprehensive studies on this complex system, but there is some information available, which can be used in future studies. Each of these groups have their characteristics and reasons for not getting vaccinated. The US Census Bureau surveyed "vaccine hesitants" and made the results available at their website.[19] The Census information shows that the primary factors contributing vaccine hesitancy were concerns about the vaccines' side effects, mistrust in the vaccines, mistrust in the government, belief that they themselves do not need a vaccine, desire to see the long-term effects of the vaccines, and disbelief that COVID-19 was a big threat. The Census bureau information also shows that younger people, males, those with less education, and those who lacked health insurance coverage were more likely to be hesitant.

An important factor that affected the variations in the vaccination rates in the United States was people's political positions. Aggregate analyses show that those who voted for Trump in the 2020 election were less likely to get vaccinated, compared to this who voted for Biden.[20]

Another important group who was initially skeptical about the vaccines were African Americans. Several studies showed that this group had lower levels of vaccination (e.g., Rungkitwattanakul et al., 2021; Sharma et al., 2021). This was partly a result of the lack of access to vaccines particularly by those with lower incomes. They were not sufficiently informed about the availability of the vaccines (that vaccines were free of charge and available many local pharmacies) and at least some did not have the means of transportation to reach vaccination centers.

But there was a more important reason: mistrust among African Americans in the medical profession. This mistrust developed as a result of the publicly known mistreatments of some African Americans.[21] In the Tuskegee Syphilis Study between the 1930s and 1970s, hundreds of African Americans with syphilis were not treated with available drugs for experimental reasons.[22] When it became known publicly, mistrust in medical professionals became widespread among African Americans. In 1951, Henrietta Lacks was treated for her cervical cancer at Johns Hopkins University, when a doctor snipped cells from her cervix without her consent and in the following six decades her cells were cultured and used in medical experiments.[23] Mistrust of the government, of pharmaceutical companies, and of the medical profession to the past collective experiences of African Americans were among the major factors cited in a small-sample survey conducted among the patients at a hospital in the United States (Rungkitwattanakul et al., 2021).

Now, let us look at the information in the above paragraphs from a complex systems perspective. Complex systems may be integrated to varying degrees. (Remember von Bertalanffy's definition of a system.) Giddens's (1984) definition of social systems as "situated activities of human agents, reproduced across time and space" (p. 25) is particularly useful here.

Consider the examples of the COVID-19 vaccine development, manufacturing, and delivery processes. There were multiple actors involved in them: federal agencies, state governments, nonprofit and private actors, such as biotechnology and pharmaceutical companies, logistics companies like UPS and FedEx, local pharmacies, and others.[24] Then to what degree did these actors constitute a system or systems (how integrated they were to constitute a system)? Applying Giddens's definition, we can say that the activities of these human agents (actors) were situated in the historical economic and political contexts of the COVID-19 pandemic and they were reproduced across time (as long as the pandemic continued) and space (across scientific communities; supply chains of the vaccine manufacturers; and local, national, and international communities).

Also, the examples of the Israeli study I cited earlier (that vaccine hesitancy was lower among those who received their information from family and friends and from mass media, compared to those who received their information from social media)[25] and the vaccine hesitancy among African Americans (that they were influenced by the stories they had heard from their parents and peers about the earlier mistreatments of African Americans) illustrate the characteristic of systemic relations. In both cases, the groups who mistrusted the COVID vaccines did so because of the information they received from their trusted sources (e.g., family members, community leaders, the social media, and specific mass media outlets like Fox News). These pieces of information and misinformation about the vaccines were reproduced across time and space in these information environments.

### Nonlinearity

Nonlinearity is another important concept that can help us understand the effects of the interactions among the various actors in the COVID-19 vaccine hesitancy networks. The virus spreads in continued interactions with human systems, but the effects of these interactions are not proportional in all situations. For example, different variants of SARS-Cov-2 virus spread at different rates of transmission: The Delta variant was much more transmissible than the original ("novel") virus.[26] Also, the rate of transmissions is influenced by how humans interact among themselves (whether they use masks and whether they stay away from each other). Epidemiologists developed a measure of these rates of transmissions and governments around the world used it to monitor the transmissibility rates

66   *Concepts*

of SARS-Cov-2: the R-naught ($R_0$). It is a measure of "the number of people that a single infected person can be expected to transmit that disease to" in average.[27] If people use masks and keep their distances from each other, the $R_0$ will be lower. In other words, not each human contact with others has a proportionate effect on the spread of the virus. In communities where the Delta variant spread already and those communities where individuals did not use mask or keep their distances, the virus can spread faster. Because the $R_0$ was higher in such a community, the overall spread was disproportionately higher (nonlinear).

The calculations in Table 4.1 illustrate how the difference between the $R_0$ values of the original strain of SARS-CoV-2 and the Delta variant led to a big difference in their spreads in communities. (I did not include Omicron in this comparison table, because its transmissibility was not clearly determined at the time of this writing.[28]) The original virus had an $R_0$ of 2.2[29], while the Delta variant's $R_0$ was estimated to be between 7 and 8.[30] To keep calculations simple, I used 7.5 for the $R_0$ of the Delta variant. As the table shows, the difference of 5.3 in the $R_0$s in the beginning explodes into a 3,140.6 difference only after four individual contacts with others, which can happen in a matter of one day. This disproportional effect of the $R_0$s on the total infections explains why the Delta variant quickly became the dominant variant around the world by August 2021.[31] Shortly before that time, large percentages of populations had been vaccinated and the at least in the United States and other developed countries and the total infection numbers had been lowered significantly. With its nonlinear affects, Delta changed the trajectory of the COVID-19 pandemic.

Another example of nonlinearity in the COVID-19 case was that only a few "influencers" in the social media were disproportionately effective in generating and spreading the disinformation and misinformation about the vaccines. Researchers at the Center for Countering Digital Hate found that only 12 individuals were responsible for 65% of the anti-vaccine contents in social media, particularly in Facebook, Instagram, and Twitter.[32] They were most effective in Facebook, the most influential social media platform in the world: A 73% of the disinformation content originated from these 12 influencers on this platform.

Arguably, there were also "influencers" who spread correct (scientific) information about the vaccines during the pandemic. There is no particular study on this topic that I am aware of, but it would be reasonable to

*Table 4.1* Effects of the $R_0$ Values of the Original SARS-CoV-2 Virus and the Delta Variant

|  | $R_0$ | First Round | Second Round | Third Round | Fourth Round |
| --- | --- | --- | --- | --- | --- |
| Original SARS-CoV-2 | 2.2 | 2.2 | 4.8 | 10.6 | 23.4 |
| Delta Variant | 7.5 | 7.5 | 56.3 | 421.9 | 3164.1 |

speculate that few nodes were disproportionately more effective in the distribution of the correct information about the COVID-19 pandemic and the vaccines. Probably, the Director of the US Centers for Disease Control Dr. Anthony Fauci (Director of the US National Institute of Infectious Diseases and Chief Medical Adviser to the President) and the COVID-19 dashboards of the Johns Hopkins University, *New York Times*, and CNN[33] were the most important influencers (central nodes) in the network of disseminating scientific information in the United States.

This disproportionality is a result of a property of large networks, like the World Wide Web and social media: a scale-free power-law distribution (see Chapter 3). According to the power law, few nodes are connected to a large number of other nodes and most of the other nodes are connected to smaller number of nodes. According to Barabási and Albert (1999), the mechanism that creates these lopsided distributions is *preferential attachment*: As the networks expand by the addition of new nodes, these new nodes "attach preferentially to nodes that are already well connected." In the COVID-19 misinformation case, once those 12 influencers establish themselves, they became more preferred sources of information and the pieces of information they generated were spread disproportionately more than others.

### Self-organization

A major political and philosophical debate throughout the pandemic was whether it would be better for governments to make decisions about masking, social distancing, and vaccinations or let people make their own decisions. In other words, could human societies self-organize in the face of a pandemic or should an external force (e.g., the state) be involved? A general argument in favor of self-organization in this case would be that individuals should be free to choose because they can make intelligent choices, given accurate information, without the interference of the state.

The correlations between the variations in the mask mandates among the US states and the variations in the infection rates provides some answers to the question. Those states without the mandates (some of which banned the mandates imposed by local governments and school districts) and those counties without mandates had higher levels of infections.[34] So, do these results mean that self-organization does not work in the case of a pandemic?

To answer this question, we can adopt Elinor Ostrom's (2005) conceptualization of self-organization in general and, particularly, the attributes of appropriators and resources in self-organization that she identified. As I noted earlier, self-organization is not a categorial designation, according to Ostrom: People may be able to organize themselves more or less depending on the conditions. Among the conditions of self-organization she identified, the following are the most relevant to the COVID-19 case.

Ostrom shows that for a self-organization to be successful, the indicators of the resources available to individuals (e.g., effectiveness of masks and

68   *Concepts*

vaccines) should be reliable and valid and that system should be sufficiently small so that the participants can develop accurate knowledge of the boundaries of it. In the COVID-19 case, scientists and governmental agencies, such as US CDC (Centers for Disease Control), did develop such indicators (e.g., $R_0$). But that was not sufficient because the pandemic was not a small system. It was a global phenomenon and it had multidimensional implications (e.g., public health and economic dimensions). The information about the pandemic was vast and dynamic and disseminated through multiple channels (CDC, FDA, the president, state governors, local doctors, pharmacies, mass media, influencers on social media, etc.), which provided conflicting pieces of information to the public.

What compounded the problem was the systematic disinformation and misinformation campaigns in the social media and some mass media (e.g., Fox news). As the Israeli study I cited above shows, social media played a significant, possibly the biggest, role in the dissemination of disinformation and misinformation. Ostrom cites *common understanding* of the system among its participants and how their actions affect the system as another condition for self-organization. In the COVID-19 case in the United States, the disinformation and misinformation campaigns were likely fueled by the lack of common understanding among citizens of the scope and severity of the pandemic, its consequences in communities, and the consequences of their actions for the spread of the virus, as I mentioned above.

From the discussion above, we can reach the conclusion that in the vast scale of the pandemic, self-organization was not possible and external interventions by governments were necessary to curb its spread. There is another way to look at the problem of self-organization from a complex systems/networks perspective. Barabási and Albert (1999) demonstrate that *preferential attachment* is actually a mechanism of self-organization in large networks. They also show that preferential attachment creates lopsided power law distributions. So, the vast spread of the misinformation on the social media platforms was self-organizational. The problem was that the results of this self-organization were not beneficial to communities and larger societies.

## Summary

This is a long chapter, because I intended to show that complexity theory includes multiple concepts, all of which have implications for understanding governance processes and networks. Many of these concepts and implications have not been utilized in the governance networks literature, but a few authors began to utilize them in the last decade (see Table 1.1 and Figure 1.3 in Chapter 1).

This chapter began with a definition of complexity. Then I discussed the key concepts of complexity theory: systems, nonlinearity, self-organization, emergence, and coevolution. The discussion on systems shows that they can be conceptualized and studied in degrees: A set of relationships may be more or less of a system. I use the terms system and networks interchangeably in this book, because with the exception of some technical definitions, they both refer to same kinds of relationships. The concept of nonlinearity can help us understand the effects of the relationships in systems/networks for collective outcomes. The discussions on self-organization show that this is a highly relevant concept to governance networks: These networks can be self-organizational at varying degrees and of different forms. Elinor Ostrom's elaborate conceptualization of the conditions of self-organization can be used to study these degrees and form empirically. Governance networks, like all other social systems, coevolve with other social and natural systems.

In a separate section, I illustrated the relevancy of these concepts with examples from the COVID-19 pandemic. The coevolutions of the viruses, human immune systems, and social (economic, political) systems are illustrative of the macro-level processes in systems. After the illustrations of coevolution, I discussed how systems can be defined in the COVID-19 vaccine development and delivery examples, how nonlinearity can help us understand the effects of the transmissibility of viruses, and how self-organization applies to vaccine and mask mandates.

## Notes

1 Ilya Prigogine can be cited as the foremost theorist of dissipative structures in physical systems, particularly thermodynamics (Nicolis & Prigogine, 1989; Prigogine, 1996; Prigogine & Stengers, 1984). There is a discussion of this concept in my earlier book (Morçöl, 2012); I do not focus on it in this book.
2 For descriptions of agent-based simulations, see Gilbert (2020); for cellular automata, see Ilachisnki (2001); for fractal geometry, see Falconer (2014).
3 Nearly Half of the Republicans Say They Don't Want a Covid Vaccine, a Big Public Health Challenge. *New York Times.* nyti.ms/3diXX7h
   Despite Ample Shots and Incentives, Vaccine Rates Lag Far Behind in the South. *New York Times.* https://nyti.ms/3cvENKk
4 In a blog post at Harvard's School of Public Health, these terms are defined as follows.
   *Misinformation:* inadvertently drawing conclusions based on wrong or incomplete facts.
   *Disinformation:* the deliberate spread of falsehoods to promote an agenda.
   (Katherine J. Igoe, Establishing the Truth: Vaccines, Social Media, and the Spread of Misinformation. www.hsph.harvard.edu/ecpe/vaccines-social-media-spread-misinformation/)
5 Steven Mello. "More COPS, Less Crime." www.princeton.edu/~smello/papers/cops.pdf
6 Ostrom uses the terms "self-governance" and "self-organization" interchangeably. See her specific reference to both concepts in Ostrom (1990, p. 26).
7 See her YouTube videos: Elinor Ostrom on the Myth of the Tragedy of Commons (www.youtube.com/watch?v=ybdvjvIH-1U) and Ending The Tragedy of The Commons (www.youtube.com/watch?v=Qr5Q3VvpI7w).

## 70   Concepts

8   His term "edge of chaos" is similar to Prigogine's "far from equilibrium." Both authors refer to the conditions that are not at equilibrium, conditions in which systems are in dynamic states and inclined to change. Kauffman points out that biological systems are typically in nonequilibrium states.

9   Gillis, J. (2010).

10   Harvard School of Public Health, "What Will It Be Like When COVID-19 Becomes Endemic?" www.hsph.harvard.edu/news/features/what-will-it-be-like-when-covid-19-becomes-endemic/

   Despite Omicron, Covid-19 Will Become Endemic. Here's How. www.vox.com/future-perfect/22849891/omicron-pandemic-endemic

11   Newly Discovered Bat Viruses Give Hints to Covid's Origins. *New York Times.* https://nyti.ms/3DH7U8E

12   Investigations into the Origin of COVID-19 (Wikipedia entry). https://en.wikipedia.org/wiki/Investigations_into_the_origin_of_COVID-19

13   Nova episode: The Viruses That Made Us Human. www.pbs.org/wgbh/nova/article/endogenous-retroviruses/

14   Pandemic Population Change Across Metro America: Accelerated Migration, Less Immigration, Fewer Births and More Deaths. www.brookings.edu/research/pandemic-population-change-across-metro-america-accelerated-migration-less-immigration-fewer-births-and-more-deaths/?utm_campaign=Metropolitan%20Policy%20Program&utm_medium=email&utm_content=128487676&utm_source=hs_email

   COVID-19 is Hitting the Nation's Largest Metros the Hardest, Making a "Restart" of the Economy More Difficult. www.brookings.edu/blog/the-avenue/2020/04/01/why-it-will-be-difficult-to-restart-the-economy-after-covid-19/?utm_campaign=Brookings%20Brief&utm_source=hs_email&utm_medium=email&utm_content=85686670

15   Reopening America: The Restaurant Sector Must Adapt and Innovate to Survive. www.brookings.edu/research/reopening-america-the-restaurant-sector-must-adapt-and-innovate-to-survive/?utm_campaign=Brookings%20Brief&utm_medium=email&utm_content=90187907&utm_source=hs_email

   With Department Stores Disappearing, Malls Could Be Next. *New York Times.* https://nyti.ms/2ZChA23

   Amazon's Profit Soars 220 Percent as Pandemic Drives Shopping Online. *New York Times.* www.nytimes.com/2021/04/29/technology/amazons-profits-triple.html

16   Pfizer–BioNTech COVID-19 Vaccine. https://en.wikipedia.org/wiki/Pfizer%E2%80%93BioNTech_COVID-19_vaccine

   Oxford–AstraZeneca COVID-19 Vaccine. https://en.wikipedia.org/wiki/Oxford%E2%80%93AstraZeneca_COVID-19_vaccine

17   US Coronavirus Vaccine Tracker. https://usafacts.org/visualizations/covid-vaccine-tracker-states/

   COVID-19 Vaccination in the United States (Wikipedia entry). https://en.wikipedia.org/wiki/COVID-19_vaccination_in_the_United_States

18   Coronavirus in the U.S.: Latest Map and Case Count. *New York Times.* www.nytimes.com/interactive/2021/us/covid-cases.html.

19   How Do COVID-19 Vaccination and Vaccination Hesitancy Rates Vary Over Time? www.census.gov/library/stories/2021/04/how-do-covid-19-vaccination-and-vaccine-hesitancy-rates-vary-over-time.html

Complexity 71

20 Red States Are Vaccinating at a Lower Rate Than Blue States. www.cnn.com/2021/04/10/politics/vaccinations-state-analysis/index.html
Least Vaccinated U.S. Counties Have Something in Common: Trump Voters. *New York Times.* https://nyti.ms/3x0v9bj
21 How to Overcome Vaccine Distrust Among Black Americans. https://thehill.com/opinion/healthcare/531892-how-to-overcome-vaccine-distrust-among-black-americans?utm_campaign=Brookings%20Brief&utm_medium=email&utm_content=104919855&utm_source=hs_email
22 The U.S. Public Health Service Syphilis Study at Tuskegee. www.cdc.gov/tuskegee/timeline.htm
23 "Henrietta Lacks": A Donor's Immortal Legacy. www.npr.org/2010/02/02/123232331/henrietta-lacks-a-donors-immortal-legacy
24 US Centers for Disease Control, How Vaccines Get to You. www.cdc.gov/coronavirus/2019-ncov/vaccines/distributing.html
Pfizer, Manufacturing and Distributing the Covid-19 Vaccine, www.pfizer.com/science/coronavirus/vaccine/manufacturing-and-distribution#:~:text=continuous%20temperature%20monitoring.-,Our%20distribution%20is%20built%20on%0a%20flexible%20just%2Din%2Dtime,ground%20transport%20to%20dosing%20locations
UPS Operates First Ever U.S. Drone COVID-19 Vaccine Delivery. https://about.ups.com/us/en/our-stories/innovation-driven/drone-covid-vaccine-deliveries.html
Delivering the First Wave of COVID-19 Vaccines. www.fedex.com/en-us/healthcare/vaccine-shipping.html
25 The Game is Not Yet Over, and Vaccines Still Matter: Lessons from a Study on Israel's COVID-19 Vaccination. www.brookings.edu/blog/up-front/2021/09/13/the-game-is-not-yet-over-and-vaccines-still-matter-lessons-from-a-study-on-israels-covid-19-vaccination/?utm_campaign=Brookings%20Brief&utm_medium=email&utm_content=159977144&utm_source=hs_email
26 CDC, Delta Variant. www.cdc.gov/coronavirus/2019-ncov/variants/delta-variant.html?s_cid=11559:%2Bdelta%20%2Bvariant:sem.b:p:RG:GM:gen:PTN:FY21
27 Understanding Predictions: What is R-Naught? https://globalhealth.harvard.edu/understanding-predictions-what-is-r-naught/
Challenge 4: Modeling Disease Spreading and Flattening the Curve. https://medicine.yale.edu/coved/modules/covid/challenge4/
28 CDC, Omicron Variant—What You Need to Know (December 20, 2021). www.cdc.gov/coronavirus/2019-ncov/variants/omicron-variant.html
29 University of Minnesota. Data Suggest nCoV More Infectious Than 1918 Flu, But What Does that Mean? www.cidrap.umn.edu/news-perspective/2020/01/data-suggest-ncov-more-infectious-1918-flu-what-does-mean
30 The CDC Said the Delta Variant Is As Contagious As Chickenpox. That's Not Accurate. www.wabe.org/covid-delta-variant-transmission-cdc-chickenpox/
31 What We Know About the Dangerous Delta Variant. *New York Magazine.* Intelligencer. https://nymag.com/intelligencer/article/covid-b-1-617-2-delta-variant-what-we-know.html#:~:text=Delta%20has%20become%20the%20dominant%20strain%20in%20the,early%20May%20and%209.5%20percent%20in%20early%20June.

## 72  Concepts

32 Shannon Bond, Just 12 People Are Behind Most Vaccine Hoaxes On Social Media, Research Shows. https://www.npr.org/2021/05/13/996570855/disinformation-dozen-test-facebooks-twitters-ability-to-curb-vaccine-hoaxes Just 12 People Are Behind Most Vaccine Hoaxes On Social Media, Research Shows : NPR - NPR.org. The majority of anti-vaccine claims on social media trace back to a small number of influential figures, according to researchers. Chandan Khanna/AFP via Getty Images hide caption www.npr.org

33 Johns Hopkins Coronavirus Resource Center. https://coronavirus.jhu.edu/ Track Coronavirus Cases in Places Important to You. New York Times. www.nytimes.com/interactive/2021/us/covid-cases-deaths-tracker.html Tracking Covid-19 Cases in the US. CNN. www.cnn.com/interactive/2020/health/coronavirus-us-maps-and-cases/ Tracking Covid-19 Vaccinations Worldwide. CNN. https://edition.cnn.com/interactive/2021/health/global-covid-vaccinations/

34 Guy GP Jr., Lee FC, Sunshine G, et al. Association of State-Issued Mask Mandates and Allowing On-Premises Restaurant Dining with County-Level COVID-19 Case and Death Growth Rates—United States, March 1–December 31, 2020. MMWR Morb Mortal Wkly Rep 2021;70:350–354. DOI: http://dx.doi.org/10.15585/mmwr.mm7010e3external icon. Ginther DK, Zambrana C. Association of Mask Mandates and COVID-19 Case Rates, Hospitalizations, and Deaths in Kansas. JAMA Netw Open. 2021;4(6):e2114514. doi:10.1001/jamanetworkopen.2021.14514 Lower COVID Rates in States That Mandated Masks. www.webmd.com/lung/news/20210415/lower-covid-rates-in-states-that-mandated-masks

# Part II
# A Complex Governance Networks Conceptualization

# 5 Introduction of the Conceptualization

The question now is how to connect the concepts presented in Part I (Chapters 2–4) to each other in a complex governance networks conceptualization. I propose the *micro–macro problem* as the central concept to use in doing so. Then what is the micro–macro problem? It is the problem of how the actions of individual actors (micro units) generate collective outcomes (macro structures, such as social institutions, systems of rules) and how, in turn, these collective structures affect individual actions.

In this chapter, I demonstrate why and how the micro–macro problem is relevant and important. In the following three chapters (Chapters 6–8), I will elaborate on the elements of this concept: the characteristics of micro units in Chapter 6, how micro actions lead to macro outcomes/structures in Chapter 7, and how macro structures affect individual actions in Chapter 8.

To better understand the relevancy of the micro–macro problem to the complex governance networks conceptualization, let us remember the implications of governance studies/theories, network theories and social network analysis, and complexity theory. Governance theorists challenged the traditional ways of thinking in public policy and administration and raised questions about a series of important issues, including whether governments can control multicentered (or "polycentric") governance processes and how autonomous policy/administrative actors can/do work together effectively in these processes. They offered a few conceptual answers to the questions they raised. We have learned from governance theorists that collective problem solving has to involve multiple actors in today's societies and that governance processes are multicentered. Even if societies were ever monocentric at one point in human history, they have become polycentric and their problems have become more complex in the late 20th century.[1]

Governance networks researchers have studied the implications of these government conceptualizations empirically. They applied mathematical network theories, more specifically social network analysis, in their analyses. They measured the properties of the actors and their connections to each other governance networks and the structural properties of these networks. Governance networks scholars also made some advances in conceptualizing network effectiveness and accountability, two primary areas

DOI: 10.4324/9781003053392-7

## 76 *A Complex Governance Networks Conceptualization*

of concern in traditional public administration. (I will discuss these issues particularly in Chapters 9 and 10.)

Meanwhile, complexity theorists/researchers were developing methodological tools to apply their concepts like nonlinearity, self-organization, and emergence in empirical investigations. They developed tools like agent-based simulations and applied them at increased frequencies in the natural and information sciences, mathematics, ecology/environmental studies, urban studies, and others in the last several decades. Only in the 1990s, these tools entered into the realm of public administration and policy studies, particularly through the works of pioneers like Kiel (1994) and Comfort (1994, 1999). The conceptual and methodological tools of complexity theory did not gain much traction in the governance networks literature in the 1990s and the first decade of the 2000s; these tools appeared in the literature and they were integrated with the other concepts of governance networks in the 2010s. The analyses of the journal publications in the Web of Science I presented in Figure 1.3 (Chapter 1) confirms these observations. In a parallel development, the frequency of the book-length applications of complexity theory concepts and tools increased in the 2010s (e.g., Gerrits, 2012; Geyer & Rihani, 2010; Morçöl, 2012a; Rhodes, Murphy, Muir, & Murray, 2011; Teisman, van Buuren, & Gerrits, 2009).

These brief summaries suggest that the three theory streams (governance, governance networks, and complexity) have logical connections and conceptual overlaps with each other, as some authors also recognize (Kapucu & Hu, 2020; Kettl, 2002; Koliba, et al., 2019). Then the question is, how to integrate them into a complex governance network (CGN) conceptualization.

My answer is the micro–macro problem. This problem is explicitly or implicitly recognized particularly in two analytical approaches I mentioned above: social network analyses and agent-based simulations. In both approaches, researchers aim to find the connections between the properties of and actions by micro units (individual actors) and macro structural properties. How they do that is a topic of the following chapters. The following conceptual introductions of the problem will help set the stage for the more detailed and technical discussions in the subsequent chapters.

## The Micro–Macro Problem and Collective Problems of Human Societies

The micro–macro problem is about how the properties of and the relations between actors in a network/system (i.e., the micro level) affect and the macro-level (systemic) structures and how in turn these structures affect the properties of and relations between actors. In the context of collective problem solving, this is the problem of how the actions and relations of individual actors generate collective outcomes and how, in turn, the collective outcomes (social institutions, systems of rules) affect individual actions and relations.

*Introduction of the Conceptualization*   77

To clarify why this problem is important, let us consider a major collective problem all human societies are facing: the climate crisis. To solve this collective problem, should all micro units (all individual humans, eight billion of them) be intelligent (capable of processing information at the highest levels)? Should they be fully informed about the nature of the problem (climate crisis) and the macro-level impacts of their individual actions on the problem? For example, should all humans be fully informed about the mechanisms of global warming (the greenhouse effect, carbon cycles on the planet, impacts of industrial production and individual consumption, etc.) to be able to prevent the climate crisis? Should they all be also altruistic (i.e., they should care about their communities and entire humanity more than their own individual and immediate interests)? Let us also consider the opposite hypothetical scenario: What if none of the actors is intelligent, informed, or altruistic? Would then there be no solutions to collective problems, like the climate crisis? Another possibility: What if some individual actors are more intelligent, more informed about the collective problem, and/or more altruistic than others? Then should these individuals be in charge of solving the problems?

The reader will recognize that the questions in the above paragraph, or some variants of them, guided philosophers and decision makers (leaders, politicians, social activists, etc.) in their questioning and devising solutions to collective problems in human history. Think about Garret Hardin's (1968) "Tragedy of Commons" conjecture, which I cited in Chapters 2 and 4 and will come back to in Chapter 11. In Hardin's conjecture, it is not clear whether the individual actors (herders) are intelligent and informed, but they are certainly selfish. Their short-sighted and selfish behaviors lead to the destruction of their common pasture: a negative collective (macro) outcome. The lesson one can draw from Hardin's conjecture is that left to their own devices, people are not capable of solving their collective problems. That is because they are selfish, unintelligent, and/or uninformed. Then, by inference, this collective problem can be solved only by an external actor, the government.

An inevitable question then is, could "the government" be unselfish, intelligent, and fully informed so that it can solve a collective problem? Some philosophers explored that possibility. Plato's "philosopher king" is an example. In his *Republic*, which he wrote around 375 BC, Plato depicts an ideal/hypothetical ruler who has the absolute knowledge of what needs to be known to rule a society, which he has obtained through philosophical study.[2] About two millennia after Plato's conjecture, French scholar Pierre Simon Laplace (1749–1827) proposed a more scientific version of it: Laplace's demon. In his reasoning on whether the laws of nature can be known fully, he articulated this conjecture. Laplace's demon is an intellect that is capable of knowing the past, present, and future of everything in the universe with perfect precision, down to the properties and movements of every single atom.[3] Then, one can infer, this all-knowing demon should be able to solve collective problems. If a government, or some other entity,

## 78 A Complex Governance Networks Conceptualization

possesses the capabilities of Laplace's demon, it can solve problems like Hardin's Tragedy of Commons and the climate crisis.

One may react to these hypothetical questions and conjectures intuitively and rightfully say that they do not depict real-life humans or societies. That is exactly what Elinor Ostrom's criticism of Hardin's "Tragedy" is: This conjecture does not represent real-life individuals or their relationships. Real humans are not entirely selfish or fully altruistic; they are not all-knowing and fully capable intellects or fully ignorant either. Their intellectual capabilities, levels of information, and motivations vary. Then the questions whether individual actors can solve their collective problems and whether they need an external interference by a knowledgeable, powerful, and organized actor (i.e., a government) to solve the problems should be answered in the context of each specific problem. According to Ostrom, whether and to what extent humans can solve their collective problems without external interference depends on certain conditions; she made some generalizations about the conditions of self-organization, as I noted in Chapter 4.

Another important theorist to mention here is the libertarian philosopher Friedrich Hayek (1973, 2103). Hayek is more optimistic about the capability of individual human actors in solving their collective problems without external interference. He compares two kinds of social order—spontaneous social orders (self-generating and endogenously determined systems) and externally designed orders (e.g., designed by a government)—and concludes that the former are superior to the latter. That is because spontaneous orders are the products of complex interactions of multiple minds, which have better capability to capture/match the complexity of their environments. In contrast, the cognitive capability of an external singular power (a government) is limited. In the end, Hayek recognizes that both spontaneous and designed orders are necessary in real life, but the former should play larger roles.

The reader can see allusions to the micro–macro problem in Plato's, Laplace's, Hardin's, Ostrom's, and Hayek's thinking. Plato's, Laplace's, and Hardin's conjectures are extreme simplifications obviously, but they are still helpful in the sense that they raise questions about the respective roles of individual actors and governmental actors in collective problem-solving processes. These conjectures address an important aspect of the micro–macro problem: the connections between the capacities and motivations of individual minds and collective outcomes. Ostrom redresses the abstractness of the problem Hardin poses and reminds us of the importance of the variations in the cognitive capacities, information levels, and motivations of individual actors in collective problem solving. She also proposes a conceptual framework (conditions of self-organization), which can help us understand these variations and their collective consequences. Hayek points to a possibility: that the minds of multiple regular individuals (even though they may not be fully intelligent, informed, or altruistic) are better than the singular mind of the government, in solving collective

Introduction of the Conceptualization   79

problems. The micro–macro problem helps us understand these issues, and more, in a coherent conceptual organization, as we will see in the following chapters.

## A Brief Background of the Micro–Macro Problem

The term "micro–macro problem" first coined and used by Coleman (1986), to the best of my knowledge. In this book, I adopt his formulation of the problem and adapt it to the context of collective problem solving in general, and complex governance networks in particular. Some aspects of Coleman's formulation is outdated (it is almost four decades old), but the core ideas are still very much relevant today. The following brief background is based on Coleman's analysis and narrative of the history of this conceptual problem. In my account, I will focus on the most relevant parts of his formulation for the purposes of this book. I recommend his seminal article (Coleman, 1986) for a more detailed history and a discussion of the implications of this problem for sociology, economics, law, and social action.

Coleman finds the first articulation of the micro–macro problem in sociologist Talcott Parsons's attempt to ground social theory in theory of social action in his seminal work *The Structure of Social Action* (1937). In his book, Parsons aimed to theorize the connections between purposive individual actions (micro level) and collective ("macrosocial") consequences of those actions (macro level). Parsons was not the first who attempted to theorize collective consequences of purposive actions, Coleman reminds us. Similar attempts can be seen in the works by Thomas Hobbes, Adam Smith, John Locke, Jean Jacques Rousseau, and John Stuart Mill in the 17th, 18th, and 19th centuries. They all aimed to how purposeful actions of individuals are connected to the functioning of political and economic systems. But Parsons articulated the problem most cogently and posed it as the central problem of sociology. He later abandoned his theoretical efforts.

This abandonment was unfortunate, according to Coleman, because it led to divergent theoretical and research orientations in sociology (i.e., methodological individualism of behaviorism and methodological holism of functionalism), which deprived the discipline of an integrative framework. The micro–macro problem was not abandoned completely, however. There some partial theoretical attempts related to this problem. Coleman cites the works of sociologists Robert Merton and George Homans, which brought back the problem of the macrosocial consequences of purposeful individual action to the attentions of sociologists. He also notes that the problem was reformulated and posed under different names by others: the "agency–structure problem" (Simmel's sociology), the "transformation problem" (European sociology), the problem of "collective action" (Olson), and the problem of "social choice" (Arrow). I can add that a group of political economists followed up on these works and developed the rational

80  *A Complex Governance Networks Conceptualization*

choice research tradition (e.g., V. Ostrom, 1999a, 1999b; E. Ostrom, 1990, 2005) and that critical theorist Bob Jessop (1990, 2001, 2004, 2008, 2016) placed the "agency–structure problem" in the center of his theory of the state and state power.

Coleman's most important and enduring contributions to these related literatures are to bring a conceptual cohesion by articulating the central questions of the micro–macro problem and pointing to the methodological problems in answering them. He poses the two central questions as "how the purposive actions of the actors combine to bring about system-level behavior, and how those purposive actions are in turn shaped by constraints that result from the behavior of the system" (p. 1312). In my earlier works (e.g., Morçöl, 2012a), I added one more question and reformulated Coleman's two questions. In this book, the following three chapters (Chapters 6–8) are structured around these three questions. They are:

1. Micro properties: What are the properties of micro units (e.g., individual actors)? Are they intelligent, rational, etc.? (Chapter 6).
2. Micro-to-macro processes: How do actions of and relationships among micro units (e.g., individual actors) lead to the creation/aggregation/emergence of macro processes and structures? (Coleman's first question, Chapter 7).
3. Macro-to-micro processes: Once the macro structures emerge, how do these macro structures and processes affect the beliefs, motivations, and actions of individual actors? (Coleman's second question, Chapter 8).

These questions are important, but they are simplifications. The micro-to-macro and the macro-to-micro processes are not actually two separate stages; they do not follow clear and linear paths. They happen simultaneously and in various combinations in real life. Researchers need to disentangle these combinations with their simplifications to make sense of complex realities. The conceptual tools of the micro–macro problem can help us to make sense of complex human systems in general, and complex governance networks in particular. I will address these complexities particularly in Chapter 8.

Coleman's second important contribution is to point out the methodological developments in sociological research in the mid-20th century among the reasons for the lack of consistent theoretical development of the micro–macro problem. He cites particularly survey research and statistical analyses, which became increasingly popular in this period, and notes that they rely on the assumption that units (individuals) are independent of each other. As such, they are not suitable to study the macrosocial consequences of the characteristics of independent individuals and their actions. He notes that more sophisticated methods are required to study the interdependencies among individual actors and their macrosocial consequences and cites "network analyses" as a possible methodological solution.

There have been major methodological advances since the publication of Coleman's seminal article in 1986. Social network analyses (SNA) have become more sophisticated in factoring in interdependencies among individual actors and studying the connections between the properties and interactions of network actions on one hand and the properties of network structures on the other. Also, survey methods have been adapted to collect data about the interdependencies of individual actors in social network analyses (Borgatti et al., 2018, pp. 52–59). Agent-based simulations (ABS) offer additional methodological capabilities to study the macrolevel consequences of the interdependencies among individual actors dynamically. I will cite such examples of SNA and ABS applications in Chapter 7.

## Why the Micro–Macro Problem is Important for Understanding Social Systems

The micro–macro problem may not be directly relevant to the complex systems studies in the natural sciences, but it is essential in conceptualizing social systems. Take the example of Prigogine and Stengers's (1984) theory of thermodynamic systems. These systems are complex (because of the nonlinear patterns in their evolutions). A researcher of thermodynamic systems does not have to be concerned about the micro–macro relations in these systems. That is because the individual atoms of the same kind (e.g., oxygen atoms) behave the same way under same conditions.

Here is a simple example: Two hydrogen atoms and one oxygen atom combine to generate a water molecule, once enough heat is applied.[4] This will happen when the experiment is done in the United States, Chine, Nigeria, or anywhere else. The atoms behave the same way in all places, because they do not have different personalities, nor do they carry different cultural values depending on where they are located. This is why it was sufficient for Prigogine and Stenger to measure the macro (system-level) properties of thermodynamic systems at the macro level only.

The same is not true for humans. Unlike an oxygen atom, or a hydrogen atom, an individual person is unique. Social systems are composed of individuals who do have personality traits and they carry cultural values. These differences among humans make studying their systems even more complex than studying thermodynamic systems. Schelling's (2006) description of social systems illustrates this complexity.

> People are responding to an environment that consists of other people responding to their environments, which consists of people responding to an environment of people's responses.... These interactions between

82  *A Complex Governance Networks Conceptualization*

individuals and their environments, which are consisted of other individuals, constitutes a system.

(p. 14)

In Chapter 4, I stressed that complexity is not a function merely of the large numbers of the elements of a system; more important, it is function of the variations among the elements and thus the variety in the relations among them. Because each individual human is unique, the variety of their relations and the relations between individuals make human systems much more complex than thermodynamic systems. This higher degree of complexity requires a different approach/framework to study human systems. The micro–macro problem should be the core problem of such a framework, I argue in this book.

Consider the example of demographic changes in human societies. *New York Times* published a report that the ongoing trend of the decline in birth rates around the world would lead to significant changes in human lives in the middle of the 21st century.[5] This trend could ease the burden on the natural environment, as humans' demands for energy and food are likely to decrease. It could also decrease the number of workers whose contributions to retirement systems sustain the incomes of retirees. These are macro-level trends, which can be measured as aggregates. That is what demographers and economists do. But the trends are also the aggregated results of individual (micro-level) decisions (e.g., decisions to marry or not and how many children to have), which in turn are affected by macro-level phenomena, such as macro economy. A growing economy generates employment opportunities for individuals to sustain their lives and allows/encourages more of them to participate in the labor force. When both parents work that increases family income, but also decreases the ability to have more children because of the increased cost of raising a child (childcare, healthcare, education expenses).

The above description of demographic changes is, of course, incomplete, but it illustrates that it is not sufficient to study macro trends (e.g., population increase, vaccination rates) only and that it is necessary to understand micro- and macro-level processes and the relations between these levels. The micro–macro problem is about those relations.

### The Micro–Macro Problem and Policy Process Theories

Some public policy process theorists recognize the micro–macro problem, at least implicitly. For example, although punctuated equilibrium theorists study policy processes at the macro level, they make micro-level assumptions about individual human behaviors. They assume that individuals are "bounded rational," which affects macro-level punctuated equilibrium processes (Baumgartner et al., 2018). These theorists do not specify how boundedly rational behaviors lead to macro patterns like punctuations in the equilibrium of societies, however.

*Introduction of the Conceptualization* 83

The micro–macro relations are more explicitly addressed in Elinor Ostrom's (1990, 2005) institutional analysis and development framework and Paul Sabatier and Hank Jenkins-Smith's (1993) advocacy coalition framework. Both frameworks include conceptualizations of the actions of actors (micro-level) and those of macro-level structures (institutions or advocacy coalitions), but neither framework explicitly focuses on the mechanisms of the relations between the two levels. In the following chapters in this book, I will do that.

## Micro, Macro, and Other Levels

One more issue I want to briefly touch on is whether two conceptual levels (micro and macro) are sufficient to study complex human systems. Human systems are more complex than this dichotomous conceptualization and there may be multiple levels of conceptualization and analysis. Ostrom (2005) recognizes that are four levels in institutional analysis: operational, collective-choice, constitutional, and metaconstitutional levels (pp. 58–62). Also, complexity theorist Axelrod (1997) conceptualizes the micro–macro transformations in social systems at multiple levels. He demonstrates how collective political actors emerge from the actions of individuals and then they become actors in larger social processes. Koliba and his colleagues (2019) devote an entire chapter to "meso-level theories" of governance networks, in addition to the micro and macro levels they conceptualize (pp. 399–418).

These conceptualizations are interesting and potentially useful, but there is no agreement among the theorists on what those specific levels are. For example, it is not clear what specifically the meso-level is and how it could be delineated conceptually and empirically from the micro and macro levels. The definitions of the levels are specific to the theories in which they are defined. In this book, I use the dichotomous conceptualization of micro and macro as the generic template. This dichotomy may be supplemented with other levels in given contexts.

## Summary

This chapter was about making the case for the micro–macro problem as the core problem of studying social systems, particularly complex governance networks/systems. After briefly summarizing the three theory streams discussed in the previous chapters (governance, networks, and complexity) and the two groups of conceptualizations that can be identified in the literature related complex governance networks (social-ecological systems and the micro–macro problem), I provided the basic conceptualization and questions of the micro–macro framework. The next three chapters (Chapters 6–8) are about the details of this framework. This chapter ended with a brief discussion of multilevel conceptualizations of governance systems (e.g., micro, meso, and macro levels).

## Notes

1 Graeber and Wengrow's (2021) account of human history shows that societies have never been fully monocentric.
2 Wikipedia entry, Philosopher king. https://en.wikipedia.org/wiki/Philosopher_king
3 Laplace's conjecture is better known as the basis of deterministic thinking in science: the thinking that all events in the universe are caused by knowable precedents. An inference that can be drawn from this conjecture is that it is possible for the intellect to know all the details of all the events in the universe. The following extract from Laplace's *A Philosophical Essay on Probabilities* points to this possibility.

> We may regard the present state of the universe as the effect of its past and the cause of its future. An intellect which at a certain moment would know all forces that set nature in motion, and all positions of all items of which nature is composed, if this intellect were also vast enough to submit these data to analysis, it would embrace in a single formula the movements of the greatest bodies of the universe and those of the tiniest atom; for such an intellect nothing would be uncertain and the future just like the past would be present before its eyes.
>
> *Source*: Wikipedia entry, Laplace's Demon.
> https://en.wikipedia.org/wiki/Laplace%27s_demon

4 A. M. Helmenstine, How to Make Water from Hydrogen and Oxygen. www.thoughtco.com/making-water-from-hydrogen-and-oxygen-4021101
5 Cave, Bubola, and Sang-Hun (2021).

# 6 Micro Units

This chapter is about the first question of the micro–macro problem: What are the properties of micro units (e.g., individual actors)? In the previous chapter, I asked more specific questions: Should all micro units (all individual humans, eight billion of them) be intelligent (capable of processing information at the highest levels)? Should they be fully informed about the nature of the problem (e.g., climate crisis) and the macro-level impacts of their individual actions on the problem? Should they all be also altruistic (i.e., they should care about their communities and entire humanity more than their own individual and immediate interests)? Together, these questions constitute what can be named as the *rationality problem*, which has three elements as the questions suggest: the level of intelligence (cognitive capacity to process and construct information) of an actor, the level of information the actor has, and the predisposition of the actor toward others and self (other-regarding versus self-regarding).

In this chapter, I briefly review the answers philosophers and cognitive and social theorists and researchers provided to these questions. The review presented in this chapter will prepare the groundwork for the next chapter, which is about how the actions of and relationships among micro units (e.g., individual actors) lead to the creation/aggregation/emergence of macro processes and structures.

The rationality problem has kept philosophers for millennia. As early as in the classic works of Aristotle and Plato, one can find answers to questions about how human mind works and whether it is capable of making rational decisions. The rationality problem is an extension and specific formulation of this tradition. It is a product more specifically of the Enlightenment philosophy of the 17th and 18th centuries (Honderich, 1995). A core assumption of these philosophers was that the human mind is capable of thinking rationally, and hence scientifically. The logical positivists of the early 20th century refined this assumption by showing how language and logic can be used in scientific inquiry.

The assumption that the human mind is (or can be) rational has been the basis of various theories and models in economics, decision sciences, and related areas of study, like policy analysis. It has had its critics as well. For example, Herbert Simon (1947, 1979, 1986) argued that human rationality

DOI: 10.4324/9781003053392-8

## 86 *A Complex Governance Networks Conceptualization*

is limited and formulated an alternative to the notion of comprehensive, or full rationality: "bounded rationality." Meanwhile, some behavioral and cognitive psychologists argued that we should look at human cognition differently, beyond the simplistic rational versus irrational dichotomy. They demonstrated with empirical evidence that cognitive biases make human thinking processes highly complex (Edwards & Tversky, 1967; Friedland & Robertson, 1990; Hogarth & Reder, 1986; Kahneman, 2011).

The assumption that humans can make rational decisions has endured despite all these criticisms. A core assumption of rational choice theories is that humans act as rational actors in the sense that they try to maximize their benefits and minimize their losses, not only in the marketplace, but also in politics and other social realms (Lichbach, 2003). Policy process theorists are aware of the limitations of this rational actor assumption, but they apply some forms of it in their studies. Some complex systems researchers also used bounded rationality in their agent-based simulations, but complexity theorists also offered conceptual advancements in modeling agents (concepts like "reactive agents" and "cognitive agents") (Sawyer, 2005, p. 148). I will come back to the conceptualizations of policy process theorists and complexity theorists later in this chapter. Before that, I present a brief summary of the rationality assumption in history and controversies about it.

### Rationality of Actors/Agents

The rational actor assumption is that a utility-maximizing rational actor analyzes decision choices objectively using a set of decision criteria (a set of preferences, a decision algorithm, or a utility function) and selects the best alternative. Once the preferences are set, the rational actor analyzes the facts of the decision choices independently of their own values. The rational actor is capable of collecting all the pertinent information to predict the consequences of all decision options. The decision-making process is deductive: Using a pre-determined preference set, the rational actor rank-orders all the available paths of action and chooses the best one. The chosen alternative is clear to all those who are concerned: It does not have any ambiguities in meaning—it does not allow multiple interpretations—and its outcomes can be evaluated for their effectiveness empirically.

MacDonald (2003) observes that this "rationality assumption" has three components: purposive action, consistent preferences, and utility maximization. Rational actors are purposeful in their decisions and actions, rather than being motivated by their habits, traditions, or understanding of what is socially appropriate behavior. They have consistent preferences that can be ranked clearly. These actors will select the best option in the sense that it will provide them with the maximum utility for their purposes. The three components of the rationality assumption are built on two underlying assumptions: that individuals are self-interested and that they have the cognitive capability of maximizing their utilities and they use these capabilities in their real-life decisions.

As I noted earlier, some versions of rational choice theories (Lichbach, 2003), including Elinor Ostrom's (2005) institutional analysis and development framework include all three components of the rationality assumption. MacDonald (2003) points out that in the most orthodox version of rational choice theories—including neoclassical economics—it is assumed that all individuals are purposive, consistent in their preferences, and utility maximizing in all kinds of different settings. In other words, in this version, the rationality assumption applies universally. The rational choice assumptions, its components, and underlying assumptions have been criticized from a variety of angles, which I summarize in the next section.

A related assumption is about how rational individual choices and behaviors relate to macro structures. This issue is important to emphasize here because it will be the topic of next two chapters: micro to macro and macro to micro processes. MacDonald (2003) observes that in most versions of rational choice theory, "macrosocial outcomes are [conceptualized as] the sum of discrete, intentional acts by preconstituted actors" in the sense that it "is the purposive, intentional, self-propelled behavior of individuals that aggregate into outcomes" (p. 558). Macro structures do not factor into the purposes or preferences of rational actors. In other words, the rationality assumption detaches micro and macro levels.

## Criticisms of the Rationality Assumption

The most common theme in the criticisms of the rational actor assumption is that it offers a decontextualized and universal description of the decision-making process. Since the 1960s, the critics have argued that the decision-making process is not uniform for all individuals or social situations, because one can identify multiple forms of rationality in different social, political, and historical contexts. Landau (1969) points out that rationalities are defined by their respective systems and there are as many rationalities as there are systems. Dreyfus (1984) observes that there are "deliberative" forms of rationality, which recognize the role of intuitive understanding and the complexity of relationships among human beings, as well as the rationality of the rational decision-making model, what he calls "calculative rationality." Snellen (2002) identifies four types of rationalities—legal-procedural, political, economic, and scientific rationalities—and argues that public administrators must meet the requirements of all four in the current postmodern era.

Stone (1997) and Ventriss (2003) highlight the socially and politically constructed nature of rationality and point out that different rationalities shape our views of the world differently. The Habermasian critical theorists Fischer (1990) and Forester (1993) argue that the "instrumentalist and formal rationality" undergirds most scientific and technological

## 88 *A Complex Governance Networks Conceptualization*

endeavors and offer broader definitions of rationality. Fischer proposes a "comprehensive rationality," which would include practical and emancipatory interests as well. Similarly, Forester puts forth a theory of "practical rationality," which would be sensitive to social and political contexts and intimately linked to the questions of freedom and justice.

There has been an ongoing debate between neoclassical economists and cognitive [or behavioral] psychologists on the issue of rationality. Neoclassical economists insist that the rationality assumption has general validity, but some concede that parts of the model may need to be modified or abandoned (Tversky & Kahneman, 1986). For example, these theorists argue that the core assumptions that decision choices and criteria (utility function) are independent of each other and the choices and criteria can be described in objective terms can be maintained. But some theorists have reservations about the assumptions that decision choices can be transitive on all decision criteria and that the connections between decision choices and that decision outcomes can be known in their entirety (Arrow, 1951).

The most well-known and most comprehensive criticism of the rationality assumption was formulated by Herbert Simon. At the core of his criticism is his observation that the human mind has limitations. Like the critical social and political theorists, Simon (1986) stresses that the rationality of a certain behavior can be judged only in the context of its premises or "givens," which include its social situation, the goals of the decision maker, and the computational means available to them.

Simon (1979) points out that empirical tests showed that the empirical predictions of what he calls the "classical theory of omniscient rationality" failed, because this theory did not take into account the incompleteness of decision-relevant information and the limits of the computational capabilities of individuals. Newell and Simon (1972) showed that decision-making and problem solving are dynamic processes: Individuals use personal problem spaces and individual heuristics to organize complex and massive incoming stimuli to make decisions; personal problem spaces change as the experiences and thus the aspiration levels of individuals change. In his model of "bounded rationality," Simon describes a process in which decision makers engage only in a limited search for alternatives within the dynamics of their personal problem spaces. In this model, decision makers "satisfice," not optimize, in their selection of choices: They select the first satisfying choice, rather than comparing all possible choices.

Simon (1979) observes that in spite of the heavy criticism it received, the (comprehensive) rationality assumption has been revived as a result of the advances in computer technology and the development of mathematical models in the 1950s and 1960s. This new generation of researchers created elegant models and factored in the developments in the statistical decision theory and game theory. Howard Raiffa's statistical decision theory recognized uncertainties in decision-making and utilized Bayesian statistical models. Game theory factored in the uncertainties created by multiple actors in decision-making. The notion of "subjective expected utility" was developed to accommodate the uncertainties recognized by these theories and became the basis of a renewed rational decision-making theory.

This "neoclassical shift," as Simon (1979) calls it, has important implications. The subjectivity of goals or preferences has been accepted by the rational decision-making models all along. What is new is the recognition that the rational actor may not be able to pick the best possible decision alternative because of the uncertainties in predicting future states of affairs. The notion of "expected utility" signals the abandonment of the notion of perfect maximization in decision-making, but, Simon stresses, it also helps keep up the hope that actual decision-making processes can still approximate the ideal state of (comprehensive) rationality. These neoclassical revisionists assume that the "imperfections" in the decision process could be alleviated. However, Simon argues, his and other behavioral theorists' studies showed that such "imperfections" are in fact ineradicable because of the limitations of the human mind.

Not surprisingly, the problems in factoring uncertainties into the decision-making models and recognizing the actual nature of individual decision-making created a split among neoclassical theorists. According to Grafstein (1993), the debate among them is about whether rationality is in the behavior or in the outcome of a behavior. In other words, do actors really act rationally, or does it really matter whether they act rationally or not as long as the outcome of a decision is in the best interest of the decision maker and in accord with his/her goals and preferences?

MacDonald (2003) points out that the answers to this question reflect two implicit epistemological positions held by rational choice theorists: scientific realism and instrumentalist empiricism.[1] Scientific realists take the rational actor assumption for real; they attribute an ontological status to rationality. Instrumentalist empiricists see the rational actor assumption as a "useful fiction"; even if individuals do not act rationally, what matters is whether or not rational choice models can make correct predictions about the consequences of the human economic and political behavior.

In either case, the rationality assumption is unable to avoid the logical problems of its own making. If the scientific realist position is taken, there is no guarantee that rational decision makers will make decisions that will maximize their benefits, because they work with limited information about the consequences of their choices and uncertainties (these limitations and uncertainties are recognized by the "neoclassical revisionists," as Simon, 1979, points out). Then what would be the point in attributing rationality to a process that does not guarantee the best outcome? If the instrumentalist empiricist position is taken, rationality should be sought in the outcomes of decisions and actions: As long as expected utilities are maximized, the decision should be considered rational.

The problem is, by definition, utility is subjective—it is defined in the context of one's values, which are outside the domain of empirical verification. Then who is going to make the determination whether or not a particular expected utility is maximized? If it is the decision maker

90    *A Complex Governance Networks Conceptualization*

himself/herself who should make this determination, then every subjective assessment by the decision maker should be considered rational. In this syllogistic reasoning, rationality becomes circular: What is rational is what the decision maker says it is. If that is the case, then what Landau (1969) says is correct: There are as many rationalities as there are systems (or, individuals).

## (Bounded) Rationality in Policy Process Theories

Simon's concept of bounded rationality has been used widely in policy process theories, but in some applications it is implicit. In punctuated equilibrium theory, the advocacy coalitions framework, and the institutional analysis and development framework, the theorists make the most explicit references to this concept. In the first two, the utilization of bounded rationality is basic and limited. Elinor Ostrom is more elaborate in its applications of the concepts in her institutional analysis and development framework.

In punctuated equilibrium theory, the assumption that individuals are boundedly rational is extended to posit that governmental organizations also are boundedly rational in their decision-making processes (Baumgartner et al., 2018). These theorists posit that the boundedness of individual actors' decision-making processes is one of the reasons for the occasional punctuations occurring in the policy systems, which are in equilibrium states most of the time. They also observe the boundedness of rationality in governmental decision-making, particularly in the tensions between the parallel processing and serial processing in governmental decision-making. In the former, the information is processed in a parallel manner (multiple issues are processed in separate departments of the government concurrently) . In the latter, each issue is taken up one at a time (serially) and incrementally. Occasionally, Baumgartner and his colleagues observe, the parallel and serial processing processes become incompatible; then "punctuations" (sudden and significant changes) occur in policy processes.

In the advocacy coalition framework, one of the key assumptions is that policy actors come together and form coalitions based on their common belief systems (Jenkins-Smith et al., 2018). These beliefs systems are boundedly rational in the sense that the actors are purposeful but they have limited cognitive capacities to process information.

Elinor Ostrom adopts Simon's notion of bounded rationality, but she is not ready to give up on the possibility of full (comprehensive) rationality. This dual approach to rationality creates a tension that is evident in her writings. On the one hand, she stresses that the bounded rationality assumption should be substituted for the "extreme assumptions such as unlimited computational capability and full maximization of net benefits" (1999, p. 45) and that the results of her and her colleagues' research are consistent with the assumption of bounded rationality (2005, p. 118).

On the other hand, she thinks that the rationality assumption is still the best assumption under some conditions (2005, pp. 99–133) and a "useful starting point" for her analyses (p. 103).

Ostrom (2005) acknowledges that the messiness of reality forces theorists to modify the assumptions of rational choice (p. 103). She points out that because individuals use different mental models, receive various feedbacks from the world, share different cultures, and have different emotional states, their behaviors are more complex and context-dependent than these assumptions suggests (pp. 105, 112, 119).

The "attributes of a particular community" (i.e., culture) and institutional structures constitute the context in which complex individuals make their decisions and act, according to Ostrom (1999, pp. 57–58; 2005, passim). But this context is external to individual actors. They are only "external inducements for action" (Ostrom & Parks, 1999, p. 292). They do not shape individual preferences or values. The relationship between an individual actor and an institution may be one of mutual influence, according to Ostrom and Parks, but even then, the two are external to one another.

## Complexity Theory and Rational Actor

The debates on the rationality assumption and the concept of bounded rationality have affected complexity theorists as well. Some complexity researchers adopted the bounded rationality assumption and used it as a generic framework in their empirical studies and simulations. But some criticized this assumption and developed more refined conceptualizations.

Epstein's (2006) argument shows why complexity theory undermines the pure and complete rationality assumption (p. 26). Complete rationality is not possible because "optimization is computationally intractable"; even if it were, the cost of computing it would be so large that such an attempt would be overwhelmed by the cost (p. 26). Therefore, the agents in simulations can, at best, be conceptualized as bounded rational (p. 27).

Other complexity theorists have gone beyond criticizing the rationality assumption and settling on the bounded rationality assumption. They refined the conceptualizations of micro agents.

Instead of using the concept of rationality, some theorists define agents in terms of their mental pictures of their environments. There are two types of agents (actors, micro units) in complex systems: *reactive agents* ("dumb" agents who do not have any mental models of their environments) and *cognitive agents* (those agents who do have some mental models of their environments). Reactive agents do not have any internal representation of the world and they simply react to external impulses, whereas cognitive agents are intentional and deliberative agents who have beliefs about their environments, their actions, and their impacts (Sawyer, 2005). Cognitive agents have "internal models" (or "schema"), which help them anticipate future events and thus guide their actions (Holland, 1995, pp. 31–34).

## 92 *A Complex Governance Networks Conceptualization*

They have the "reflexive capacity of actors and (sub)systems" in receiving, encoding, transforming, and storing information and using it to guide actions (Teisman, Gerrits, & van Buuren, 2009, p. 9).

Complexity theorists acknowledge that real-life agents do not fall into one of these dichotomous categories; they fall somewhere between being reactive or cognitive. As Miller and Page (2007) point out, the level of sophistication of an agent is an unresolved problem in complexity theory. The question is: To what extent agents should be modeled as rational, informed, and able to act in the way they desire to act in agent-based simulations? (p. 239).

The problem of modeling agents is even more complex than this gradational conceptualization. As I noted earlier in this chapter, cognitive/behavioral psychologists identified various biases in human decision-making processes. Newell and Simon (1972) theorized that humans use personal problem spaces and individual heuristics in decision-making and that these spaces change as their experiences change. All these conceptualizations suggest that cognitive processes are complex and that not all individuals are alike. Cognizant of these conceptualizations, complexity theorists operationalize agents as heterogeneous (their motivations and behaviors are not all the same), adaptive, and interactive micro units in their agent-based simulations (Axelrod, 1997; Holland, 1995).

The problem of how to model these heterogenous agents is not easy to solve, however. In their discussion of the problem of "generalized attributes," Miller and Page (2007, pp. 238–239) highlight the conceptual problems in modeling the heterogeneity of agents. They note that some researchers generalize the attributes of agents (i.e., treat them as homogenous: they are alike in their beliefs, preferences, and abilities), others build heterogeneity into their simulations. Miller and Page point out that although it is easier technically to homogenize agents in simulations, we should be aware that "the introduction of just a bit of heterogeneity into homogenous world may substantially alter the system's behavior" (p. 239).

All in all, it is important to recognize the heterogeneity of individual agents/actors and the complexity of their interactions in collective action processes, such as governance processes. How their actions affect collective outcomes and structures is even more complex, which is the topic of the next chapter.

## Summary

This chapter was about how micro units (individual actors, agents) can be conceptualized in the micro–macro problem. I began with an overview of the rational actor assumption (the assumption that individuals are, or can be, comprehensively/fully rational). This assumption has been criticized from a variety of theoretical angles, which I summarized briefly. The most well-known criticism came from Herbert Simon. He proposed an alternative conceptualization ("bounded rationality"), which is based on the assumption that human cognition is limited. His conceptualization undergirds several theories of public policy processes. The criticisms formulated by behavioral and cognitive psychologists (that human cognition is only limited, but also biased) are less well-known, but they are as important.

Complexity theorists have not developed a common conceptualization of micro units (agents, actors) whose perceptions, preferences, and behaviors they simulate in their studies. Some simply adopted the bounded rationality assumption. More important, some complexity theorists developed more refined concepts, such as reactive agents versus cognitive agents. They recognize that this dichotomous conceptualization is a simplification; it does not capture the heterogeneity of human perceptions, preferences, or behaviors. How to conceptualize micro units (agents, actors) remains an open question in complexity theory.

## Note

1 MacDonald's (2003) categorization refers to the epistemological debates among European, particularly British, scholars in the 1970s. Keat and Urry (1975), Bhaskar (1975), and Benton (1977) made a distinction between "theoretical realism" (or just "realism")—their own position—and "positivism." They argued that the former accepts the existence of the referents of scientific concepts, whereas the latter, based on the Humean empiricist epistemology, is not concerned about the ontological status of their concepts as long as they help make accurate predictions.

# 7 Micro to Macro

Let us return to the rationality problem posed in the beginning of the previous chapter: Are individual humans intelligent and knowledgeable of the collective problems they face, so that they can think through and analyze the problems, plan to solve them, and implement their plans? In other words, are they rational? (Remember that this was another way of asking the first question of the micro–macro problem: What are the properties of micro units (e.g., individual actors)? As I noted in the previous chapter, several theorists and researchers argued and empirically demonstrated that humans are not comprehensively rational (capable of picturing problems and their solutions in their entirety) due to the limitations of their cognitive capabilities and the biases in their perceptions.

Let us also remember the second question of the micro–macro problem: How do actions of and relationships among micro units (e.g., individual actors) lead to the creation/aggregation/emergence of macro processes and structures? Before we can answer this question, we need to remember more general questions cognitive scientists and decision-making theorists asked. These questions are about whether micro-level cognitions (rationality, intelligence, cognitive maps) "match" macro-level structures. In other words, can individual actors have full, or partial, knowledge of the collective processes and structures, of which they are parts? In Herbert Simon's and his colleagues' pioneering works, this question was formulated as follows. What is the extent to which the "personal problem spaces" and "individual heuristics" of humans (Newell & Simon, 1972) match the macro structures and processes they are involved in and participated in the creation of?

The last part of this question (participating the creation of) is about whether and how macro structures emerge from the actions and interactions of micro units (individuals). And that is what we want to get at. But before we do that, let us look into the first part (the extent to which micro problem spaces (e.g., individual heuristics) match macro structures). This investigation will help us prepare for the second part. If individual actors/agents (micro units) can have the full knowledge of the consequences of their and others' actions and interactions, then they can solve their collective problems—rationally and intelligently. Then they can design good (just,

DOI: 10.4324/9781003053392-9

equitable) societies rationally, for example. (This was possible, according to the Enlightenment philosophers.) If they have no knowledge, or very little knowledge of the consequences, can their actions lead to the emergence of macro structures (the second part of the above question)? In other words, do macro structures emerge regardless of whether individual actors are knowledgeable of the consequences of their actions?

The first part of the question is can individual actors have full knowledge of the consequences of their actions? For example, can we know fully and accurately how human interactions enable the transmission of the SARS-CoV-2, how these transmissions lead to illness and consequent hospitalizations and deaths, and how mask wearing and vaccinations can prevent these transmissions from happening? If the answer were affirmative, we could solve the COVID-19 pandemic problem relatively easily. During the writing of this book (summer through winter of 2021), various vaccine companies had manufactured enough doses of the vaccine for at least half of the world's population and they were in the process of manufacturing more. The "vaccine hesitancy" and the defiance of some people to wear masks in the United States—the country hardest hit by the pandemic—and many other countries indicate that not all humans had the full knowledge of virus transmission mechanisms and the effectiveness of vaccines and masks at that time.

The vaccine hesitancy and the resistance to wearing masks can be attributed to the worldviews of rural populations, past collective experiences of particular social groups (e.g., the vaccine hesitancy among African Americans due to their mistreatments by the medical community), and the active disinformation and misinformation campaigns in the social media and parts of mass media).[1] Then, can some humans (e.g., scientists, medical doctors) know at least parts of the transmission and illness processes and mechanisms and can some (some politicians and citizens) act to reduce transmissions and illness by mask wearing and getting vaccinated? If the answer is yes—public health scientists know, it is—then collective problem solving is possible, but it still is quite a complex process.

To better understand this complexity, we can look into complexity theorists' conceptualizations and findings. Ban-Yam (2002) argues that it is very difficult, if not impossible, for individual humans, even sophisticated scientists, to *fully* understand complex collective behaviors, but at least some individuals, or groups of individuals, can develop *partial* understandings of these behaviors. It is not possible to understand collective behaviors fully, not only because of misinformation and disinformation—as in the case of the COVID-19 pandemic—or even because of lack of education. That is because of the emergent nature of complex systems. Even with the best of intentions and high levels of intelligence and education, it would not be possible to model complex collective behaviors completely, he concludes.

Bar-Yam cites two general methods used to study complex macro-level behaviors. The first method is to study the macro properties of a complex system and then develop simulation models to understand or predict its

96 *A Complex Governance Networks Conceptualization*

future behavior. This is the macro-level modeling approach—also known as systems dynamics modeling. The second method is to break down systemic properties into their components to study them. This can be done in two ways. First, it can be done in a reductionist manner, by trying to understand the properties of the systems in terms of the properties of its components and adding them up (aggregating them). I discuss the issue of aggregation versus emergence in the next section. Second, the researcher may use models to study the complex dynamics of micro to macro relations, which is the main topic of this chapter. The models in this second group are called agent-based models. Bar-Yam argues that neither systems dynamics models (macro-level only), nor reductionist models are sufficient to understand complex collective behaviors. The dynamic agent-based models are better. As I discuss in the last section of this chapter, however, these models are not easy to build at the level sophistication that will be necessary to simulate entire complex systems. In the last section, I discuss some applications of systems dynamics modeling and agent-based modeling, particularly in the case of the COVID-19 pandemic.

Complexity theorists also demonstrate that even when at least some individuals may understand the properties of complex systems—even when there is some degree of the match between the cognitive maps of individual agents/actors (e.g., degree of knowledge of collective problems) and the macro structures and outcomes (e.g., the evolutionary pattern of the pandemic)—that will not necessarily determine the effectiveness of their collective actions. That is because the causal link between the actions of individuals and their collective outcomes is not straightforward. In other words, even if an agent, or a group of agents, strategize in a sophisticated manner, that will not necessarily bring about successful collective outcomes. Even if the cognitive map of an agent, or that of a group of agents, matches the emergent macro structures and process, that will not guarantee that social problems can be solved. In Epstein's (2006) words:

> [I]ndividual rationality is neither necessary nor sufficient for the attainment of macroscopic efficiency.... [A] society of autonomous agents [may arrive] at [economic optimality] even though the overwhelming majority do not optimize individually.... [T]he invisible hand does not require rational fingers.

> (p. 144)

To unpack what Epstein means, let us remember the simplistic, but heuristically useful, dichotomy of reactive agents versus cognitive agents (see Chapter 6). Complexity researchers show that the actions of reactive agents (with no cognitive maps) may be effective at a macro level. Take the example of ants. Schelling (2006) describes how ants work without an external (or central) coordination and only in reaction to the behaviors of the other ants in their immediate environments. Each ant has a very limited capacity to process the information about its environment, and only its

*Micro to Macro* 97

immediate environment. Still, some collective solutions emerge from the interactions among these ants: They can successfully build their nests and find their paths to search for food (p. 21). Although each ant is a reactive agent (with very little cognitive capacity), an ant colony is "intelligent" as a whole, he concludes.[2]

Also consider viruses, such as SARS-CoV-2, as examples of reactive agents. Their only "purpose" is to replicate. They need animal or human hosts to replicate in them. They do not plan or strategize to be successful; they do not have any cognitive maps of their environments (e.g., information about animal or human hosts in which they can replicate). Their success (effectiveness in adapting to their environments) depends on accidental mutations. During their replication processes, occasionally, viruses mutate (i.e., their generic codes are altered accidentally). Some of these mutations make the new virus "variants" more successful (adaptable to their environments).

In the COVID-19 pandemic, three major mutations were very successful. The first one was the "novel" SARS-CoV-2 virus, which was a mutation of the original virus that had existed in an animal host. The host was probably a bat species or pangolins, but that is not known with certainty.[3] It had mutated successfully enough to survive in human bodies, which increased its chances to spread much faster because the very high-level interactions among humans. (Just from our own experiences, we can know that humans come close to each other and interact in numerous ways every day.) The second successful mutation was the "Delta variant." It was a result of the mutation in a single amino acid in the SARS-CoV-2 spike protein, which enabled the virus to attach itself to human cells, and consequently penetrate them, more effectively.[4] The result of this accidental mutation was that the infectiousness of Delta variant quickly surpassed those of all the other variants of SARS-CoV-2 in the summer of 2021 and became the dominant variant around the world. In the United States, before the Delta became dominant, the new COVID-19 cases were in decline; the variant quickly reversed the trend to cause a fourth wave of the pandemic. The Omicron variant was even more successful because of the multiple mutations in its spike protein. It outcompeted the Delta variant and became dominant in the winter of 2021–2022 in the other countries (del Rio et al., 2021).

Obviously, humans are more intelligent than ants and viruses. They can develop cognitive maps of their immediate environments and their collective structures and processes (societies, communities, nations, histories, etc.). They can strategize and plan to achieve collective outcomes, at least to some degree. As I noted earlier, not all humans had equally accurate and comprehensive maps of the SARS-CoV-2 coronavirus or the COVID-19 pandemic. (Some were simply deceived by misinformation and disinformation and some others were merely ignorant.) In very simplistic terms, some had better cognitive maps than others. Human agents were heterogenous.

In many cases, humans may have relatively accurate maps of their own immediate environments and strategize and act to maximize their individual

## 98   A Complex Governance Networks Conceptualization

interests, as in maximizing their own profits in commercial markets in the short term. Then do these maps and actions lead to effective collective outcomes, for communities and larger societies? Adam Smith (1902)[5] thought so. In his conceptualization of the relations between individual wealth and societal wealth, he stresses the role of an "invisible hand" in generating positive/effective collective outcomes. He states:

> As every individual…endeavors as much as he can both to employ his capital in the support of domestic industry [i.e., the economy of his household], and so to direct that industry that its produce may be of greatest value; every individual necessarily labors to render the annual revenue of the society as great as he can. *He generally, indeed, neither intends to promote the public interest, nor knows how much he is promoting it.* By referring the support of domestic to that of foreign industry, he intends only his own security; and by directing that industry in such a manner as its produce may be of the greatest value, *he intends only his own gain, and he is in this, as in many other cases, led by an invisible hand to promote an end which was no part of his intention…. By pursuing his own interest he frequently promotes that of the society more effectually than when he really intends to promote it.* [italics added]
>
> (pp. 160–161)

The most important point in this quote is that Smith delinks individual intentions/plans and collective outcomes. Individuals do not need to intend or plan to contribute to public goods/public interest. They can do so simply by acting in their own interests. They do not even need to know that they are contributing to something other than their own interests. Another important point in Adam Smith's quote is that there is an "invisible hand" (a hidden social mechanism that works independently of the intentions of individuals) and these mechanisms link the products of individual actions to public goods and public interest.

Other theorists made similar observations. For example, Vincent Ostrom (1974) also delinks individual rationality, intentions, and acts one the one hand and good collective outcomes on the other. In his view, there is no linear causal path from individual motivations and behaviors to collective outcomes. He also argues that individual actors do not have to have "other-regarding" motivations (e.g., altruistic motivations) to generate desirable collective outcomes. The actions of self-regarding and (boundedly) rational individuals can also lead to such outcomes. He poses the links between the individual intentions/rationality/actions and collective outcomes as the "collective action problem."

Smith's and Ostrom's arguments remind us of an important question: Could individual acts lead to "public bads" (negative collective outcomes, such as air pollution and global warming), as well as public goods? The conceptual works by complexity theorists Schelling (2006) and Epstein and Axtell (1996) and their simulations answer this question affirmatively. They demonstrate that individual actors' selections of where they live (particularly their inclinations to live together with others like themselves) lead to neighborhood segregation in urban areas, with all the negative consequences. In his classic formulation of the micro–macro problem, Coleman (1986) also suggests that the micro to macro relations do not always generate positive (desirable) macro outcomes.

In all these conceptualizations and argumentations—from Adam Smith's to Herbert Simon's and complexity theorists'—there is one common understanding: Micro-level knowledge of macro structures is not necessary for the emergence of macro structures. There are links between micro-level actions and interactions and macro structures, but those links are not simple or linear. What those links are and how they work are the micro to macro problem. This was the second question of the micro–macro problem: How do actions of and relationships among micro units (e.g., individual actors) lead to the creation/aggregation/emergence of macro processes and structures? In Coleman's (1986) classic formulation, the micro–macro problem is:

> ...the process through which individual preferences become collective choices; the process through which dissatisfaction becomes revolution; through which simultaneous fear in members of a crowd turns into a mass panic; through which preferences, holdings of private goods, and the possibility of exchange create market prices and a redistribution of goods; through which individuals' task performance in an organization creates a social product; through which the reduction of usefulness of children to parents leads families to disintegrate; through which interest cleavages lead (or fail to lead) to overt social conflict.
>
> (p. 1321)

Coleman's formulation should be amended. Her refers to only one aspect of the micro–macro problem: micro to macro processes. It is the topic of this chapter. The second aspect is about how collective (macro) structures, such as social culture and institutions, affect individual knowledge, intentions, and actions (the third question of micro–macro problem posed in Chapter 5). That is topic of the next chapter.

In the following sections, I discuss three conceptual issues that are necessary to understand the micro to macro processes: aggregation versus emergence, irreducibility, and mechanisms of emergence.

## Aggregation or Emergence?

To understand the mechanisms of the micro to macro processes, we need to make a conceptual distinction between *aggregation* and *emergence*. Aggregation is an additive process and it suggests a reductionist thinking (a whole is equal to the sum of its parts). Emergence connotes holism (a

100 *A Complex Governance Networks Conceptualization*

whole is more than the sum of its parts). It is not settled among complexity theorists whether there is really a difference between the two and, if there is a difference, how they can be discerned in practice.[6]

Before a discussion of the conceptualizations by complexity theorists and their empirical studies, let us return to Adam Smith's (1902) "invisible hand." We can surmise from the quotation form his work in the previous section that probably he did not mean an additive process by "invisible hand," but he does say so specifically. It is not clear whether in his view public goods/public interest are aggregated or emergent. How Smith's views evolved and how they affected his followers are beyond the scope of my discussions here. But I can make two observations. First, in neoclassical economics and the theories of political economy, such as rational choice theory, the issue of aggregation versus emergence is not even taken seriously. Second, at least in my reading of their works, these theorists make an explicit, or implicit, assumption: that collective outcomes, such as public interest, merely accumulate (aggregate) from individual interests. In this aggregation process, the whole is equal to the sum of its parts.

MacDonald's (2003) interpretation confirms my reading or the theories. He states that in rational choice theories, "macrosocial outcomes are the sum of discrete, intentional acts by preconstituted actors.... [It] is the purposive, intentional, self-propelled behavior of individuals that aggregate into outcomes…" (p. 558). This aggregative view is clearly stated by Cochran and Malone (1995): " '[P]ublic interest may be understood as the entirety of…individual preferences expressed as choices" (p. 5). Rational choice theorist Lichbach (2003) thinks that macro-level entities, such as society and culture, do not have "independent status[es] apart from the individuals who constitute them" (p. 32). (His argument relates to a concept I will discuss in the next chapter: irreducibility.) This aggregative view was adopted by the British Prime Minister Margaret Thatcher, who said in an interview: "There is no such thing as society. There are individual men and women, and there are families."[7]

This aggregative view has its skeptics and critics, but there is no clear alternative conceptualization. Herbert Simon and his associates (1992, p. 49) raise doubts about this additive view of micro to macro processes. They point out that there is so much we do not know about these processes and they should be the topic for the future scholars to study. Elinor Ostrom (1999, 2005) acknowledges that the additive view of interest aggregation is not adequate, but she does not offer a specific alternative.

Complexity theorists do take the issues of aggregations versus emergence seriously, but they do not offer a unified and coherent perspective. Sometimes they use the two terms vaguely and interchangeably, but mostly they recognize the special and different characteristic of emergence. Holland (1995) states that aggregation "concerns the emergence of complex large-scale behaviors from the aggregate interactions of less complex agents" (p. 11). Axelrod (1997) asks, "How can new political actors *emerge* from an *aggregation* of smaller political actors?" [emphases added.] (p. 124). Miller and Page (2007) define emergence in terms of aggregation of localized behavior that is disconnected from its origins (p. 44).

In Sawyer's (2005, pp. 95–97) sociological treatise and Holland's later work on emergence (1998), it is conceptualized more cogently. Sawyer stresses that that emergence differs from aggregation in the sense that aggregate properties are reducible, whereas emergent properties are irreducible. In other words, if a whole is aggregated, then its properties can be decomposed. (If one adds up the properties of its components, one will end up with the aggregated total.) Emergent properties are decomposable (irreducible) because they are "nonlocalized": They cannot be identified in the components, but they are "distributed spatially within the system" (p. 96). Also, the interactions among the components are nonlinear. The decomposability of systemic properties—because of their nonlocality and the nonlinearity of the interactions among the components—is the basis of defining them as emergent.

Holland (1998) argues that emergence is a real property of complex systems in nature and it can be studied scientifically. Then how would we able to identify it if we see it? His answer is in his characterization of "emergent macro properties": They persist despite continual turnover in their constituents (p. 7). For example, biological organisms, such as humans, have persistent collective structures and behavioral patterns, despite the fact that they are open systems (i.e., they constantly exchange matter and energy with their environments). Humans breathe air in, drink water, and eat food and breathe air out, perspire, and defecate, but they can maintain their bodily integrity.

Another example is social institutions, which can be conceptually separated from organizations. They are long-lasting social organizational forms. They are not designed, but they emerge from the relationships among actors; once they emerge, they are maintained by the reworking of these relationships (Lejano, 2008, pp. 494–495). And these emergent structures can maintain their integrity for long periods of time. Take the Catholic Church as an example. Arguably, it is the largest and longest lasting institution in human history.[8] During its roughly 2,000 years of history, hundreds of millions of individuals populated its hierarchical structures and made and maintained its many rules, which are codified in the Cannon Law.[9] Individuals came and went, some of the rules have changed, but the institutional structure and patterns of behavior persisted over millennia. It is safe to say that institutions like the Catholic Church are examples of emergent social structures.

What makes a macro structure persist despite the turnover in its constituents? One conceptual answer to the question is *irreducibility*, which I discuss next. Some answers to the question can also be found in the *mechanisms of emergence* complexity researchers identified and the empirical studies on emergence. I will discuss these mechanisms in the following sections.

## Irreducibility

Anderson's (1972) definition of irreducibility is that not all phenomena in nature can be explained in terms of the fundamental laws of lower-level phenomena (pp. 393–396). In his interview with Waldrop (1999, pp. 82–83), Anderson illustrates the irreducibility of systemic properties with the example of the water molecule. It is composed of two hydrogen and one oxygen atoms. When billions of water molecules are together, they collectively acquire a new property: liquidity. The property of liquidity is irreducible to those of the properties of hydrogen or oxygen molecules. Understanding the formula of the molecule ($H_2O$) will not help us understand how liquid water behaves. For example, at $0°$ Celsius, or $32°$ Fahrenheit, liquid water undergoes a phase transition and becomes solid. When this transition happens the basic structure of water molecules ($H_2O$) does not change, but the way they are organized does: They form themselves into an orderly crystalline array, what we call ice.

Kauffman (1995) illustrates emergence with examples from biology. Once live organisms emerge, their complexity cannot be understood in terms of the rules governing the functioning of the molecules they are made of.

> Life ... is an *emergent phenomenon* arising as the molecular diversity of a prebiotic chemical system increases beyond a *threshold of complexity* [edge of chaos].... [L]ife is not located in the property of any single molecule—in the details—but is a *collective property of systems* of interacting molecules. Life ... emerged whole and has always remained whole. *Life ... is not to be located in its parts, but in the collective emergent properties of the whole they create....* No vital force or extra substance is present in the *emergent,* self-reproducing whole. But the collective system does possess a stunning property not possessed by any of its parts. It is able to reproduce itself and evolve. The collective system is alive. Its parts are just chemicals. [emphases added]
>
> (p. 24)

Not all complexity theorists agree with the view that emergence in the sense of irreducibility should be part of complexity theory. Epstein (2006), for example, has deep reservations about these concepts because of their philosophical underpinnings. He states that emergence in the sense of irreducibility is rooted in the mysticism of the British emergentist philosophers of the 1920s. These philosophers were "unmistakably anti-scientific— even deistic," according to Epstein, because they "claimed *absolute unexplainability* for emergent phenomena" [emphases in original] (p. 32). He quotes the deist philosopher Lloyd Morgan, who said: "Emergent evolution is from first to last a revelation and manifestation of that which I speak of as Divine Purpose" (Quoted in Epstein, p. 3).

## Micro to Macro   103

He also points out that emergentism is not compatible with agent-based modeling, a primary methodological tool of complexity theorists. He states:

> Classical emergentism holds that the parts (the microspecification) cannot explain the whole (the macrostructure), while to the agent-based modeler, it is precisely the generative sufficiency of the parts (the microspecification) that constitutes the whole's explanation! In this particular sense, *agent-based modeling is reductionist*. Classical emergentism seeks to preserve a *"mystery gap"* between micro and macro; agent-based modeling seeks to demystify this alleged gap by identifying microspecifications that are sufficient to generate—robustly and replicably—the macro (whole). [emphases added]
>
> (p. 37)

Is there really a "mystery gap" in the concepts of emergence and irreducibility? Does irreducibility necessarily mean that natural systems, at least some of them, are unexplainable and therefore they should be the products of a divine purpose and intervention? Some complexity theorists answered this question directly or indirectly. Kauffman (1995), for example, says that "fundamental holism and emergence are not at all mysterious" (p. 24). According to Sawyer (2005), emergentism does not have to be deistic. In his view, the emergentism of those sociologists who founded the discipline is nonreductive and ontologically materialistic (p. 29). He calls this understanding "nonreductive materialism" (p. 65). In this view, both the macro- and micro-level properties are real; one is not an epiphenomenon of the other. There are micro–macro–micro transformations, but each level maintains its separate existence.

But then, one might ask, (how) do macro and micro levels maintain their separate existences while interacting with each other? Holland (1998) offers an answer. He first recognizes the separation of micro and macro levels: Because the whole is not a simple sum of its parts, the "regularities in a system's behavior...are not revealed by direct inspection of the laws satisfied by the components" (p. 225). In other words, persistent macro patterns obey macro laws, and they "do not make direct reference to the underlying generators and constraints" (p. 239). Then he addresses the question, whether or not the properties of a system cannot be reduced at all to those of its components. Holland suggests "we *can* reduce the behavior of the whole to the lawful behavior of its parts, *if* we take the non-linear interactions into account" [emphases in original] (p. 122). Reduction is possible in science; after all it has worked for centuries. But he offers a different version of reduction.

> The laws of chemistry are indeed *constrained* by the laws of physics and, in this sense, chemistry is reducible to physics.... [But, on the

104  *A Complex Governance Networks Conceptualization*

other hand,] [t]he macrolaws that govern the interactions of molecules are formulated and used without reference to the laws of particle physics. [emphasis added]

(p. 245)

It can be concluded from Holland's treatment of irreducibility that the lower-level laws still do apply at higher levels, but only as constraints. For example, if we want to understand social phenomena, we cannot reduce it completely to individual human psychology or biology, but we need to understand that individual biology and psychology are constrains for social (collective) behavior. But are micro-level laws (e.g., laws about psychology and biology) merely constraints for macro-level laws (laws about the social, collective behaviors), or are there mechanism that link these levels to each other?

## Mechanisms of Emergence

If the emergence of macro patterns and structures is not an unexplainable mystery, then its mechanism should be identifiable. One generic mechanism is nonlinearity. I discussed nonlinearity as a characteristic of the relations among the components of complex systems in Chapter 4. In that chapter, I defined nonlinearity as disproportionality in the relations among the components of a complex system and noted that positive and negative feedback loops are nonlinear. Nonlinearity is essential to understand emergence mainly because it makes aggregation (as addition) impossible. Remember the aggregative conceptualizations by neoclassical economists and rational choice political economists. If the relations among the components of an economic, or political-economic, system are nonlinear, then one cannot add up the interests of individual actors to calculate the public interest. The concept of emergence suggests that actually public (collective) interest is more than this simple arithmetic operation of addition.

Complexity theorists identified two specific mechanisms of emergence: differential persistence and preferential attachment. Holland (1998) observes that *differential persistence* is the primary mechanism of the emergence of hierarchical organizations. The basic principle behind this concept is that persistence pays in determining what comes out next. Those components of a system whose properties and behaviors made them more successful in the past will persist and play a larger role in shaping the future patterns in the behavior of the system. Examples can be found in the Darwinian evolution: "[T]he patterns that persist long enough to collect resources and produce copies are the ones that generate new variants" (p. 227).[10] His conceptualization indicates that differential persistence is not uniform in all systemic processes. In fact, different patterns persist at different rates and forms. Some patterns persist only as long as they do not encounter other patterns, in which case they may dissolve. Others persist by undergoing dissolution or transformation into other patterns. Still

*Micro to Macro* 105

others persist and maintain their forms regardless of the other systems they encounter (p. 227).

Think of the SARS-CoV-2 virus as an example of the second form: transformation into other patterns. Its basic structure and mechanisms of infection (e.g., transmission through tiny particle through air and the specific spike proteins that enabled the virus to attach itself to human cells) persisted long enough to generate new and more successful variants (e.g., the Delta and Omicron variants). The basic structure and mechanism of infection of the virus remained the same, which is why its "variants" are still the variants of SARS-CoV-2, but they were different enough to be called variants. The Delta variant was more successful in the sense that it was more transmissible than the original SARS-CoV-2; that was because of the mutations in its spike protein that helped it attach itself to human cells more easily and because of its ability to travel through air more easily.[11] Omicron was even more successful because of the further mutations in its spike protein and its ability to replicate much faster once it is in the human body.[12]

The primary mechanisms that human social systems developed to break the patterns of SARS-CoV-2 and its variants were the COVID-19 vaccines. The epidemiological prediction was that if a sufficient percentage of humans were to be vaccinated, that would break the patterns of the virus by making the immune systems of individuals resilient against it and thus slowing its replication in the body and stopping the transmissions from one individual to the next. This targeted state of affairs was called "herd immunity." There was no certainty about whether and when human societies would reach a sufficient level of herd immunity against SARS-CoV-2 at the time of the writing of this book.[13] So, it was not clear whether the virus would keep transforming itself to develop newer variants or its patterns would "dissolve."

The second specific mechanism of emergence is *preferential attachment*, which I briefly mentioned in Chapter 3. Barabási and Albert (1999) demonstrate that this is the primary mechanism of the emergence of "scale-free networks," whose degree distribution follows a "power law."[14] In this kind of distributions, a few nodes have a large number of connections to other nodes, whereas a large number of nodes have very few connections.

Take the example of the connections between the websites (nodes) on the Internet. There is a power law distribution among them. (See the information at the "Internet Map."[15]) The connections between the websites (micro units) constitute the scale-free network of the Internet (macro structure). The ratios of the number of the connections Google, Facebook, YouTube, and Yahoo vastly outnumber the connections other website have. For example, in my searches on the Internet Map in June 2021, I found that more than 50% of all users of the Internet visited Google.com at that time, roughly 40% visited Facebook.com, close to 30% visited YouTube, and 25% Yahoo.com. Among the other better-known websites, IMDB.

106  *A Complex Governance Networks Conceptualization*

com (Internet Movie Database) was visited by a little over 2%, nytimes.com (*New York Times*) by over 1%, and Samsung.com by less than 0.5%. The website of my institution Penn State University (psu.edu) was visited by about 0.05% of the Internet users (a ratio of 1,000 to 1, between Google's and Penn State's websites).

Several researchers observed power distributions in the systems they analyzed. Price (1965) showed that citations of academic journal articles followed this pattern. Barabási (2002) found a power distribution in the "hub" system of the flight connections of airlines (pp. 70–71). For example, the Atlanta, Memphis, New York, Cincinnati, Detroit, Minneapolis/St. Paul, and Salt Lake City, airports serve as the hubs in the Delta Airlines system. More Delta flights land in and depart from these airports; travelers make their connections to hundreds of other airports in the United States and the rest of the world at these airports.

Two genetic mechanisms of the emergence of power law distributions are growth and preferential attachment (Barabási & Albert, 1999, pp. 87–88). Growth plays a role in the sense that as a network expands existing nodes have more time than the newcomers to acquire links: If a node is the last to arrive, no other node has the opportunity to link to it; if a node is the first in a network, all subsequent nodes have chance to link to it. Thus, growth offers a clear advantage to the senior nodes. Seniority alone is not sufficient to explain the power laws, however. Preferential attachment also plays an important role. Some existing nodes, not necessarily the most senior ones, may have been connected to larger numbers of nodes, for whatever reason. Because new nodes prefer to link to the more connected nodes, early nodes with more links will be selected more often than their younger and less connected peers. As more and more nodes arrive and keep picking the more connected nodes to link to, the first nodes will inevitably break away from the pack, acquiring a very large number of links. They will turn into "hubs."

Preferential attachment is another name for the "rich-get-richer" phenomenon. Bianconi and Barabási (2001) refined this concept as "fitter-gets-richer." They observe that what determines how many links a particular node gets is not only its prior links, but also its "fitness." Those with better fitness to their environments attract more new connections. The cumulative effects of these processes at the individual node level "determine the system's large-scale topology" (p. 436).

There are some criticisms of the applicability of scale-free networks, preferential attachment, and power law distributions. The critics argue that too many phenomena are described as scale-free or power-law and that preferential attachment may not be the mechanism of emergence even in the networks that are actually scale-free (M. Mitchell, 2009, pp. 253–255). These criticisms have some merit, but as the empirical applications of Barabási and his colleagues' concepts in some areas, including governance studies, show, they do have validity.

## Modeling the Micro to Macro Processes

There are some empirical applications that show that power law distributions emerge because of preferential attachment. In their studies of German cities, Helbing and his colleagues (2009) identified power law distribution in the urban supply networks (numbers of doctors, pharmacies, and petrol stations) and traffic flows. Rosenkopf and Padula's (2008) analyses of the alliance networks in the mobile communications industry show that preferential attachment is a major mechanism in the evolutions of these networks. More specifically, network evolution is an endogenous process and pairs of firms with direct or indirect ties in existing alliance networks are more likely to form future alliances, as are firms with more extensive histories of alliance formation. In their study of the governance networks in 10 estuaries in the United States, Berardo and Scholz (2010) found that coordination in these networks emerged from "the uncoordinated selection of popular partners by individual actors seeking better payoffs" (p. 645). In other words, they found, preferential attachment to the "popular" actors can generate a coordinated structure in a network. In their study of the neighborhood councils' governance network in Los Angeles, Musso and Weare (2014) also found evidence of preferential attachment. Using an exponential random graph model, they found that the councils preferred to connect with others whom they trusted, those that were geographically close, those they found to be like themselves (homophily), and that these connections led to the emergence of the structure of this governance network.

Berardo and Scholz (2010) and Musso and Weare (2014) used social network analyses (SNA). SNA methods can be used to investigate "how large-scale systemic transformations emerge out of the combined preferences and purposive actions of individuals.... [These methods link the] changes in microlevel choices to macrolevel structural alterations" (Knoke & Yang, 2008, p. 6). Another methodological approach is agent-based modeling (ABM). This approach is used to study the dynamics of micro–macro relationships and transformations in complex systems (e.g., Johnston et al., 2008; Zia et al., 2006).

The advantage of ABM over SNA is that the former is dynamic, but the latter is not. SNA applications "snapshots" of network relations and macro properties at given times. ABM applications simulate system dynamics over time. The advantage of SNA applications is that they use data about real human beings (or other units of analysis), whereas in ABM applications researchers make some assumptions and generalizations about human behaviors. Often, they use abstractions like "reactive agents" and "cognitive agents" (see the earlier discussions in the previous chapter) and enter "average" behavioral characteristics into simulations, rather than information about actual behaviors. In that sense, ABM applications are "artificial" (hence an earlier name used for them: "artificial life simulations").[16]

108  *A Complex Governance Networks Conceptualization*

The ABM approach can also be compared with systems dynamics modeling (SDM). As I mentioned earlier in this chapter, SDM methods are used at macro-levels to simulate complex system behaviors with the purpose of predicting their future behaviors. ABM, on the other hand, is used to simulate micro–macro relations. Bar-Yam (2002) suggests, and I agree, that the SDM approach is not sufficient to understand complex collective behaviors. The ABM approach is much more challenging, but if it can be implemented, it will yield better results.

Consider the example of modeling COVID-19 dynamics. Several macro-level simulations had been conducted on these dynamics at the time of the writing of this book. In their international study, Bubar and his colleagues (2021) modeled the effects of the variables of vaccine prioritization strategies, transmission rates, age demographics, contact structure, and R-naught (replication rate of the virus) to predict the mortality rates from COVID-19. Using data from South Korea and nonlinear macro-level modeling, Kwuimy and his colleagues (2020), simulated population numbers in various stages of the infectious disease progression. They found that a combination of government response to the pandemic and public reaction could effectively stop Covid-19. Matraj and his colleagues (2020) simulated multiple scenarios of combinations of the rates of deaths, symptomatic infections, and hospitalization to predict optimal vaccine allocation. They found that when the effectiveness of a vaccine was 50% or above, that would be enough to substantially mitigate the COVID-19 pandemic, given that a high percentage of the population was optimally vaccinated and that vaccines were allocated to older age groups first.

These macro-level simulations yielded very useful results, but micro–macro models, like ABMs, are more detailed and realistic in capturing system dynamics. As Vardavas and his colleagues (2021) point out, these "population-based models" (PBMs) depict disease dynamics at the system level and they can be useful for exploring and comparing macro governmental intervention policies. They are not good at capturing individual-(micro-) level disease transmission or vaccination dynamics, however. ABMs can factor in a range of "epidemiological heterogeneities" that affect transmission patterns, such as individual belief systems about the spread of infections and the efficacy of vaccines, which are affected by the individuals' interactions with family and friends. The authors point out that ABMs yield better tools than PBMs in targeting interventions in local communities. They propose that the most effective methodological approach would be to combine these two modeling approaches.

It is a major methodological challenge to combine these modeling approaches. Hartnett and his colleagues (2020) demonstrate that innovative approaches like "deep generative modeling" can help overcome these methodological challenges. Real-life social network data and advanced SNA methods, such as deep-neural networks, can be used to inform simulations at multiple levels. This approach not only combines the ABM and PBM approaches, but also it can help reduce the "artificiality" or ABMs. The

*Micro to Macro* 109

authors illustrate this with examples of the transmissions of diseases, like influenza.

Another example is the interactive TRACE model a team of researchers from Brookings Institution and Washington University in St. Louis developed. TRACE is an ABM that includes macro-level system parameters, like base-line cases and policy interventions. This model can be sued to test the effects of policies on COVID testing and social distancing on the rate of disease spread.[17] It includes interactions among simulated individuals and aim to estimate the number of infections at any point in time and the cumulative infection rate over the course of the entire time period. The results of the simulations are not static. Instead, the researchers made available a dashboard where users can change macro-level parameters to estimate the number of infections in different time periods and cumulatively.[18]

These recent advances show that it is not only possible to study micro to macro processes in complex systems in general, but also such studies can be very useful in understanding governance networks. As Vardavas and his colleagues (2021) and Ogibayashi (2021) argue, these studies are not merely academic. They can be used to devise effective policy interventions into complex systems like mitigating COVID-19 pandemic.

## Summary

This chapter was about how emergence happens. The question is, do micro-level behaviors and interactions lead to the generation of macro-level patterns and structures? If so, how? To answer these questions, I revisited some general conceptualizations and propositions by Adam Smith, Herbert Simon, and Vincent Ostrom. Then I summarized complexity theorists' views on the concept of emergence.

In the sections that followed, more specific topics are covered. A key conceptual issue that should be clarified is the difference between aggregation (reductionist approach) and emergence (holistic approach). If one adopts the holistic view of emergence, then the process of how micro behaviors and interactions affect the emergence of macro processes and structures becomes an important area of investigation. One may argue that macro structures exist independently and their properties are irreducible to those of micro units (e.g., individuals) and investigate the phenomena at the two levels separately.

One may also argue that there are mechanisms that connect the levels and then aim to find out what they are. In a section of this chapter, I summarized the two mechanisms that have been identified by network and complexity researchers: differential persistence and preferential attachment. There are some empirical studies on governance networks in which the researchers identified preferential attachment. In these studies, the researchers used social network analyses and agent-based simulations. These examples and examples from the literature on modeling the COVID-19 pandemic were the topics of the last section.

## Notes

1 Empirical evidence showed that Republicans were more hesitant to getting vaccinated.
We've Reached the "Red Covid" Phase of the Pandemic. www.cnn.com/2021/09/28/politics/red-covid-republican-states/index.html
2 Your Ant Farm Is Smarter Than Google, *Time*, May 27, 2014. https://time.com/118633/ant-intelligence-google/.
3 Zheng-Li Shi, Origins of SARS-CoV-2: Focusing on Science. *Infectious Dis Immunity* 2021; 1(1): 3–4. www.ncbi.nlm.nih.gov/pmc/articles/PMC8057312/
4 "The Mutation that Helps Delta Spread Like Wildfire," *Nature*, August 20, 2021. www.nature.com/articles/d41586-021-02275-2
5 Adam Smith's *Wealth of Nations* was originally published in 1776.
6 I provided a historical account of the thinking on emergence and discussed the contemporary conceptualizations of these mechanisms by complexity theorists extensively in my earlier book (Morçöl, 2012, chapter 3). Here I summarize some of the more relevant parts of those discussions.
7 Thatcher said this in an interview with *Women's Own* magazine in 1987. She was asserting that individuals should not relying on government for solving their problems. The full text is as follows:

> I think we've been through a period where too many people have been given to understand that if they have a problem, it's the government's job to cope with it. 'I have a problem, I'll get a grant.' 'I'm homeless, the government must house me.' They're casting their problem on society. And, you know, *there is no such thing as society. There are individual men and women, and there are families.* And no government can do anything except through people, and people must look to themselves first. It's our duty to look after ourselves and then, also to look after our neighbour. People have got the entitlements too much in mind, without the obligations. There's no such thing as entitlement, unless someone has first met an obligation [emphases added].
>
> (*Women's Own Magazine*, October 31, 1987;
> http://briandeer.com/social/thatcher-society.htm)

8 Catholic Church. https://en.wikipedia.org/wiki/Catholic_Church
9 The Catholic Church Is All About Rules! https://catholicstand.com/catholic-church-rules/
Canon Law. www.usccb.org/beliefs-and-teachings/what-we-believe/canon-law
10 Differential persistence, a concept of evolutionary biology, has been applied in other areas that were influences by evolutionary theories in biology, most notably evolutionary archeology (e.g., Leonard, 2001; Murrell, 2007; O'Brien and Lyman, 2002).
11 Why Is the Delta Variant More Transmissible? www.verywellhealth.com/delta-variant-more-transmissible-covid-5195084
Two studies suggest that newer variants of the coronavirus are better at traveling through the air. www.nytimes.com/live/2021/10/02/world/covid-delta-variant-vaccine#two-studies-suggest-that-newer-variants-of-the-coronavirus-are-better-at-traveling-through-the-air
12 Michaeleen Doucleff, A Tantalizing Clue to Why Omicron is Spreading So Quickly. December 15, 2021. www.npr.org/sections/goatsandsoda/2021/12/15/1064597592/a-tantalizing-clue-to-why-omicron-is-spreading-so-quickly

13 Kamran Kadkhoda, Herd Immunity to COVID-19: Alluring and Elusive. *Am J Clin Pathol*. 2021 January 5 www.ncbi.nlm.nih.gov/pmc/articles/PMC7929447/

14 The article on scale-free networks in Wikipedia notes that neither concept nor the name of scale-free networks was invented by Barabási and Albert. It is noted that in 1965 Derek de Solla Price showed that

> the number of links to papers—i.e., the number of citations they receive—had a heavy-tailed distribution following a Pareto distribution or power law, and thus that the citation network was scale-free. He did not however use the term "scale-free network", which was not coined until some decades later. In a later paper in 1976, Price also proposed a mechanism to explain the occurrence of power laws in citation networks, which he called "cumulative advantage" but which is today more commonly known under the name preferential attachment.

15 *Source*: http://internet-map.net/

16 I discussed the strengths and shortcomings of SNA and ABM in my earlier book (Morçöl, 2012a, pp. 210–243).

17 Testing Responses Through Agent-Based Computational Epidemiology (TRACE),

> www.brookings.edu/testing-responses-through-agent-based-computatio nal-epidemiology-trace/?utm_campaign=brookings-comm&utm_source=hs_ email&utm_medium=email&utm_content=88190463

> Developing Policies for Effective COVID-19 Containment: The TRACE model. www.brookings.edu/blog/up-front/2020/05/15/developing-policies-for-effective-covid-19-containment-the-trace-model/?utm_campaign=brookings-comm&utm_source=hs_email&utm_medium=email&utm_content=88190463

18 TRACE Model Dashboard. https://brookings-csdp.shinyapps.io/TRACE-dash/

# 8 Macro to Micro
## Background and Conceptualizations of Downward Causation

The third question of the micro–macro problem is, once macro structures emerge, how do these structures and processes affect the beliefs, motivations, and actions of individual actors? (Chapter 5). This question has implications for governance processes. An explicit, or implicit, assumption in public policy and public administration studies and practices is that the actions of governments or combinations of governmental and nongovernmental actors can affect social systemic (macro) structures (e.g., constitutional institutions) and cultural norms (e.g., collective racist beliefs and practices), which in turn can influence individual (micro) behaviors.

Take the example of anti-discrimination laws. Their common principle in these laws is that no group of individuals should be discriminated against based on their ethnicity, religion, gender, or sexual orientation in employment decisions (e.g., hiring, promotion, firing decisions), housing decisions (e.g., no "redlining" in financing housing purchases), etc. These laws set up macro structures—usually called "institutions"—that are expected to influence individuals' behaviors and perhaps even their beliefs and attitudes. Do they do that?

These laws can influence and change individual behaviors, because if they are not obeyed, punitive actions can be taken against the rule violators. A manager who discriminates against minorities in their hiring, promotion, or firing decisions can be removed from their position, for example. Another, and arguably more important, question is, whether such laws are internalized by individuals so that their principles ("e.g., "do not discriminate") become their own "values"?

In other words, do macro-level properties have causal effects on micro-level beliefs/values and behaviors? This is what sociologists call *downward causation* or *social causation?* The degree of causation by macro structures on micro behaviors and beliefs is interpreted differently by different theorists.

The term "downward causation" was coined by Donald Campbell (1974), a well-known social science methodologist. He defined the term in its most abstract form: "all processes at the lower levels of a hierarchy are restrained by and act in conformity to the laws of the higher levels" (p. 180). Sawyer's (2005) description of social causation is more specific: In

DOI: 10.4324/9781003053392-10

social systems, "the system's organization has a significant influence on the functions of its components" (p. 96).

To what degree the higher levels restrain lower levels, or a system's organization influences the functions of its components, has been conceptualized differently by different theorists. In Sandra Mitchell's (2009) interpretation, macro properties of systems "place *constraints* on the behavior of their constituent parts" [emphasis added] (p. 33). According to Sawyer (2005), a "system's organization has a significant influence on the functions of its components" (p. 96). Then the question is how much macro properties *penetrate*, or *determine*, micro-level properties or behaviors (p. 26). Luhmann (1995) proposes the strongest interpretation of downward causation. In his adaptation of autopoiesis theory of biological systems (Maturana & Varela, 1980) to social systems, he conceptualizes downward causation as almost complete domination of individual values and behaviors by systemic properties. He argues that no individual person exists independently of their society. In fact, elements of a system (e.g., individuals in a society) are *constituted* by their system. He states: "Elements are elements only for the system that employs them as units and they are such only through this system" (p. 22).

This spectrum of interpretations can be observed in the works of public policy and political scholars. In most rational choice theories, there is no mention of the macro to micro effects. The reader will remember from the previous chapter that Adam Smith, one of the most important predecessors of rational choice, suggested that micro behaviors (e.g., individual choices in markets) can affect macro properties (e.g., collective wealth of a nation), but he did not mention any effects in the opposite direction. A major problem with his conceptualization is that the process always starts with utility maximizing rational actors who do not have any histories or cultural affiliations that could affect their beliefs/values, which in turn could affect their decisions and behaviors. In other words, they decide and behave as "preconstituted actors" and "it is the purposive, intentional, self-propelled behavior of individuals that aggregate into outcomes; structures neither constitute this behavior nor constitute the actors" (MacDonald, 2003, p. 558).

This rational choice view was modified or challenged by some political economists. For example, Vincent and Elinor Ostrom recognized the importance of institutions in *circumscribing* individual behaviors (i.e., the weakest view of downward causation). Vincent Ostrom (1974) stressed the importance of institutional arrangements in mediating the relationship between individual motivations and actions on the one hand and (good and bad) collective outcomes on the other. Elinor Ostrom acknowledges that individuals receive various feedbacks from their environments and adjust their behaviors to their contexts. In her institutional analysis and development framework, the "attributes of a particular community" (i.e., culture) and institutional structures constitute the context in which complex individuals make their decisions and act (Ostrom, 2005, passim). In

114 *A Complex Governance Networks Conceptualization*

her conceptualization, the attributes of a community and institutional structures function only as "external inducements for action" (Ostrom & Parks, 1999, p. 292); individuals do not internalize them, as in Sawyer's (2005) or Luhmann's (1995) interpretations of downward causation.

Policy feedback theory, a relatively recent addition to policy process theories, focuses on the macro to micro effects in policy processes specifically. In their summary of the evolution and this theory, Mettler and SoRelle (2018) describe it as a study of how prior policies affect institutions, culture, power relations, and social constructions of policy problems, which in turn affect individual values and behaviors and future policies. For example, how does the definition of citizenship in a country affect individuals' participations in elections and thus future public policies? Consider how the recognition of African Americans as citizens of the United States with the Fourteenth Amendment changed electoral politics and affected subsequent public policies in this country. Similarly, the Nineteenth Amendment granted women the right to vote and subsequently had changed the politics and policies.

Policy feedback theorists study also how public policies can facilitate the creation of interest groups in a society, which can influence future policies. Consider the effects of the Social Security Act of 1935 in the United States, which created the federally supported retirement system in this country. This act not only created the Social Security Administration, which has become a governmental institution, but also a strong constituency of retired people, who have become a very strong interest group in the country's politics. Policy feedback researchers investigate the effects of past policies on such macro cultural and institutional structures and the effects of the structures on individual behaviors and found some empirical support for their propositions (Mettler and SoRelle, 2018).

Recent literature on "public values" in public administration also brings up conceptual issues related to the macro to micro effects. This group of authors argue that (macro) "public values shape the structure of society" (Nabatchi, 2012, p. 700) and that public administration, which is the carrier of these values, has "constitutive effects" on individual behaviors (Cook, 2014a, 2014b). These propositions have not been tested empirically, to the best of my knowledge, but they can be valuable starting points in future studies to answer questions like (how) do political institutions and/or the actions of public administrators affect individuals' values and behavior?

Can complexity theory help us understand the macro-to-macro effects (downward causation)? Can its tools like agent-based models be used to empirically investigate these effects? I must stress that there is very little interest in answering these questions among complexity researchers. A brief overview would be helpful here.

I cited S. Mitchell's (2009), Sawyer's (2005), and Luhmann's (1995) conceptualizations earlier. Schelling's (2006) conceptualization of language is another example (pp. 39–40). He posits that language is an adaptive behavior. He notes that what language a person speaks depends on others

*Macro to Micro* 115

who are around the person, particularly their family. A language changes through mutual adaptations in the interactions among multiple persons. The grammar and vocabulary change over time (the former at a slower pace than the latter). The vocabulary of slang changes at a faster pace, as every younger generation invents new words and usages and as they spread fast. (Think of the social media abbreviations like "LOL" and "OMG.") These new words become the "environment" of a new person, who absorbs and transmits them to the next generation, which may modify them and supplements them with other words.

A conceptual challenge for complexity researchers is how to refine these general descriptions. Remember that in their interpretations, Sawyer (2005) and Luhmann (1995) conceptualized downward causation as how the properties of macro structures are internalized by individuals (not merely how they circumscribe individual behaviors, as Elinor Ostrom suggests). Sawyer (2005) formulates the conceptual problem as how, and to what extent, do individuals' pictures of the world "contain representations of the emergent macropatterns" (p. 26).

This is not only a conceptual problem but also a methodological one. More specifically, the problem is how one can build agent-based models that would include representations of social structures in individuals' internal cognitive models. Epstein (2006) notes that this can be done through "feedback between macrostructures and microstructures, as where newborn agents are conditioned by social norms or institutions that have taken shape endogenously through earlier agent interactions" (pp. 51–52). Some complexity researchers have taken on this challenge in their simulations (e.g., Axelrod, 1997; Bednar & Page, 2007; Cohen, Riolo, & Axelrod, 2001) to varying degrees of success. As the authors recognize, some technical problems remain in such applications, which can be addressed in future studies.

Downward causation can be studied also with social network analysis (SNA) models. In the limited SNA applications in this area, downward causation is called "network effect" or "social influence." Marsden and Friedkin (1993) point out that some key concepts of SNA can be used to estimate network effects. For example, the structural positions of actors in a network are determined by the structure of the network, such as the size and cohesion of the network, which can be measured with SNA measures like network size and density. How close two actors are depends partly on how big the network is. The proximity of two actors, in turn, can help us understand their interactions.

The intensity and frequency of these interactions can have consequences, such as "behavioral contagion" (i.e., individual actors emulating other actors' behaviors) (Centola, 2020). Think of the "contagion" of vaccine resistance during the COVID-19 pandemic. I am not aware of any specific studies on this specific topic. But the consistent results of the two surveys on vaccine resistance in the United States and Israel, in 2019 and 2021, respectively (see Chapter 3), suggests that social media posts were the most

116　*A Complex Governance Networks Conceptualization*

important media of behavioral contagion. Those who received their news primarily from their family members and mass media were more likely to get vaccinated, while those got their news from social media were less likely to get vaccinated. The network effects of social media on vaccine hesitancy or resistance can be investigated using SNA tools like network size, density, and cohesion in future studies.

## Structuration

Complexity theorists and researchers theorized and demonstrated that macro patterns and structures, such as collective human behaviors, social institutions, and cultural norms, emerge from individual (micro) actions and discovered the mechanisms of these micro to macro processes (Chapter 7). They also made some progress in conceptualizing how macro patterns and structures affect micro behaviors (this chapter). But there is much more to be done to understand the macro-to-macro processes.

To make progress in conceptualizing and empirically studying the micro–macro problem in general, we need begin with a recognition that the micro to macro and macro to micro processes are abstractions. In real life, they do not happen in a clear sequence; instead, they happen together and dynamically. Then is there a conceptualization that can help us understand and model the micro to macro and macro to micro processes together? Complexity theorists do not offer one. There is a social theory that complexity researchers can adopt: Anthony Giddens's (1984) structuration theory.

Giddens's elaborate theory includes sociological nuances, which are not necessary to discuss in detail here. I presented an extensive summary of this theory and the debates on it my earlier book (Morçöl, 2012a, pp. 84–89, passim). Here, I briefly summarize the key aspects of his theory.

The gist of Giddens's (1984) theory can be summarized as follows. The reproduced *actions of intentional and knowledgeable actors* constitute *social systems*, which exhibit *structural properties*. To unpack this proposition, let us first remember the conceptualizations of individual cognition and decision-making by complexity theorists, particularly the conceptualization of reactive agents versus cognitive agents (Chapter 6). In Giddens's proposition, the actors are cognitive, not reactive. They can develop cognitive maps of their environments (the natural phenomena surrounding them and the cognitive maps and actions and reactions of other individual agents). Their actions together constitute a social system.

Both structures and systems are macro-level phenomena, but Giddens differentiates the two. Structures are social constructions (rules, principles, and values that are accepted commonly by the members of a society). Systems are situated *activities*. Structures and systems (ideas and actions) are connected in the sense that rules, values, and principles can influence a social system's behaviors. These influences can be observed in the "structural properties of systems."

*Macro to Micro* 117

What is particularly important in Giddens's (1984) theory is how he connects the micro- and macro-level phenomena to each other. Structures are at the macro-level because they are held commonly by the members of a society. But they do not have independent existence; instead, they are ideas (social constructions) that reside in the minds of individual actors. These ideas influence the behaviors/activities of individuals, which in turn create and reproduce social systems. Once Giddens differentiates between structures (collective ideas) and systems (collective actions) conceptually, he ties them back together. He states that structures do not exist independently of actions; instead, they are "instantiations" of practices (actions), "memory traces orienting the knowledge of human agents" (p. 17). These instantiations, memory traces, enable and/or constrict future behaviors of actors (p. 25). Giddens calls the whole of these complex processes "structuration."

Let us remember the debates among complexity theorists whether emergent phenomena (structures) have independent existence and irreducible (Chapter 7). The reader will notice that Giddens's structuration theory closes the "mystery gap" between micro and macro levels complexity that theorist Epstein (2006) is concerned about. The issue of whether macro-level phenomena have independent existence (i.e., they have ontological status) is important to revisit when considering Giddens's structuration theory, because this issue has implication for complexity theory in general and how complexity researchers should conceptualize macro to micro relations (downward causation) in particular.

Sawyer's (2005) critique of Giddens's theory helps us understand the issue of independent existence and its implications. It is important to stress that Sawyer critiques Giddens from a structuralist sociological perspective, which has its roots in the works of Émile Durkheim in the late 19th and early 20th centuries.[1] He embraced the notion that social structural properties emerge and they cannot be reduced to individual actions to ground the discipline of sociology and differentiate it from psychology. Sawyer argues that Giddens rejects this differentiation. This is not merely a rejection of sociology as a separate discipline, but, more importantly, a denial of the existence of *social causation* (or *downward causation*), according to Sawyers. How so?

To answer this question, we need to look into Giddens's theory more closely. He argues that there is no separation between social structures on the one hand and individuals' ideas and actions on the other. He uses the term "duality of structure" (instead of a "dualism") to depict the relationship between structures and individuals. He uses the term to mean: "[T]he *structural properties of social systems are both medium and outcome of the practices they recursively organize.* Structure is not 'external' to individuals" [emphases added] (p. 25). Instead, structures are internalized by actors, which in turn enables or constructs their own actions and other actors' actions in the future (p. 310).

## 118   *A Complex Governance Networks Conceptualization*

What is the problem with this conceptualization, according to Sawyer? He argues that Giddens's duality of structure ignores the fact that not all structures emerge from the actions of cognitive actors who are guided by their internal cognitive maps. Sawyer cites agent-based simulations that demonstrate that social structures can emerge from the interactions of reactive agents, that by definition have no cognitive maps, and that the existence of those structures can constrain the actions of such agents (p. 161). Indeed, as Epstein (2006) reminds us, in agent-based simulations "individual rationality is neither necessary nor sufficient for the attainment of macroscopic efficiency.... [A] society of autonomous agents arrives at [economic optimality] even though the overwhelming majority do not optimize individually" (p. 144).

As I argued elsewhere (Morçöl, 2012a), this indeed is correct, but real human beings are not reactive agents, dumb machines, or simple robots. They are more like cognitive agents, who are intentional and deliberative and have beliefs about their environments, their actions, and their impacts. So, the results of simulations with reactive agents do not tell us much about the real mechanisms in human societies. The dichotomous conceptualization of reactive versus cognitive agents may still be useful, however. The term "cognitive agent" does not necessarily mean that they are fully cognizant of their natural environments or the social structures that emerged from their prior actions. The comprehensiveness and accuracy of their internal representations is limited, as Simon's (1979, 1986) work on the boundedness of their rationality and behavioral/cognitive psychologists work on cognitive biases (Edwards & Tversky, 1967; Friedland & Robertson, 1990; Hogarth & Reder, 1986; Kahneman, 2011) demonstrated amply. In my earlier work, I proposed that it will be more useful if the concepts cognitive agents and reactive agents are considered as a dimension, representing different degrees of comprehension and accuracy in agents' cognitive maps the world.

Sawyer (2005) also argues that Giddens's concept of duality of structure can be the basis for rejecting downward (social) causation. Think of the scenario in which social norms, cultural values, or institutions having no impact on individuals' cognitive maps of the world or their actions. Sawyer argues that Giddens's concept at least dilutes the power of social causation. I think Sawyer's challenge here should be taken seriously, but Giddens's nuanced conceptualization does not necessarily deny social causation. It can help us understand the complexity of macro to micro effects.

According to Giddens (1984), social structures can affect actors in two ways. First, structures not only constrain but also enable actors' acts. He gives the example of language: It constrains and enables individuals' thinking and actions (p. 170). Without language we cannot think, but the language we have learned to use can constrain the way we think. In a similar vein, Bart Kosko (1993), a leading theorist of "fuzzy logic," contends that the "bivalent" ("either or") language of modern sciences have been restraining scientific advances. Instead, he argues, we should adopt a "multivalent" language to open up new venues for advances. Indeed, the multivalent language of fuzz logic has enabled advanced in the designs of some consumer goods, such as washing machines and vacuum cleaners, and improving the operational efficiency of subway systems.[2]

Giddens also posits that social structures constrain individual actions to varying degrees. He identifies three types of constraints on individual actions in a society: material constraints, (negative) sanctions, and structural constraints (pp. 174–179). Material constraints are physical and biological: Human actors cannot defy the laws of physics, such as gravity, or limits of their biology. They cannot defy the gravity by flapping their arms to fly, for example. Bu they can collectively design flying vehicles to stretch the limits of these constraints. Negative sanctions are constraints that derive from punitive responses to individual actions by authorized agents of a government (e.g., an arrest by a police officer) or by the representatives of social groups the individual belongs to (e.g., banishment by a leader of a religion). Negative sanctions involve application of power, either in the form of applying physical power or using the force of communally accepted authority. It is not easy to escape the arrest by a police officer, but in some cases, it is possible to change the laws that led to one's arrest, together with other individuals, in a democratic process. If an individual is banished from a religious group, they may be able to join another one or live without joining one. Structural constraints can be defined in the context of an action. In a capitalist economy, a worker may not have any choice other than selling their labor to earn their livings. These constraints vary across time and geography. In some economies, workers may not have any options other than selling their labor to employers, but in others they may be able to change their statuses in the society by starting their own businesses and freeing themselves from the constraints of being a worker.

Giddens uses term "span of time-space distanciation" to explain the variations in the constrains on individual actors. She posits that the greater the distanciation, the more resistant social structures are to change and more constraining on individuals (p. 171). In other words, those structural rules that are more distant, in terms of time and geography, to a particular individual will be more external (constraining) to them. Those that are closer to the individual will be more internalized.

Think about public policies made at the federal and local levels of government in the United States. Giddens's uses the concept distanciation to suggest that those structural rules made in a distant past or in a distant location will be more external (constraining) to individuals, whereas those rules made in closer locations and by closer actors can be seen as less constraining and accepted and absorbed more easily. Take the example of the national polls that show that Americans find their local governments and the rules they make closer to them, as opposed to the ones made by the federal government.[3] Also, think about the process of vaccinating the population during the COVID-19 pandemic. The resistance to vaccinations in some parts of the populations in the United States was surely fueled by

120   *A Complex Governance Networks Conceptualization*

the national politics of the time,[4] but the studies on the unvaccinated also showed that the "resistance" or "hesitancy" among them in the United States and elsewhere diminished once they began to be influenced by actors closer to them. Instead of the distant "government" making the rules and imposing them on these actors, now they were being persuaded by their family members, friends, personal physicians, etc.[5]

Giddens's structuration theory enables the researchers of complex social systems (e.g., governance systems/networks) to conceptualize the highly complex micro–macro–micro processes in these systems. His concept of the duality of structures (structural properties are both media and outcomes of the practices they recursively organize, they are not "external" to individuals, and they are both constraining and enabling) demystifies social structures. They cannot exist independently of individuals' perceptions and actions, unlike the structures in nature. This is important because it reminds us that there are differences between natural systems and social systems.[6] They both may be complex systems but different kinds. Giddens's notion that structural properties are both mediums and outcomes of actors' practices is compatible with Holland's notion that the properties of emergent structures can be reduced to those of individuals if nonlinear relations are taken into account.

Sawyer's (2005) objections to Giddens are still important. His argument that macro structures should be clearly separated from micro (individual) actions has some merit. Are some social structures so separate from individual actors (i.e., "external to them"), so that they feel alienated from the structures? Conceptualizing (some) social structures as "external" can help us understand some social processes, such as in the vaccine hesitancy examples cited above. To the extent that the "vaccine hesitants" felt that the rules of vaccination were made by structures that were distant to them (e.g., the US federal government), these structures were "external" to them and thus alienating.

The issue of to what extent macro structures are external to individual actors in governance processes should be studied empirically and conceptualized better. I propose the following questions for such studies and conceptualizations:

To what extent emergent properties are external to individual actors? To what extent emergent properties are independent of the properties of individual actors? To what extent do they constrain (or enable) actors' behaviors (social causation)? To what extent are social structures internalized by individuals?

(Morçöl, 2012a, p. 91)

There is a conceptual and methodological reason to study macro structures as external to individual actors: It is more practical. There are those who study macro structures and processes only and make only

*Macro to Micro* 121

passing references to micro-level processes. Punctuated equilibrium theory is an example. As I noted in Chapter 5, this group of theorists make the assumption that individual actors are boundedly rational and make an inference from this to the punctuations at the macro level, but they do not study the micro–macro connections specifically (True, Jones, & Baumgartner, 2007). The theorists of the institutional analysis and development framework (E. Ostrom, 1990, 2005) and the advocacy coalition framework (Jenkins-Smith et al. 2018) do try to connect the micro and macro levels, but both fall short of providing elaborate theories of the connections. Ostrom aims to understand particularly the effects of macro structures on individual policy actors (this chapter's topic), but her conceptualization is not elaborate on how that happens. The advocacy coalition framework theorists are focused on the micro to macro processes (how individual actors form coalitions to influence macro policies), but they ignore how macro policies affect micro behaviors. Policy feedback theorist do focus on macro to micro processes, but, as they acknowledge, their conceptualizations are not sufficiently advanced to provide us a comprehensive picture yet (Mettler & SoRelle, 2018).

The theoretical power of Giddens's structuration theory has been recognized by some who adopted complexity and/or network perspectives in governance studies, but their applications remained mostly conceptual. Klijn (2001) cites Giddens to underscore the interrelationship between the stability (structure) and dynamism (process) of networks and the role of actors. Through their sustained interactions, actors create policy network structures: rules and resources that (will) have a structuring effect on future interactions in the network. Zaheer and Soda (2009) note that prior network structures both enable actors to create or recreate future structures and constrain their actions. Actors' purposive actions may form and dissolve network links and their experiences and knowledge of past network connections motivate and enable the actors to take such actions. These are important conceptual contributions and their propositions deserve to be investigated in empirical studies.

## Summary

In the previous two chapters, I summarized complexity theory conceptualizations of micro units (individual actors) and how macro structures emerge from the actions of these actors. I cited the conceptual refinements and empirical studies on these topics in recent decades. This chapter was about whether and how those macro structures affect micro behaviors. It is a conceptually sound proposition that macro structures (e.g., cultural norms and social institutions) can affect individual beliefs, attitudes, and behaviors (downward causation, social causation). This proposition has been adopted and conceptually refined by sociologists (Sawyer, 2005), public policy theorists (policy feedback theory), and

## 122  *A Complex Governance Networks Conceptualization*

complex systems theorists (Epstein, 2006). It is difficult to empirically investigate, however, and very few studies have been conducted, as I noted in this chapter.

Giddens's (1984) theory of structuration offers a sophisticated alternative. Giddens posits that micro and macro levels are not separate from each other. Macro structural properties do not exist independently of actors, but in their memories and knowledge. Structures are created and reproduced through social practices, which he calls the structuration process. In this process, structural properties are both the media and outcomes of the practices they recursively organize. Structural properties both enable or constrain future behaviors of actors. Giddens's elegant and sophisticated theory is difficult to operationalize and investigate empirically and therefore such empirical studies are rare, as I noted in this chapter.

Downward causation and structuration are promising conceptualizations for the advancement of complexity theory applications in social sciences, in general, and complex governance networks, in particular. There remains substantial conceptual and empirical works to fulfill that promise however.

## Notes

1  Émile Durkheim. https://en.wikipedia.org/wiki/%C3%89mile_Durkheim
2  Fuzzy logic. https://en.wikipedia.org/wiki/Fuzzy_logic
3  Americans' Trust in Government Remains Low. https://news.gallup.com/poll/355124/americans-trust-government-remains-low.aspx
4  Red States Are Vaccinating at a Lower Rate than Blue States. www.cnn.com/2021/04/10/politics/vaccinations-state-analysis/index.html

   For COVID-19 Vaccinations, Party Affiliation Matters More Than Race and Ethnicity. www.brookings.edu/blog/fixgov/2021/10/01/for-covid-19-vaccinations-party-affiliation-matters-more-than-race-and-ethnicity/?utm_campaign=Brookings%20Brief&utm_medium=email&utm_content=165955443&utm_source=hs_email
5  A New Poll Shows Why Some Vaccine-hesitant Americans Decided to Get the Covid-19 Shot. www.cnn.com/2021/07/13/politics/poll-covid-19-vaccine-decision/index.html

   The Game is Not Yet Over, and Vaccines Still Matter: Lessons from a Study on Israel's COVID-19 Vaccination. www.brookings.edu/blog/up-front/2021/09/13/the-game-is-not-yet-over-and-vaccines-still-matter-lessons-from-a-study-on-israels-covid-19-vaccination/?utm_campaign=Brookings%20Brief&utm_medium=email&utm_content=159977144&utm_source=hs_email

   Why Many Black Americans Changed Their Minds About Covid Shots. https://nyti.ms/3oWEwqY
6  There is a long history of the debates on whether or not natural and social phenomena require different forms of investigation. The roots of this debate are in the hermeneutic critique of positivist science in the 19th century. An extensive discussion of this topic is beyond the scope of this book.

# Part III
# Implications of the Complex Governance Networks Conceptualization for Key Issues in Governance

# 9 Wicked Problems and Effectiveness

This chapter is about two related concepts: wicked problems and effectiveness. They are related, in the sense that they are inherently contradictory. If public (collective) problems are wicked, then the implied conclusion will be that they are unsolvable, let alone being solved effectively. Effectiveness is a core issue in the theories and practices of both public policy and public administration. In both fields of study, the question is how to solve, or contribute to the solution of, public problems. The academic studies in these fields and the related practices are about whether and how we can solve public problems effectively. It is important to make the connection between the concepts of wicked problems and effectiveness particularly in the context of understanding complex governance networks. The developments in the areas of study on governance, networks, and complexity, which I presented in the previous chapters, will help us do so.

In the first section of the chapter, I discuss wicked problems. After pointing to the extent of the literature on wicked problems and summarizing the background and basic propositions of this conceptualization, I will show that what the authors keep referring to is the complexity of collective problems. Some make passing references to the complexity theory literature in their assessments of the wickedness of the problems they address, and some mention how governance networks may help counter the wickedness of public problems and be effective in doing so, but there is no systematic application of complexity theory or a comprehensive understanding within the framework of governance networks.

There is also a literature on the effectiveness of governance (or policy) networks. These authors demonstrate that these networked relations and structures can be effective in solving, or ameliorating, collective problems. I discuss this literature in a separate section.

## Wicked Problems

Rittel and Webber (1973) popularized the term "wicked problems." What they meant were those policy and planning problems that did not fit into the conceptual and mathematical models of their time. Since then, the concept has been used in a very large number of publications and in a wide

DOI: 10.4324/9781003053392-12

126  *Implications of the Complex Governance Networks Conceptualization*

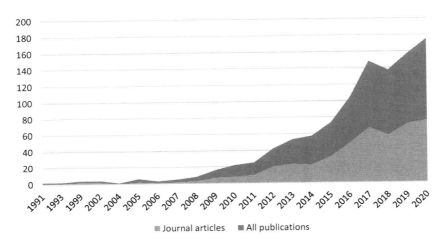

*Figure 9.1* Publications on "wicked problems" in the Web of Science.

range of fields of study. Crowley and Head (2017) note that the Rittel and Weber paper was the most-cited paper in *Policy Sciences*, a leading journal of policy processes and analysis, at the time of their review of the literature.

A Google Scholar search I conducted in June 2021, using the keyword "wicked problems," yielded more than 55,000 entries. A parallel search in the Web of Science, which is more restrictive of the publications it includes than Google Scholar, the same keyword yielded 634 total publications between 1991 and 2021. Of those 634 resulting from the search, 458 were journal articles. As Figure 9.1 shows, there was an exponential growth in the numbers of total publications and journal articles, particularly in the 2010s. These publications covered a large variety of areas: environmental studies, urban and regional planning/studies, education research, public administration, health policy, economics, information sciences, political science, and sociology.

These numbers and this figure clearly point to the enduring and increasing influence of the concept of wicked problems in the literature in the last half a century. Its influence goes beyond the literature that used the term directly. There is a broader literature that has been inspired by or at least related to the wicked problems conceptualization. Crowley and Head (2017) observe that similar concepts, like "messy problems," "intractable problems," "unstructured problems," "contested problems," "recalcitrant problems," "undisciplined problems," "uncontrollable problems," and the like have also been used in the literature.

The concept of wicked problems is popular also in the governance and collaborative networks literatures I cited in this book. Some of the authors I cited use it to mean problems that have no clear definitions or clear solutions and whose elements have complex interdependencies (e.g.,

Emerson & Nabatchi, 2015; Klijn & Koppenjan, 2016; Koliba et al., 2019). These "wicked problems," the authors argue, make it more difficult, if not impossible, to solve policy problems rationally and effectively. In this literature, the term is used either interchangeably with "complex problems" (e.g., Koppenjan & Klijn, 2004, p. 1), or there are implicit references drawn between the two.

Indeed, public policy and administration problems, and governance network processes, are complex, but is "wicked problems" really a good concept to signify this complexity? It is important to point out that in the governance literature, and broader literatures, this term usually refers to the multiplicity of actors involved in policy and administrative processes, the uncertainties in the knowledge processes about these processes, and the difficulties in addressing the problems. The reader will recognize that these are among the issues the researchers of complex systems and governance networks address in their studies, but their characterizations of the complexity of problems do not suggest that they are "wicked" in the sense that they are unsolvable.

In some parts of the literature, the term "wicked problems" is used particularly to criticize "rational" linear planning methodologies, which are supposed to yield straightforward solutions to well-defined problems. With their criticisms, these authors aim to make the case that participatory (more democratic) methods of policymaking and planning are necessary. This was also the original meaning of the term, as Rittel and Webber (1973) intended. They showed that many of these problems cannot be defined easily, in a way that all stakeholders would agree on them, and clear solutions could be found and implemented. They categorized any problems that would fit this description as wicked.

As I showed in the previous chapters of this book, after the advances, in the last half a century, in the conceptualizations of complex systems and governance networks and the methodological advances in studying these systems and networks, the term wicked problems has no longer a high degree of validity or usefulness. It is not only complexity theory that leads us to reach this conclusion. There are some public policy scholars who argue that as well.

I will summarize these leads and criticisms in a section later in the chapter. Before that, a background and overview of the concept will be useful.

### What Are Wicked Problems?

The most important aspect of Rittel and Webber's (1973) conceptualization of wicked problems is that they formulated it when they criticized the "rational" and "instrumentalist" methodologies in planning, system design, and policymaking, which were fashionable in the 1960s. They cite specifically the practices like the policy analysis methodologies developed at the RAND Corporation and the PPBS budgeting system, which was applied

128  *Implications of the Complex Governance Networks Conceptualization*

for a short while in the US federal government in this period. These methodologies and practices are flawed, Webber (1983) argues, because they are based on the faulty assumptions that there can be widespread consensus on goals, that a causal theory of the policy problem can be developed, and that the future can be predicted using this theory. They are flawed also because their users fail to make an effort to understand the social context (values, norms, and history) in defining and trying to solve policy problems.

Rittel and Webber (1973) specifically state that when they use the term "wicked," they do not do so in ethical terms. For example, they do mean that these problems are "evil." Instead, they use the terms descriptively, in a meaning akin to "malignant," "vicious," "tricky," or "aggressive" (p. 160). They argue that these terms better characterize social problems, particularly policy and planning problems. Rittel and Webber did not merely offer a concept but a serious conceptualization. They identified 10 "distinguishing properties" of wicked problems.

1. There is no definitive formulation of a wicked problem.
2. Wicked problems have no stopping rule.
3. Solutions to wicked problems are not true-or-false, but good-or-bad.
4. There is no immediate and no ultimate test of a solution to a wicked problem.
5. Every solution to a wicked problem is a "one-shot operation"; because there is no opportunity to learn by trial-and-error, every attempt counts significantly.
6. Wicked problems do not have an enumerable (or exhaustively desirable) set of potential solutions, nor is there a well-described set of permissible operations that may be incorporated into the plan.
7. Every wicked problem is essentially unique.
8. Every wicked problem can be considered to be a symptom of another problem.
9. The existence of a discrepancy representing a wicked problem can be explained in numerous ways. The choice of explanation determines the nature of the problem's resolution.
10. The planner has no right to be wrong (pp. 161–167).

One can find justifications for characterizing public (collective) problems with these 10 properties. They may sound "about right." They are generic and vague enough to be applied to various fields and examples. But do they really have validity in specific applications? Do these "distinguishing properties" increase the analytical power of our studies? In other words, do they help us better understand a phenomenon, or do they justify being dismissive of the possibility that we can understand the complexity of our collective problems, at least to some degree? The reader will remember from the earlier chapters that the developers and users of complexity and network theories, and the associated analytical methods, aim to do just that: better understand the complexity of reality and our problems. So, these theories and methods are philosophical antitheses of the notion of wicked problems.

The notion of wicked problems and the 10 "distinguishing properties" may also have unintended consequences. They may justify arguments like a scientific understanding of policy problems and their solutions is not possible because of the insurmountable subjectivities in human knowledge and the unsolvable political power relations in societies. In other words, if the term wicked problems are used to justify anti-science stances and fatalistic conclusions, it will be highly problematic.

Take the example of the COVID-19 pandemic. Indeed, there were gaps and uncertainties in scientists' knowledge of how the SARS-CoV-2 virus works to affect human organisms at the beginning of the pandemic. There was no definitive formulation of the problem (#1 on Rittel and Webber's list); no immediate or ultimate solution to it (#4); and because every human body is unique, there was no universal solution to curing or treating COVID-19 cases (#7). The knowledge of the problem and its solutions got better over time, however. Vaccines and some therapeutic drugs were developed and they helped brought down the number of infections and deaths over time. Many gaps and uncertainties remained during the course of the pandemic in scientists' understanding of the mechanisms of how SARS-CoV-2 infects human bodies and how the disease progresses.

There were also gaps and uncertainties also in the knowledge of vaccine delivery during the pandemic. There was no clear definition of the problem of "vaccine hesitancy" or ("vaccine resistance") (#1), nor were there clear solutions for overcoming the problem (#4). Public health researchers and policymakers gained a better understanding of the problems over time. For example, they learned that the anti-vaccine propaganda was more effective in the counties that voted for Trump in the 2020 election and that some African Americans were more resistant because of their collective memories of the past mistreatment by health professionals. In general, it was understood that many "vaccine hesitants" were driven by complex mixture of concerns, including vaccine side effects, mistrust of "the government." There were still major knowledge gaps, however. As the retiring director of the US National Institutes of Health, Dr. Francis Collins, admitted in an interview in December 2021, the biggest and most important gap was in his organization's knowledge of how humans can be vulnerable to the misinformation and disinformation campaigns in the social media.[1]

Consider the broader example of pandemics in human history. They plagued human societies for millennia. (Remember the Antonine Plague of the years 165–180 AD, which was mentioned in Chapter 1.) Even after one pandemic subsides and the virus causing it mutates to become less lethal for humans, another one emerges. These observations do no mean that neither the scientific knowledge of viruses nor the social scientific knowledge of public health (how pathogens spread in societies and how mitigation measures can be modeled and designed) is invalid or useless. I cite examples

# 130   *Implications of the Complex Governance Networks Conceptualization*

of modeling the COVID-19 pandemic and the roles they played in mitigating its effects in Chapter 4.

### *The Uses of the Term Wicked Problems in the Literature and Its Criticisms*

As I noted earlier in this chapter, wicked problems is an increasingly popular concept in the literature. Its applications have moved away its original definition by Rittell and Webber (1973). In the literature, the 10 "distinguishing properties of wicked problems" are rarely cited. Instead, the term has become a catch phrase used to refer vaguely to the socially constructed nature of collective (public) problems and their complexity. These usages have been criticized by some authors.

Some among the adopters of wicked problems mean it to highlight the social contexts of policy problems and to support their general conclusion that planning and policymaking processes must take into account the subjectivities in human knowledge. In some of these applications, the authors use the term to point to the socially and/or cognitively constructed nature of policy problems and make the case that participatory, discourse-based, and argumentative approaches are necessary in policy analysis (Crowley & Head, 2017, p. 542).

In many of the sources the term is cited, the authors make implicit references to the complexity of public problems. For example, according to Van Bueren and her colleagues (2003), what makes collective action problems wicked are the various forms of uncertainty in defining and solving them: the cognitive uncertainty (lack of scientific knowledge about them), strategic uncertainty (because of the involvement of multiple actors), and institutional uncertainty (that decisions are made in different places in organizations). In their analyses of the case of the Dutch zinc industry, they aim to show that because of these uncertainties decisions can be handled adequately only by "enhancing and intensifying interactions between stakeholders" in networked relations (p. 194).

Ferlie and his colleagues (2011) argue that wicked problems exist in the policy networks in the UK. What they mean by that is there are multiple stakeholders in these networks and policy solutions are coproduced. Similarly, Head and Alford (2015) find wickedness in the complexity of policy problems and the multiplicity of stakeholders. In Head's (2019) conceptualization, policy problems are wicked because of their dynamism the uncertainties in knowing them. He refers to complexity theory, collaborative governance conceptualizations, and constructivist perspectives as possible theoretical lenses through which wicked problems can be understood.

The concept of wicked problems is used also in the literature on information systems, particularly in the areas of digital government and social media. In their conceptualization, Kim and Zhang (2016) use the term to refer to the complexities generated by digital government initiatives and social media usage. Schoder and his colleagues (2014) also observe that information science problems are wicked in the sense that they are complex. The complexity of these problems arises from multiple challenges in systems engineering (functionality, technical design, and modeling), measurement, data handling, semantic analyses of textual content, linking humans and computers, and commercialization of applications.

The main problem with most of the applications of the term "wicked problems" in the literature is that they are based on casual conceptualizations. The authors either select a few of Rittel and Webber's (1973) 10 "distinguishing properties of wicked problems" in their conceptualizations, or they do not mention them at all, as in the examples I cited above. Instead, they point to the social construction processes in policymaking and/or the complexity of the processes and call them "wicked."

If the intent is to highlight the complexity of collective problems, then this complexity should be defined rigorously. As I demonstrated in Chapter 4, complexity theorists offer conceptual tools to do exactly that. By doing so, they demonstrate that complexity is not a residual category that can be used to refer to the "unknown" or "unknowable," a category that is the categorical opposite of what is perfectly and entirely known or knowable. This point is important to emphasize, because Rittel and Webber's original characterization of wicked problems, particularly some of their "distinguishing properties" of wicked problems, suggest that such problems are beyond the realm of finding possible solutions. The following "properties" do suggest that. There is no definitive formulation of a wicked problem (#6). Wicked problems have no stopping rule (#2). There is no immediate and no ultimate test of a solution to a wicked problem (#4). Wicked problems do not have an enumerable (or exhaustively desirable) set of potential solutions, nor is there a well-described set of permissible operations that may be incorporated into the plan (#6). Rittel and Webber do not specifically say that, but in many of the applications of their concept, the "uncertainties" and "dynamism" of policy problems are used to mean, explicitly or implicitly, that they are unsolvable.

In his analyses of the political literature on the climate crisis, Mann (2021) finds the idea of "wicked problems" profoundly problematic. That is because this term "tends to produce a sense of helplessness because wicked problems are, by their definition, unsolvable," and it is used by some social scientists as a "rhetorical fence" to avoid the physical reality of the climate crisis (p. 257). He also criticizes its uses by "fossil fuel interests" to suggest that environmental problems are "hopelessly complicated" (p. 257). Mann argues that climate crisis is solvable by deliberate and concerted policy actions.

In his elaborate conceptual analysis of the uses of "wicked problems" in the literature, Peters (2017) argues that the concept has become a "fad in contemporary policy analysis" and notes that many public policy problems are labeled "wicked" casually in the literature. In these casual applications of the term, the authors refer to the multiplicity of the actors involved in policy problems and their social and political complexity, instead of

132　*Implications of the Complex Governance Networks Conceptualization*

applying Rittel and Webber's (1973) original 10 "distinguishing properties of wicked problems" in a systematic manner.

Peters argues that by not applying the original "distinguishing properties," these authors stretch the meaning of the concept to fit the examples in their analyses. Many of them tend to use the concept to underscore the importance and difficulty of the problems they analyze, but these vague applications lack any analytical capacity and consequently they become almost meaningless. Even when a policy problem has some of Rittel and Webber's "distinguishing properties" (for example, they may not have clear definitions and policy interventions may have unintended consequences), these characteristics alone do not make the problems wicked. They may simply suggest that new methods of understanding them and methods of policy interventions are needed. (I would add to Peters's argument that the conceptual and mathematical tools of complexity theory do provide such methods.)

Peters also objects to the normative uses of the concept, which was not intended by Rittel and Webber. In these normative uses, the authors suggest that social problems must be solved through centralized and forceful action (i.e., by the central government). Peters acknowledges that central and forceful interventions may be necessary in some, or many, cases, but that does not necessarily apply to all cases. He cites particularly Elinor Ostrom's works on polycentricity, which demonstrated that people have the capacity to solve difficult problems in localized and decentralized ways and that there are various configurations of actors and institutional arrangements that can be applied in solving such problems (see Chapter 4).

The conclusion I draw from the above review of the literature on wicked problems is that even though Rittel and Webber had good reasons to formulate this concept in the context of the developments and debates in the 1960s and 1970s, the concept lost its usefulness in the following decades, particularly because of its casual usages in the literature. These casual usages do not say much other than suggesting that public policy problems are difficult to solve and that they are socially constructed, as Peters (2017) stated.

Then, should we stop trying to solve them, or make progress in alleviating them? That possible negative connotation of the usages of wicked problem is particularly problematic, because it may lead to a sense of hopelessness in the face of big collective problems like the climate crisis, as Mann (2021) points out. This negative connotation is also in contradiction with a historically key concern of public administration and public policy studies: effectiveness.

## Effectiveness

The concern for effectiveness has always been an undercurrent in the theory and practice of public policy and administration. Societies and their autocratic rulers or democratically elected representatives all want public policies to be designed so that they will be effective in solving a public problem, and once the policy is formulated, it should be executed effectively by public administrators. Practitioners know from their experience and scholars observe in their studies that it is not easy to define or achieve effectives in policymaking or administration, however. These experiences and observations led long-running debates in the literature, which I briefly summarize in the next subsection. The studies on governance network underscore the complexities in accomplishing effectiveness in solving public problems, but they also show that it is possible to do so with an understanding of the complexities, which I summarize in the subsection that follows the next one.

### Effectiveness in Public Policy and Administration

Effectiveness is one of the two core problems in public administration, the other one being the problem of accountability, which is the topic of the next chapter. One can observe how central these two problems are in the history of governments in human societies. Since the beginning of the state (Fukuyama, 2011 (pp. 19–22) set its date to the 3rd century BC), army commanders and civilian administrators wanted their units and personnel to be effective in reaching their goals. Both democratic and un-democratic governments desire effectiveness in their administrative units, whatever their goals may be: conquering a new territory, enhancing the power of the ruler, or providing a public service to their subjects or citizens.

Effectiveness (and its concomitant efficiency) has been a core concern for the European and American public administration scholars from the beginnings of their studies in the early 20th century. German sociological theorist Max Weber's (2010) conceptualization of the "ideal typical bureaucracy" (that it is an impersonal, orderly, rule-bound, and hierarchical system), which he proposed in the 1910s, was one of the earliest statements about how governments could be organized to function effectively. The bureaucratic organization of the state should work effectively, according to Weber, to ensure that democracy, capitalist economy, and modern culture could function in the early 20th century (pp. 214–216). American management theorist Frederick Taylor (1947), who influenced management studies in general, formulated his principles of scientific management with the purpose of finding the "one best way" of organizing work tasks to achieve effectiveness and efficiency. Leonard D. White (1939) noted that the objective of public administration was "efficiency."

The topic of efficiency was the primary area of contention in the Simon versus Waldo debate of the 1940s and 1950s. In their contemporaneous books and journal articles, Simon (1946, 1952) and Waldo (1948, 1952) crystallized the issue. Simon argued that efficiency had to be the guiding principle of public administration research, even though he recognized the limits of the rationality of human mind in trying to accomplish that. Waldo argued that efficiency was the core problem of business administration but

## 134 *Implications of the Complex Governance Networks Conceptualization*

not public administration. He further argued that efficiency in itself could not be a value, partly because there were different types of efficiency.

In the 1960s and 1970s, as the public services were delivered increasingly through goal-oriented programs (e.g., the Head Start program, whose goal was to help underprivileged children in their education), scholars devised methods of measuring the effectiveness of these programs. Rivlin (1971) identified the main problem of social service programs as one of effectiveness. She went on to identify the reasons for performance failures and described the various mechanisms of improving effectiveness: decentralization, community control, and the market model. She aimed to show that the effectiveness of these models could be measured with multiple indicators and the specific measures would have to match the difficulty of a particular problem. Program evaluation, which became a systematic field of study in the 1970s, is about measuring the effectiveness of public policies and programs. Rossi and his colleagues' classic *book Evaluation: A Systematic Approach* (2004, original publication in 1979) describes the methods of evaluating program effectiveness. They detail how social problems can be identified, how programs can be conceptualized, how program implementation ca be monitored, how program outcomes can be measured, and how the impacts of program can be assessed.

Effectiveness is also the core problem in the "performance management" literature of the 1980s and 1990s. The New Public Management school of thought was an example. The National Performance Review (Gore, 1993) was another example. The review identified the problem of public administration as that its centralized bureaucracies had matched the needs of the industrial era, but they were not good matches for the 1990s. That was because they discouraged creativity and risk taking and promoted a culture of fear and resignation. The authors of the review proposed "entrepreneurial organizations" as the solution and argued that the US federal agencies had to "reinvent" themselves. The authors also recognized that it was difficult to measure the performances of public agencies, because typically there were multiple and conflicting objectives and overlapping jurisdictions of the federal, state, and local agencies. Hence, it was difficult to devise methods of measurement that would be acceptable to all stakeholders.

The authors of the National Performance Review indicate were aware of the fact that public policies were made and administered increasingly through complex the governance networks in the 1990s. As I noted in Chapter 2, in the beginning of the 21st century governance scholars Kettl (2002) and Salamon (2002) articulated these observations in more coherent conceptualizations of governance process. The problem of effectiveness was more complex in governance networks.

### *Effectiveness of Governance Networks*

The complexity of the effectiveness problem in governance networks arises from the multiplicity of the actors involved in them and the multiple ways they interact with each other. (See Chapter 4 for a conceptualization of complexity.) These multiplicities force governance network theorists to define effectiveness on multiple dimensions and contextually.

Kapucu and Hu's (2020) comprehensive review of the literature illustrates the challenges and advances in conceptualizing network effectiveness. They point out that because of the complexity of governance networks—that there are multiple and potentially conflicting goals in them and the public agencies have overlapping jurisdictions, not to mention the increased complexity of government agencies working with nonprofits and private corporations, which have their own goals and priorities—their effectiveness cannot be measured on one dimension and using one metric. That is partly because—unlike in strictly hierarchical organizations (as in Weber's ideal typical bureaucracy)—no single authority can set an overall goal and expect that all network actors will follow it. Because of the various perspectives and priorities among network actors, it is not feasible for them to agree on how to measure the effectiveness of their network.

These multiplicities in the goals and perspectives of network members do not necessarily suggest that it would be hopeless to conceptualize and measure network effectiveness, however. Kapucu and Hu observe that there are some common elements among the conceptualizations of network effectiveness in the literature: *multidimensionality* of effectiveness, its *context specificity*, and *contingent* and *dynamic* nature. They also observe that network effectives is conceptualized in terms of *network processes* and *outcomes*. Kapucu and Hu propose an integrative framework that includes both the processes and outcomes of network activities. This framework includes contextual factors (uncertainty and changes in the network's environment, resource availability for the network, support the network members receive from the larger community), structural characteristics of networks (size, age, and composition of the network), and network functioning factors (network governance structures, network behaviors of leadership, and network management and leadership).

Some aspects of Kapucu and Hu's framework can be observed in other authors' conceptualizations. For example, Sørensen and Torfing (2009) define network effectiveness on multiple dimensions. In their conceptualization, governments play a major role in designing governance networks and setting the measures of network effectiveness. Sørensen and Torfing posit that governmental authorities can design network environments and assess their effectiveness on four dimensions: network design, network framing, network management, and network participation. For example, governmental authorities can define the objectives of networks and set clear deadlines for their tasks (design). They can coordinate goal alignment and create strong interdependencies (framing). They can provide adequate resources and reduce tensions in the relations among them (management). They can facilitate sustained cooperation among network members (participation).

136  *Implications of the Complex Governance Networks Conceptualization*

Ansell and Gash's (2008) work is a primary example of the literature on the conceptualizations of governance network effectiveness in terms of processes. They define effectiveness in terms of the success of collaboration among network actors. This success can be measured in the "immediate outcomes" of the actions of network actors.

Thomson and her colleagues' (2009) work is an example of assessing network effectiveness in outcome variables. They identify five outcome variables, all of which can be measured in the perceptions of network actors and others: perceived effectiveness in achieving network goals, quality of partners' working relationships, broadening partners' views, partner interactions, and increase in equitable influence and power used. All the variables Thomson and her colleagues identify are perceptual variables and there are no objectively measurable metrics for them, which is an illustration of the difficulties in conceptualizing and measuring network effectiveness.

Provan and Kenis's (2008) typology of network governance structures and Provan and Milward's (1995, 2001) model of network effectiveness are particularly important to cite here, because they have been applied in several empirical studies. Provan and Kenis identified three types of network structures: participant-governed networks, networks governed by a lead organization, and networks governed by a network administrative organization. In their analyses of these types, they observed that three factors affect the effectiveness of these types: level of *trust* among network participants, *number of participants*, and degree of *goal consensus* among them. An increase in each of these variables will lead to higher network effectiveness.

Provan and Milward (1995, 2001) define network effectiveness on three levels: the *participant* (individual actor or organization), *network*, and *community* levels. They posit that to evaluate effectiveness at the participant level, the following measures can be used: outcomes, legitimacy, resource acquisition, and cost. At the network level, effectiveness can be evaluated by the number of network members and their level of engagement, the extent to which the network fulfills the needs of its clients, and the degree to which the network maximizes resource utilization. At the community level, effectiveness can be measured in terms of impact on clients' well-being, total cost of service, public satisfaction with the service provided by the network, and the growth of social capital.

An example of the applications of Provan and Milward's (1995) original model, and its refinements (Provan & Milward, 2001), is Keast and Mandell's (2013) work. In their case study of six networks in Australia and the United States, they took a configurational approach and found that different configurations of network structures and network actors determined the degree of network effectiveness.

Another example the configurational approach in studying network effectiveness is Raab, Mannak, and Cambre's (2015) study on the crime prevention networks, which were composed of networks of actors (law enforcement, social service organizations, etc.) in the Netherlands. They define network effectiveness at the community level and in terms of reducing recidivism. Using qualitative comparative analyses, they investigated particularly how the configurations of network structures (network integration), network context (resource munificence and stability), and network governance mode related to network effectiveness. They found that centrally integrated networks, which had been in existence for at least three years, and those that were stable were more effective. Also, those networks that had considerable resources at their disposal or the ones with network administrative organization were more effective.

Several researchers used social network analyses (SNA) to analyze network effectiveness. Kapucu and Demiroz (2011) applied SNA methods to assess the effectiveness of disaster response networks, particularly in the cases of September 11 and Hurricane Katrina in the United States. They demonstrated that network structural factors were related to network outcomes. They also stress the importance of identifying informal networks and comparing them against the planned network structures.

Scholz, Berardo, and Kile's (2008) study on whether governance networks solve collective action problems is another example of SNA applications. These researchers tested the effects of two types of network structures on solving collective problems: small and dense networks, which can increase commitments to cooperative solutions among network members, and large boundary-spanning networks, which can enhance searches for and information exchanges among network members. They found that large boundary-spanning networks were more effective.

In his application of SNA methods in the study of the clean energy governance networks in 48 states in the United States, Yin (2017) found that governance networks with high overall "bridging and bonding social capitals" performed better in generating green jobs and renewable energy capacity. He also found that a more professional legislature facilitates faster clean energy development.

In their study of intergovernmental collaborations among local governments in Iowa, Siciliano, Carr, and Hugg (2020) examined how the changes in the structures and compositions of the intergovernmental collaborations among local governments in Iowa affected network outcomes. With their social network analyses, they found that more central and stable networks were more effective in reducing crime rates and more diverse networks were more effective in stimulating economic development.

Cantner and Graf's (2006) study of the network of innovators in Jena, Germany, is another example of social network analyses of network effectiveness. They found that the innovation networks in Jena were composed of multiple and actors of various types: individual innovators (scientists and others), various types of private firms, academic institutions, governmental organizations, politicians, etc. They asked which macro-level (network) characteristics help us predict the level of cooperation (a measure of effectiveness in innovation) in innovation networks? They answer the question

# 138 *Implications of the Complex Governance Networks Conceptualization*

with their comparisons of the matrixes of technological overlaps among the actors and cooperation among them in two different time periods in the 1990s. Their social network analyses (quadratic assignment procedure regressions) show that the technological overlap network in the earlier period and the cooperation network in the earlier period were significant predictors of cooperation network in the later time period. They conclude that the technological overlaps among network actors contributed to the effectiveness of the innovation networks in Jena.

## Summary

I began the chapter with a discussion of the concept of wicked problems. Originally formulated by Rittel and Webber (1972), this concept has been used in increasing numbers to refer to complex problems in recent decades. After summarizing Rittel and Webber's original conceptualization, I argued that the concept has been used so casually and that it has lost its analytical usefulness. The casual usages of this concept also imply that social problems cannot be defined, their characteristics cannot be known, and they cannot be solved. Complexity theory counters this implication. Complexity theorists recognize that problems are complex and their characteristic and dynamics may not be known in their entirety, but our knowledge of them can be enhanced by using more advanced conceptual and analytical tools, such as social network analyses and agent-based simulations.

The literature on the effectiveness of governance networks demonstrates that some progress has been made in conceptualizing and measuring the effectiveness of complex governance networks. All these conceptualizations are multidimensional. The complexity of the effectiveness of governance networks can be captured on multiple dimensions. There is no common conceptualization of the effectiveness of governance networks yet, but there are some common elements in the conceptualizations in the literature. There are also applications of SNA in empirically assessing these models, particularly at the whole network level. I summarized these commonalities and the applications of social network analyses last in the chapter.

## Note

1 Dr. Collins reflects on career at NIH, COVID response effort, work on genome sequencing: www.pbs.org/newshour/show/dr-collins-reflects-on-career-at-nih-covid-response-effort-work-on-genome-sequencing

# 10 Accountability

Accountability is the second key concern in the public administration practice and theory. The first one was effectiveness (Chapter 9). In a hierarchical organization, it is relatively easier to establish accountability rules and enforce them. In complex governance networks, multiple actors are in nonhierarchical, or less hierarchical, relationships and they are interdependent. The relationships among them are complex: They relate to each other in multiple ways (e.g., contractual relations and formal and informal partnerships) and these relationships are dynamic (Chapter 4). Therefore, the accountability problem in complex governance networks should be conceptualized differently, as some governance scholars also recognize (Kettl, 2002; Koliba, et al., 2019).

## Definitions and Conceptualizations of Accountability

*Merriam Webster* defines the term "accountable" as "answerable and explainable." Accountability includes "an obligation or willingness to accept responsibility or to account for one's actions, including being punished for wrongdoing."[1] This definition implies that an action and its consequences can be attributed to an actor (an individual or a group), so that the actor can be held accountable. In other words, they can answer questions about their actions and explain them.

In this abstract definition, accountability has four elements: actor, action, outcome, and a judge who will hold the actor responsible for their action and/or its outcomes. All these elements should be connected to each other, so that a system or mechanism of accountability can be established. In this system, particularly the connections between the actor, action, and outcomes should be clear, not only conceptually but also in observable evidence. Conceptual clarity and availability of empirical evidence are key issues in the accountability literatures in political science, public administration, and law. That is because to the extent that an action can be linked to a person or a group (e.g., organizational unit), that person or group can be held accountable for that action and/or its consequences. Then the person or the group can be held responsible and rewarded (for a job well done) or penalized for a misdeed or wrongdoing.

DOI: 10.4324/9781003053392-13

140  *Implications of the Complex Governance Networks Conceptualization*

The implication of this line of reasoning is that the action of an actor can be identified and the action can be connected to an outcome causally. The connection between the actor and their action will be easier to identify if a third party (a watchdog, journalist, judge etc.) has the information about that connection. The connection between the action and its consequences is more difficult to identify in complex systems, such as complex governance networks.

Then, what is causality? It is a deeply philosophical concept that has serious implications for research methodology (how to identify causal connection between variables) and practice. For our purposes here, the issue is how to establish the causal connection between one action and the outcome. Did the action cause the outcome? I discussed the philosophical underpinnings and methodological implications of causality in my earlier books (Morçöl, 2002, 2012a). I will not repeat them here. More elaborate conceptualizations of causality and their implications in philosophy and research methodology can be found in Pearl (2009) and Nadler (1993).

In this chapter, my focus is on the importance of establishing conceptual connections between an actor, their action, and its outcomes and the role of judge(s) in this process and empirically demonstrating the connections. These conceptual and empirical connections are easier to establish in orderly and hierarchical organizational systems (i.e., bureaucracies). In complex governance networks, the connections are more difficult to establish, which forces us to rethink the issue of accountability in these networks. That is because in complex systems in general the connections between an actor's action and its consequences are complex (Chapter 4). These connections are nonlinear and indirect. There are systemic interdependencies and interactions among multiple actors (not a single actor) that make it difficult to disentangle the actions of the actors from each other and the connections between the actions and the outcomes.

Before discussing the problems of accountability in complex governance networks more specifically, a review of the conceptualizations of accountability in the literature will be useful.

### An Overview of the Conceptualizations of Accountability

Historically, accountability has been defined in two ways: *internal accountability* and *external accountability*. In the first definition, an actor (individual) could hold themselves accountable by being a virtuous human. If the actor is a collective (group, organization), then the collective should have internal mechanisms to regulate the actions of its members and hold its members accountable. (Remember the concept of self-organization in complexity theory.) In the second definition, the individual actor is held accountable externally, typically by a superior of theirs in a hierarchical organization, or by a group of electors in democratic processes (think of an elected representative in a General Assembly). If the actor is a collective (e.g., an organization) it is held accountable by another collective.

*Accountability* 141

The earliest examples of the thinking of accountability as internal accountability can be found in the *Analects* of Confucius,[2] who lived between 551 and 479 BC in China. These were the times when the bureaucratic apparatus of the Chinese state, the first state in human history, was being built (Fukuyama, 2011, pp. 110–114). The Chinese bureaucracy established rules about how to collect and administer taxes; build roads, bridges, and irrigation systems; and maintain standing armies and wage war. As these administrative functions became clearer, one of the key issues was how they would function effectively (Chapter 9). Another question was how to ensure that the civilian bureaucrats and soldiers who were tasked with these functions would do what they were supposed to do (i.e., how they would be held accountable).

Confucius's general answer to these questions was that the bureaucrats and rulers had to be virtuous. In other words, for Confucius, accountability should be internal to the bureaucrat and the ruler. They should hold themselves accountable. But how would the bureaucrats and rulers know what virtuous conduct was? Where would the rules of virtuous behavior come from? Who would create and maintain them? The answer was that societies had norms and ethical rules, and individuals were expected to follow them. To the extent that they followed these ethical rules, bureaucrats and ruler would be virtuous.

Would this scheme work? Do people follow ethical rules? Could every ruler and bureaucrat be virtuous beings and hold themselves accountable? The common answer to these questions is, probably not. Then some external control and accountability mechanisms are needed.

As the states and their bureaucratic organizations grew in size and their functions were diversified, the rulers created external mechanisms of accountability. The hierarchical structure of bureaucratic organizations enabled the creation and enforcement of such mechanisms. The command-and-control mechanisms in large armies, such as the Roman legions, were primary examples of these mechanisms. They were emulated in civilian bureaucracies. The hierarchical structures and formal rules and procedures of bureaucratic military and civilian organizations enabled rulers and bureaucrats to control the activities of soldiers and civilian bureaucrats and hold them accountable for their actions.

Max Weber's ideal typical conceptualization of bureaucracy, which he formulated in the early 20th century, is an abstract mechanism of controlling bureaucrats and holding them to account. His ideal type of bureaucracy is based on "the principle of fixed and official jurisdictional areas, which are generally ordered by rules, that is, by laws or administrative regulations" (Weber, 2010, p. 196). The regular activities of a bureaucrat (i.e., their "official duties") are formulated and delimited by higher authorities in a hierarchically structured organization. The bureaucrat is expected to follow the rules and fulfill their duties. If they do not, they can be coerced to do so by their hierarchical superiors. The combination of the orderliness and clear expectations and the availability of coercive mechanisms in a bureaucratic

142 *Implications of the Complex Governance Networks Conceptualization*

organization makes it possible to hold bureaucrats accountable externally, regardless of whether they are virtuous and ethical humans or not.

As long as these hierarchical organizational forms and the rules could be maintained, external accountability mechanisms are workable. As we saw in the previous chapters of this book, complex governance networks defy hierarchies and thus they turn the accountability problem into a highly complex one.

Even before we get into a discussion of complex governance networks, there is another conceptual and practical problem of accountability that should be addressed: How can the top actor in a hierarchal system be held accountable? The chain of hierarchy ends at one point: the person at the very top of a bureaucracy. In the case of the bureaucratic organization of the state, that is the king, queen, president, prime minister, or the like. The question is, who will hold them accountable? This question has been answered in three ways historically.

The first answer is that they are accountable to no one. They know the best for everyone, therefore there is no need to hold them accountable. This is the model of absolute dictatorship. There have been numerous examples of absolute rulers, who did not have any accountability to anyone, in human history. They expropriated the properties of their subjects and ordered the killings of their subjects and war prisoners, with impunity (Graeber & Wengrow, 2021, passim).

In the second model, the ruler is considered to be accountable to a higher being, typically a deity. The ruler represents the deity and is tasked with interpreting the will and wisdom of the deity. Fukuyama (2011) argues that this understanding is the basis of the emergence of the rule of law, separately from and before the emergence of liberal democratic institutions, with which it is most closely associated today. The premise of the rule of law is that laws exist before lawmaking. Laws were made by the deity to establish order in the universe. Under the rule of law principle, the ruler is not the sovereign, but the laws are (p. 262). This notion has roots in various religious traditions, particularly Christian and Islamic beliefs (pp. 262, 278–279).

In the third model, the ruler is accountable to the public, through elections and other mechanisms (i.e., the political accountability model). People elect their representatives. If they want to remove the ruler, they can do so in another election. This is political accountability, which is most closely related to liberal democracy (see the next chapter). We know from our experiences and knowledge of governments that democratic processes are not as simple as this simplified description suggests. There are cultural and institutional mechanisms that mediate electoral processes and restrain the participation of some in the society, for example. Not all actors among the citizens of a liberal democratic society are equally powerful or informed to be able to participate in or influence electoral results equally. Some members of a community may not be allowed to vote at all (e.g.,

*Accountability* 143

non-citizens, slaves in the pro-Civil War United States, women before they earned the right to vote in 1920 in this country). Those who can vote may not have the full information about the ruler's actions to be able to form an informed opinion and they can be manipulated by others.

These brief descriptions of the three accountability models show that accountability is not a straightforward or simple process. Scholars of political science and public administration have been aware of the complexities in the accountability mechanisms in bureaucracies and democracies. A very brief overview of some of the thinking and debates in the literature will be illustrative.

Should bureaucrats be held accountable only to their hierarchical superiors, or should they be held to account (also) by the people (through elected politicians) in a democratic society? In their well-known debate in the 1930s and 1940s, Friedrich and Finer aimed to answer this question. Friedrich (1940) argued that it would not be possible for politicians to control bureaucrats and hold them to account, because modern societies required bureaucracies that were populated with bureaucrats with expert knowledge. Politicians did not have such expertise to be able to control bureaucrats and hold them to account. The best solution was to hold bureaucrats accountable professionally and morally (i.e., internally, as Confucius had suggested). Finer (1936, 1941) argued that accountability could be ensured only through an external control of bureaucracies by elected politicians.

The developments in political and public administration systems in the 1980s and 1990s brought another dimension into the discussions and debates on accountability: market accountability. The scholars of the New Public Management movement of this era argued that public agencies should be judged by their performances, which was similar to the mechanisms private corporations were judged and held to account (cited in Peters &Pierre, 1998, pp. 227–230; Shafritz & Hyde, 2017, p. 375). So, in this theory accountability was directly tied to performance.

### Multidimensional Accountability Models

In the brief history presented above, we can identify four types of accountability: internal (virtue and ethics based) accountability (Confucius), rule-based and hierarchical bureaucratic accountability (Weber), political accountability (liberal democracies), and market-based accountability (New Public Management). In the recent literature, three of these four types (the bureaucratic accountability, political accountability, and market-based accountability) have been considered in various combinations. Aware of the complexity of the issue of accountability, several scholars reconceptualized accountability in multidimensional terms.

In the recent literature on accountability, the authors recognize that accountability should be conceptualized in multiple dimensions. Beyond

144 *Implications of the Complex Governance Networks Conceptualization*

this commonality, though, there is not much agreement on what those dimensions should be. Different authors come to the problem of accountability from different angles and they highlight different issues in it.

The multidimensional conceptualizations of accountability in the literature are summarized in Table 10.1. This table is and adaptation of the framework presented in an earlier study (Morçöl & Karagoz, 2020). That framework was based on a summary of the dimensions of accountability identified particularly by Dubnick and Frederickson (2014), Haus and Heinelt (2005), Kearns (2011), Koliba et al. (2019), and Koppel (2003, 2005). Other scholars contributed to these conceptualizations and applied them in empirical studies, some of which are cited in the table. The table is not exhaustive of all the literature or all possible conceptualizations and categories of accountability, but it is illustrative of multidimensional thinking of accountability.

The first part of the table (General Principles and Methods) is an application of Kearns's (2011, p. 199) conceptualization of accountability. He posits that there are three fundamental questions to be answered: Accountability for what (purposes and principles)? Accountability to whom? Accountability through which mechanisms? These three questions are represented in the first three columns of the table.

The first column of the table represents Behn's (2001) and Koppel's (2003, 2005) answers to the first question. They identify five conceptions of accountability: controllability transparency, responsibility, liability, and responsiveness. *Controllability* is about the actions of agents by principals. It represents the original understanding of accountability in public administration: Elected officials should be able to control the actions of bureaucrats who are supposed to implement elected officials' policies. That can happen only if there are structured organizational roles and each individual knows what is expected of them (Dubnick, 2003), which fits the ideal typical conceptualization of bureaucracy by Weber. Koppel's conception of controllability includes both *bureaucratic control* ("hierarchical accountability": control of subordinates by superiors) and *political control* ("political accountability": control of elected officials and others by electors) (Romzek & Ingraham, 2000).

*Transparency* is the requirement for politicians and bureaucrats to explain their actions in regular public forums, hearings, and periodic reviews. This requires free flow of information, through media and the existence of democratic institutions that can check and balance their actions. Through transparency, politicians and bureaucrats can be held *responsible* for their behaviors, according to rules, norms, and laws. A form of responsibility is legal *liability* (culpability of officials and bureaucrats for their actions and rewards and punishment). Liability can be accomplished if there is a legal system that can operate under laws and enforce them through judiciary mechanisms to find those responsible and penalize them according to laws (Dubnick, 2003). The last conception of accountability is *responsiveness*

Table 10.1 Multidimensional Conceptualizations of Accountability in the Literature

| General Principles and Methods (Kearns, 2011) | | | Stages (Haus & Heinelt, 2005; Dubnick & Frederickson, 2011) | | |
|---|---|---|---|---|---|
| Purpose / Principle (Behn, 2001; Koppel, 2003, 2005) | To whom? (judges, "accounters") (Klijn & Koppenjan, 2016) | Mechanisms/Procedures (Bovens et al., 2014; Romzek & Dubnick, 1987) | Input | Throughput | Output / Outcome (Consequences) |
| Controllability | Government agencies | Administrative (hierarchical (bureaucratic) control | Hiring and appointments | Annual reviews | Promotion and firing |
| | Elected officials | Political (democratic) control | Elections | Recall mechanisms | Elections |
| *Transparency* | *Citizens, shareholders, elected officials, government agencies* | *Open records (sunshine) laws* Watchdog journalism | Public hearings about establishment of programs / projects | Agency meetings open to public Requests through open record laws | |
| *Responsibility* | *Professional organizations (professional standards, ethical standards)* *Procedural/financial auditing/accounting organizations* *Public* | *Professional reviews* *Procedural and financial auditing* *Reputational accountability (naming and shaming)* | | Accreditation reviews External auditing of financial statements | |

*(continued)*

*Table 10.1* Cont.

| General Principles and Methods (Kearns, 2011) | | | Stages (Haus & Heinelt, 2005; Dubnick & Frederickson, 2011) | |
|---|---|---|---|---|
| *Liability* | *Courts* | *Litigation* | Litigation against wrongdoing, abuse of power, | Litigation about the constitutionality of laws, public programs |
| *Responsiveness* | *Citizens, shareholders, elected officials, bureaucratic superiors Customers / Clients* | *Performance reporting Markets* | Periodic reporting of performance indicators Information available through ratings by institutions and other clients | |

(the actions of politicians and bureaucrats in response to the needs and desires of their constituencies, customer orientation).

The second and third columns elaborate on Koppel's five conceptions. The second column includes the answers to Kearns's (2011) second question: Accountability to whom? Who are the judges? In their survey of public administrators in Finland, Lehto and Salmien (2012) identified the following categories of judges: higher-ups in bureaucracies, elected officials, government agencies, citizens, electors in public or governing bodies, courts, professional organizations (professional standards, ethical standards), procedural/financial auditing/accounting organizations, shareholders, and customers. The table shows under which conception of accountability these judges are relevant.

The third column represents answers to Kearns's third question: Accountability through which mechanisms? Romzek and Dubnick (1987) argue that two factors should be considered to identify accountability mechanisms: "(1) whether the ability to define and control expectations is held by some specified entity inside or outside the agency; and (2) the degree of control that entity is given over defining those agency's expectations" (p. 228). Then they identify four types of accountability systems at the interplay of these factors: bureaucratic, legal, professional, and political. This typology was applied in different contexts by Radin and Romzek (1996), Romzek and Ingraham (2000), and Romzek and Johnson (2005). Bovens, Schilemans, Goodin (2014) offer an expanded the list of 11 mechanisms. This column in the table is a combination of the mechanisms in these two sources.

The second part of the table is about the stages of a policy and/or administrative process. The three stages of input, throughput, and output/outcome are relevant particularly for well-defined public policies and program, with beginnings and ends. They are used in program evaluation studies. Dubnick and Frederickson (2014) point out that these stages are applicable to studying accountability as well. Haus and Heinelt (2005) cite the stages in their conceptualization of the stages in a democratic legitimation process, which includes accountability.

The categories (columns and cells) in the table are not mutually exclusive. Romzek and Ingraham (2000) observe that there are different types of accountability and they can be applied in different combinations in different cases and under different conditions. Dubnick (2011) observes that accountability can be accomplished through various institutional configurations (e.g., constitutional configurations involving checks and balances), mechanisms (e.g., reports, inspections, performance measurement), and processes (e.g., investigations of mishaps, imposing of sanctions)" (p. 708). These observations are acknowledgments of the complexity of accountability in today's world, which is populated increasingly by governance networks.

148 *Implications of the Complex Governance Networks Conceptualization*

## Governance Networks and Accountability

Governance networks scholars observe that because these networks are populated by multiple actors and they are multicentered, they require flexibility in their operations; consequently, hierarchical (bureaucratic) accountability models cannot work for them (Goldsmith & Eggers, 2004, p. 122; Kettl, 2002, p. 72). Then what is the appropriate accountability model for governance networks? The most common answer in the literature is that accountability in and of governance networks should be conceptualized multidimensionally. So, most of the principles and methods of accountability that are summarized in Table 10.1 are applicable to governance networks.

The accountability principles and mechanisms cited specifically in the governance networks literature are summarized in Table 10.2. This table shows that the traditional mechanisms of administrative and democratic controls, litigation, and markets are the most frequently cited mechanisms in this literature. Fiscal/financial accountability (principal–agent relationship between network participants and their donors), performance reporting, professional reviews, and public reputational accountability (naming and shaming) mechanisms are also cited.

Although administrative accountability mechanisms are among the most frequently cited ones in the governance networks literature, it is not clear how such hierarchical and bureaucratic mechanism would be applied to multicentered networks. Some authors recognize this problem and propose performance (outcomes)- based mechanisms as the primary mechanisms of accountability for governance networks instead (Goldsmith & Eggers, 2004; Kettl, 2002). Goldsmith and Eggers argue that to achieve the best outcomes, leaders of these networks can set goals, align the values of network participants and create trust among them, structure incentives and risk sharing, measure and monitor performance, and manage change (p. 215). But how could that be done? Kettl (2002) proposes the principal–agent theory as the basis of conceptualizing these mechanisms (p. 86). In this theory, network actors can be held accountable through negotiated contracts and financial reward for performance outcomes.

Goldsmith and Egger's and Kettl's conceptualizations require, implicitly or explicitly, that political authorities (e.g., elected politicians in democracies) would be the principals ("accounters") in these performance-based accountability relationships. Then the question is can democratically elected politicians hold network actors to account? If yes, how? Koliba and his colleagues (2019) propose Sørensen and Torfing's (2005, 2009) "democratic anchorage" concept as an answer to these questions.

Sørensen and Torfing's conceptualization includes multiple accounters and social norms. They posit that governance networks may be democratically anchored to the extent that they are "linked to different political constituencies and to a relevant set of democratic norms that are part of the democratic ethos of society" (2005, p. 201). In this conceptualization,

*Accountability* 149

*Table 10.2* Accountability Mechanisms for Governance Networks in the Literature

*General Principles and Methods*

| Purpose / Principle | To whom? (Judges, accounters) | Mechanisms/Procedures |
|---|---|---|
| Controllability | Government agencies | Administrative (hierarchical, bureaucratic) control<br>• Kapucu and Hu (2020)<br>• Klijn and Koppenjan (2016)<br>• Koliba et al. (2019) |
| | *Elected officials* | *Political control (democratic accountability)*<br>• Kapucu and Hu (2020)<br>• Klijn and Koppenjan (2016)<br>• Koliba et al. (2019)<br>• Sørensen and Torfing (2005, 2009) |
| **Transparency** | *Citizens, shareholders, elected officials, government agencies* | *Open records (sunshine) laws*<br>*Watchdog journalism* |
| **Responsibility** | *Professional organizations (professional standards, ethical standards)* | *Professional reviews*<br>• Benner, Reinicke, and Witte (2004) |
| | *Procedural/financial auditing/accounting organizations*<br>*Public* | *Procedural and financial auditing*<br>*Reputational accountability (naming and shaming)*<br>• Benner, Reinicke, and Witte (2004) |
| **Liability** | *Courts* | *Litigation*<br>• Benner, Reinicke, and Witte (2004)<br>• Kapucu and Hu (2020)<br>• Klijn and Koppenjan (2016) |
| **Responsiveness** | *Citizens, shareholders, elected officials, bureaucratic superiors*<br>*Customers / Clients* | *Performance reporting*<br>• Goldsmith and Eggers (2004)<br><br>*Fiscal/financial accountability* (principal–agent relationship between network participants and their donors)<br>• Benner, Reinicke, and Witte (2004)<br>• Kettl (2002)<br><br>*Markets*<br>• Benner, Reinicke, and Witte (2004)<br>• Kapucu and Hu (2020)<br>• Klijn and Koppenjan (2016)<br>• Koliba et al. (2019) |

not only (elected) politicians but also "private business and civil society actors" (particularly their professional organizations), and citizens who are affected by the networks decisions and actions should be the accounters. They add that "commonly accepted democratic rules and norms ensuring

150    *Implications of the Complex Governance Networks Conceptualization*

the broad inclusion of relevant and affected actors, procedural fairness and agonistic respect among actors perceiving one another as legitimate adversaries rather than enemies" should be parts of this accountability process (2009, p. 244). How could these four criteria be met? Sorensen and Torfing's answer is "meta-governance," which I discuss in the next chapter. For now, it will suffice to say that meta-governance is about the role of governments in democratic governance processes. Governments set the stage for the actors to govern themselves and hold each other to account.

Other scholars expand Sørensen and Torfing's emphasis on democratic norms and ethos as elements of the accountability processes in governance networks; they stress that "informal mechanisms" (including these norms and ethos, but also others) in general should be factored into accountability processes. Romzek and her colleagues' (2012, 2014) contributions are the primary examples of the acknowledgment of the importance of informal accountability mechanisms in governance networks. They developed a conceptual framework of informal accountability and applied it in their studies on social service delivery networks. In this framework, the core elements of informal accountability are shared norms and facilitative behaviors (such as relationship building and champion behaviors) and informal rewards and sanctions. The authors also observe that informal accountability practices in networks are challenged, mainly because of the tensions between the formal and informal accountability systems and the differences in the rhetoric of collaboration among networked organizations.

In summary, the conceptualizations in the literature on governance networks and accountability are extensions of the general recognition in the public administration literature of the recent decades that in today's world accountability should be multidimensional. Then, what would the complex governance networks conceptualization add to this recognition? To answer this question, we need to turn to the literature whose authors took complexity seriously.

## Accountability in Complex Systems

In their multidimensional conceptualizations of accountability, most governance networks scholars recognize, explicitly or implicitly, the complexity of these networks and the complexity of their accountability problems. There are also those who approach the network accountability problem more specifically from the perspective complexity theory (e.g., Hahn, 2011; Klijn & Koppenjan, 2016; O'Connell, 2005, 2006). Before summarizing the conceptualizations by these authors, let us review how complexity affected accountability in some specific cases.

"Complex systems almost always fail in complex ways." This was an important observation in the report by the National Commission on the BP (British Petroleum) Deepwater Horizon Oil Spill and Offshore Drilling in 2010.[3] On April 20 that year, a massive oil leak occurred in the Gulf of Mexico, because of the explosion on the *Deepwater Horizon* oil drilling rig.

*Accountability*   151

The leak continued for months, until the oil well was sealed in September. It was one of the largest environmental disasters in the US history, with 4.9 million barrels of oil leaked into the ocean. It is estimated that the spill cost the Gulf Coast's economy almost $23 billion because of the lost revenues.[4]

An obviously important question is, who, or which organization, was responsible and should be held accountable for the disaster. BP, the operator of the rig, was held legally accountable. "In September 2014, a US District Court judge ruled that BP was primarily responsible for the oil spill because of its gross negligence and reckless conduct." The company ended up paying $20.8 billion in fines, the largest corporate settlement in US history. This was an example of legal accountability. But the National Commission's report reminds us that the accountability for the failure of this complex system of oil extraction should not be attributed to one cause. The report indicates that government oversight was necessary, but it had to be coupled with the oil and gas industry's "internal reinvention" and the transformation of its safety culture. The list of recommendations the commission offered are important, but perhaps the most important part of the report is the following paragraph.

> As the Board that investigated the loss of the Columbia space shuttle noted, "complex systems almost always fail in complex ways." Though it is tempting to single out one crucial misstep or point the finger at one bad actor as the cause of the Deepwater Horizon explosion, any such explanation provides a dangerously incomplete picture of what happened—encouraging the very kind of complacency that led to the accident in the first place.
>
> (p. viii)

In 2003, space shuttle *Columbia* disintegrated as it reentered the atmosphere, killing all seven crew members. Then, the National Aeronautics and Space Administration (NASA) board that investigated the accident concluded: "It is our view that complex systems almost always fail in complex ways, and we believe it would be wrong to reduce the complexities and weaknesses associated with these systems to some simple explanation" (p. 6).[5] The disaster was the second fatal accident in the Space Shuttle program, after the 1986 breakup of *Challenger* soon after liftoff.[6]

Even before these disasters, there was another big one: One of the reactors in Three Mile Island nuclear generating station in Middletown, Pennsylvania, melted down in 1979. This was the first major nuclear power plant failure in history. Who was responsible for that?

In his explanations of the Three Mile Island disaster and the failures in other socio-technical systems, Charles Perrow (1984) argues that it would be wrong to single out a person and hold them responsible for these failures, because they result from the complex interactions among the many elements (some technical and some social) that constitute these

## 152 Implications of the Complex Governance Networks Conceptualization

systems. Perrow's argument, based on his analyses of a range of socio-technical systems (e.g., nuclear power plants, space travel, air travel, dams, petrochemical plants, DNA technologies), was that those accidents in high-risk technologies like nuclear power plants and space travel are inevitable because they are complex systems. The title of the second chapter of his book was reflective of this systems perspective and foretelling: "Why We Have Not Had More TMIs—but Will Soon." An image of the *Challenger* explosion was on the cover of the second edition of his book that was published in 1999.

I will leave aside the details of Perrow's analyses. But his key insights are important to highlight because they show why we should approach accountability problems in complex systems differently than in hierarchical organizations. It is important to identify the multiple dimensions of accountability in complex governance networks, as several other authors did (see the previous section). It is more important to try to understand the interactions among the elements and events in complex systems and how these micro-level interactions lead to macro (system)-level effects. We do not have such a theory of accountability for complex governance networks yet, but the conceptualizations by Klijn and Koppenjan (2016), Hahn (2011), and O'Connell (2005, 2006) are important efforts that can be built on.

Klijn and Koppenjan (2016, pp. 235–238) recognize that the complex nature of public problems makes it difficult to formulate clear goals for networks. That is primarily because of the interdependencies among actors, not only actors (members) of governance networks, but also between the network actors and those external actors who will hold them to account ("accounters"). They propose that in such accountability situations, information provided to the actors and their accounters should be as clear as possible. The accountability mechanisms should be set up in a way that the dynamic nature of the goals of the network actors should be recognized. The designers and facilitators of these networks should understand that their ex-ante designs should be adjusted over time.

In his study of the multilevel governance network of Kristianstads Vattenrike Biosphere Reserve, a protected swamp area in Southern Sweden, Hahn (2011) investigated a key issue: how accountability works in the governance network and representative democracy relations. The governance network in this case was formed by local actors in 1989 with the purpose of watershed management. He describes the network as loosely nested in the representative democratic system, which affected its operations and how different actors in the networks and governmental entities interacted. This nestedness created the conditions for formal and informal interactions between actors. Hahn observes "the self-organized governance network is nested in the formal democratic system and, as a result, there is a complementarity and shared accountability between the network and representative democracy." He reaches the conclusion that all these created a dynamic process in which the initial perceptions and goals of the network

*Accountability* 153

actors changed. As their interactions evolved, the participants of the process developed a sense of "shared or extended accountability."

Lenahan O'Connell applied the concept of "emergent accountability" in two separate studies in Kentucky. The reader will remember from Chapter 4 that emergence is a key concept in complexity theory. O'Connell's two studies are very good illustrations of how this concept can be used in understanding the accountability problems in complex governance networks.

In his study of the workings of the intergovernmental system in Kentucky in the case of the solid waste policy, there were multiple state and local governmental entities that worked together. O'Connel's (2006) depiction shows in general terms that the networked relationships among these entities are complex. O'Connel's (2005) study of a statewide reform efforts of the social service transportation delivery system in Kentucky in the 1990s and 2000s is illustrative of this point. He states that prior to the reform effort, the transportation services were delivered by multiple governmental agencies and in a disjunctive fashion. The aim of the reforms was to combine two strategies: payment based on capitation and a broker program. By doing so, the reform created a network composed of the state, transportation brokers, transportation providers, and riders as the actors. The riders were all the participants in several social programs: Medicaid, the Human Services Transportation Delivery Program, Temporary Assistance to Needy Families (TANF), and the program for vocational rehabilitation, and services for the blind. It divided the state into 16 mutually exclusive "brokerages"; in each brokerage area where a broker is allocated a lump sum to provide transportation to those who need it. The brokers had the freedom to choose provers (taxi, van, and bus operators) and negotiate arrangements with them.

This arrangement created a complex set of accountability relations among a network of interdependent actors. O'Connell (2005) describes these relations as follows.

> The state holds the brokers accountable through the contract to broker all rides in a region (and live up to performance standards for equipment, drivers, and performance) in return for a lump-sum payment. This motivates the brokers to minimize costs. The brokers, in turn, hold riders and providers accountable by determining rider eligibility and by assigning riders to a provider. (However, if a broker or provider refuses to carry a potential rider, the latter can appeal to the state.) The brokers are motivated to eliminate all forms of waste and fraud in order to minimize their expenditures. With the brokers limiting payments to providers to only eligible trips, the providers are motivated to deny ineligible trips to riders. The riders, for their part, will hold the state and the brokers accountable by filing complaints about service quality. This motivates the brokers to maintain the quality of service and access to care. (Of course, the state officials are

154 *Implications of the Complex Governance Networks Conceptualization*

accountable to elected officials—the one aspect of the accountability environment that did not change.)

(p. 88)

This is a description of a complex system of relationships among interdependent actors. In this system, "accountability emerges from the activities of the major parties that make up a particular program's 'field.' *Each party holds some (but not all) of the other parties accountable, and the overall level of accountability emerges as they perform their specific roles*: state, broker, provider, and rider" [emphases added] (p. 92). He notes that the emergent nature of accountability in complex networks is actually a characteristic of many government programs (p. 92).

O'Connell's observation that each actor performs their specific roles (without following a centralized or overarching plan for accountability) and (system level) accountability emerges from their individual performances is the best description of the complexity theory's insight that accountability is an emergent phenomenon in governance networks. His application of complexity theory is conceptually sound, and his description of the Kentucky case is insightful. Now, the challenge is, how to conceptually refine these implications of complexity theory for emergent accountability and apply the conceptualization in future empirical studies.

## Accountability in Metropolitan Governance

Metropolitan areas are governed in complex interactions among multiple public, private, and nonprofit organizations. These actors include local (county and municipal) governments, special districts, state governments, various agencies of the federal government, various types of private businesses, and nonprofits that provide social/human services. The relationships among these actors are less hierarchical (or nonhierarchical); so administrative/bureaucratic accountability mechanisms are less applicable, or they are inapplicable. In most cases, there are no delineated geographical territories of governance networks; there may be some conceptual territories, but they usually are fuzzy. So, political accountability mechanisms are less applicable to them. The accountability mechanisms for metropolitan governance networks must be multidimensional and should recognize that their accountability emerges from the interactions among multiple actors (similar to the Kentucky case O'Connell (2005) depicted). There are very few studies on the accountability issues in metropolitan governance, and none of them applied a multidimensional accountability framework or a perspective of emergent accountability.

The accountability issues in metropolitan governance have been addressed indirectly in practice and in the academic literature. The literature recognizes that a wide range of mechanisms are used in the US metropolitan areas to coordinate and better organize the activities of the multiple actors in them for more effective and/or efficient delivery of services.

*Accountability* 155

Although accountability is not the primary concern in the descriptions in the literature, they do have implications for accountability.

In the local government system in the United States, a relatively common practice is to minimize the number of actors in governance through city–county consolidations, which centralizes governance structures and/or functions in a defined area. Examples include the consolidation of the City of Philadelphia and Philadelphia County in 1854 and the more recent consolidation of Macon City and Bibb County, Georgia, in 2012.[7] The implicit accountability solution in these consolidations is to strengthen administrative and political control mechanisms. Hierarchies are created and/or expanded, which allow for administrative accountability. In the redefined political jurisdictions, residents are enabled to hold elected official to account through elections.

There are also less hierarchical methods applied in metropolitan areas, such as regional tax sharing arrangements, creation of multipurpose metropolitan districts, interlocal agreements, and regional councils (Hamilton, 2014). Each method has its own implications for accountability. In general, they make administrative and political mechanisms of accountability less applicable, and the other mechanisms listed in Table 10.1 (transparency, responsibility, liability, and responsiveness) become more relevant. How exactly these mechanisms can work is a wide-open area of research.

There are theories and conceptualizations that can guide the studies on this topic: including the intergovernmental relations frameworks, urban regime theory, polycentrism theory, and collaborative regional governance conceptualizations. I provide brief summaries of these conceptualizations here. Extensive descriptions and historical analyses of them are provided by Hamilton (2014), Saltzstein (2003), and Stephens and Wikstrom (2000). Each of these conceptualizations focuses on certain aspects of the complex governance systems in metropolitan areas.

The intergovernmental relations frameworks are about the relations between the levels of governmental entities in a relatively hierarchical federal governmental system in the United States (federal, state, and local governments). In this relative hierarchy, administrative and political control mechanisms are possible to some degree. Urban regime theorists study how the coalitions among economic and political elites are formed (Stone, 1989). In this theory, accountability is not defined directly, but its implication is that local leaders can be held accountable politically, through influencing the political elites of the city or metropolitan area.

Polycentrism theorists offer a different perspective than both the intergovernmental relations frameworks and urban regime theories. Polycentrism theorists are not interested in questions of accountability, but their conceptualizations do have implications for accountability mechanisms. They aim is to show that governance processes can be multicentered and that multicentered governance processes can be more efficient than centralized and consolidated systems in public service delivery. In one of the most comprehensive compilations of the classical and contemporary

## 156  *Implications of the Complex Governance Networks Conceptualization*

essays written by the intellectual leaders of polycentrism by McGinnis (1999), several prominent names of polycentrism (Vincent Ostrom, Elinor Ostrom, Charles Tiebout, Gordon Whitaker, Roger Parks, and others) discuss a variety of issues, but there are only a couple of, and only indirect, mentions of accountability (pp. 307–312). Although polycentrism theorists are not concerned much about accountability, their conceptualizations suggest that those mechanisms other than administrative and political control (transparency, responsibility, liability, and responsiveness) would be more relevant for metropolitan governance.

The implications of collaborative regional governance conceptualizations for accountability are similar to those of polycentrism theories. There are very few studies that applied these conceptualizations in the area of accountability. The literature search my colleagues and I conducted in the Web of Science (see Chapter 1) shows that there were considerable increases in the numbers of studies on governance, networks, and complexity in the fields of urban and regional studies (main domain of the studies on metropolitan governance) between 1990 and 2019, and that the rate of increase accelerated in the 2010s.

A more specific presentation of the trend line in the urban and regional studies are presented in Figure 10.1. Among the 410 journal articles in the Web of Science database in urban and regional studies for the period of 1990 to 2019, only seven focused on the accountability problems in metropolitan governance. The studies were conducted in various topic areas and multiple countries: neighborhood planning in Seattle, United States (Sirianni, 2007), city-wide governance networks in Nairobi, Kenya (Hendricks, 2010), urban planning in Norway (Falleth et al., 2010), environmental policy in general (Carroza, 2015), social housing procurement in Northern Ireland (Muir & Mullins, 2015), decentralization of metro governance in Montreal, Canada (Meloche & Vaillancourt, 2015), and community supervisory committees

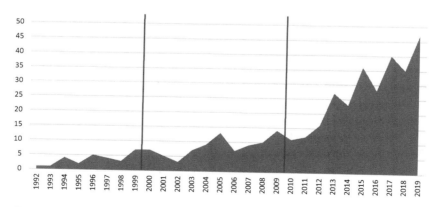

*Figure 10.1* Total number of journal publications on governance, networks, and complexity in urban and regional studies between 1990 and 2019 (Web of Science database).

*Accountability* 157

in Hangzhou, China (Zhang et al., 2019). The authors address the accountability issues in metropolitan governance from different perspectives and highlight important issues, but none of them develop or apply a multidimensional framework of accountability.

Among the recent books on urban/metropolitan governance, Saltztein (2003) and Stephens and Wikstrom (2000) do not even mention accountability issues in urban or metropolitan governance. Hamilton (2014) mentions only the accountability problems special districts (one type actors among many in metropolitan governance networks) pose to metropolitan governance practices; his discussion is limited to the challenges in holding these entities accountable democratically (through political accountability).

This review of the literature can be summed up with the observation that accountability has not been a main topic of interest in the metropolitan governance literature, but there seems to be an increased interest in it in recent years. The authors recognize the challenges the multicentered and complex governance networks pose for accountability in metropolitan areas, but they do not offer a comprehensive conceptualization to study the challenges.

The multidimensional accountability framework I proposed earlier in this chapter and O'Connell's (2005) proposition that accountability is an emergent phenomenon in complex systems applicable to metropolitan governance. There are few applications of the framework, or some aspect of it, yet. In the next section, I describe how it can be applied in a specific area of study: business improvement districts.

### Business Improvement Districts and Accountability

Business improvement districts (BIDs) are increasingly important actors in metropolitan governance. The case of BIDs illustrates how the accountability issues and challenges in metropolitan governance can be conceptualized. Several scholars, my colleagues and I among them, have studied the roles of BIDs in metropolitan governance, their effectiveness, and accountability in the last three decades. Before I discuss the accountability issues related to BIDs, a brief background and overview will be useful.

BIDs are

> designated geographic areas in which property owners are levied special assessments to finance the supplemental services delivered to the areas; (2) these areas may be governed by local governments or autonomous organizations that may be public or private in nature.
>
> (Morçöl & Gautsch, 2013, p. 243)

Why are these entities good examples of the accountability issues in metropolitan areas? To answer this question, we need to look into their history and current status and functions. Briefly, BIDs are an institutional

## 158 *Implications of the Complex Governance Networks Conceptualization*

form that is a product of the long historical evolution of local governance in the United States, and this institutional form has played increasingly important roles in local and metropolitan governance, and it has spread around the world, particularly in the last three decades.

BIDs have their roots in two historical local governance forms in the United States: special assessment districts and public authorities. For a comprehensive background information on these forms, I recommend Kathryn Foster's book (1999, pp. 7–22). BIDs combine "the distinctive revenue stream of the former with the governance structure and relative autonomy of the latter" (Briffault, 1999, p. 420). The BID institutional form we are familiar with today has evolved since the 1950s in the United States (Morçöl & Gautsch, 2013).[8] Since then, BIDs have spread to the 50 states of the United States, Washington, DC, and Puerto Rico.

There are both commonalities among the BID forms in these states and jurisdictions (institutional convergence) and differences (institutional divergence). They are "designated geographic areas in which property owners are levied special assessments to finance the supplemental services delivered to the areas" (Morçöl & Gautsch, p. 243) in all these jurisdictions. There are also differences in the management structures of BIDs: Some are managed by local governments and others by autonomous organizations (public authorities and nonprofits). In most states of the United States, two or three management structural forms coexist, but the general historical trend is toward the management of BIDs by autonomous organizations, particularly nonprofits (p. 255). This observation important, because it is an indication that the institutional forms of BIDs have been evolving toward more autonomy.

Another important observation is that in at least some large BIDs in major metropolitan areas, their management organizations have become more like general-purpose local governments (municipalities, city governments), meaning that their legal and/or de facto authorities and service areas have expanded. This development is important, given that they are legally classified as "special purpose governments" (Morçöl & Wolf, 2011). In other words, legally, BID management organizations are authorized to provide a small number of public services (such as trash collection and proving safety) in designated areas (typically downtowns and commercial corridors). But at least some large BID management organizations (like the Center City District in Philadelphia) were granted some "governmental powers," such as land-use planning, public space regulation, and operation of community courts; in others, although they do not have the legal authority to so, they exercise such powers through informal agreements (Briffault, 408, 419–20; Morçöl and Zimmermann 2008a, 41–45).

The (legal and/or de facto) increased autonomy and authority of BIDs are important because there are many of them in the United States and Canada and they have spread around the world in recent decades. The first BIDs in Canada ("business improvement areas," as they are known

*Accountability* 159

in this country) were established in the late 1960s and in the 1970s (Hoyt, 2008). By 2010, it is estimated that there were more than 1,000 BIDs in the United States and Canada (Becker, Grossman & Dos Santos, 2011). It is highly likely that these two countries have the largest numbers of BIDs in the world. BIDs have been created in some European countries (e.g., the UK, Germany, and the Netherlands) and South Africa since the late 1990s (Hoyt, 2008; Morçöl, Vollmer, & Mallinson, 2021). There are entities similar to BIDs in Australia, New Zealand, and Japan (Hoyt). The total number of BIDs around the world is not known.

The increased autonomy and authority of BIDs, together with their increased numbers and worldwide spread, are important to note. These developments indicate that BID management organizations have become important actors in metropolitan/urban governance in recent decades. Then how can they be held accountable for their decisions and actions in metropolitan areas?

There is an important characteristic of BID management organizations that should be considered, when we discuss their accountability: They never act alone. They are interdependent with other actors (local governments, other special districts, nonprofits, private corporations) in metropolitan systems/networks of governance. These interdependencies in networks increase the complexity of accountability problems. That is because it is more difficult to discern who, or what entity, would be held accountable to whom, or what entity complex governance networks, as we have seen earlier in this chapter. It is also difficult to point to what specific decisions and actions BID management organizations would be held accountable for, as my colleagues and I observed in earlier studied (Morçöl & Wolf, 2011; Morçöl and Zimmermann, 2008a).

The case of the Center City District (CCD) in Philadelphia illustrates the complexity of these accountability problems. CCD is one of the largest BIDs in the United States, and probably in the world. CCD's management organization shares its staff and offices with the Central Philadelphia Development Corporation, a membership organization of businesses (Morçöl, 2010). CCD's management organization routinely works with the city government and various nonprofit and private organizations.

The cases of the renovations and operations of several public parks in Philadelphia, such as Cret Park and Dilworth Park are good examples.[9] The CCD management organization partnered with the city government and local businesses in raising money, planning for, and re-constructing the Cret Park between 2003 and 2005. Since then, it has been operating the café it had built in the park and maintained its surroundings. Dilworth Park is particularly important to highlight because it is in a public plaza right in front of the city government building and it includes the entrances to a major station of the city's subway system. In the redevelopment of Dilworth Park, the CCD management organization partnered with the city government, the public transit authority (SEPTA), and private businesses to raise money, plan for, and reconstruct the plaza in 2014. Since then,

## 160 *Implications of the Complex Governance Networks Conceptualization*

under a long-term lease with the city government, it manages the café and the rest of the plaza and rents out space for special events, like the annual Christmas Village. The question is, who can be held to account for the redevelopments and operations of these parks in the complex web of relationships in which they have been built?

It is also difficult to determine to whom a BID management organization would be held accountable. In legal terms, it can be held accountable to the local government that created the BID with a local ordinance. That makes sense, because, on paper, local governments are supposed to oversee BID operations. In practice, however, practice they let BID management organizations operate as they wish (Morçöl & Zimmermann, 2008). Local governments can terminate BIDs legally, but they rarely do that (Briffault, 1999, pp. 388–89).

The decisions and operations of BID management organizations impact a wide range of individuals and organizations. Some authors argue that BID management organizations should also be held accountable to the property owners in their districts and other communities in metropolitan areas whom their decisions and operations impact (Briffault, 1999). Then the question is how would this be done, using which mechanisms? In some cases, BID boards are elected by property owners, but more often the initiators of a BID select board members and local governments approve them (Morçöl & Patrick, 2008; Morçöl & Karagoz, 2020). There is no legal mechanism to allow other residents (other than property owners) to participate in the elections of board members or participate in decision-making during their operations. Briffault (1999, p. 375) notes that the BID-enabling laws in most states intentionally exempt BIDs from the democratic representation rules for general-purpose governments, because they are considered special purpose districts. But, as I noted above, at least some BID management organizations (e.g., the Center City Philadelphia) have taken on expanded roles like those of general-purpose governments.

Another issue with the accountability of BID management organizations is, for what they would be held accountable. A possible answer to this question is that they should be held accountable for their performances. Mitchell (2008, pp. 95–97) proposes some criteria to assess BID management organizations' performances: the number of tasks that BIDs perform (festival organization, etc.), attracting new businesses to their district, responsiveness to the needs of property owners (measured with surveys), and contributions to city life. These are reasonable criteria, but it is a methodological challenge to measure the performances of BID management organizations on them, partly because the concepts like "contributions to city life" are quite broad and vague. It is difficult to produce more specific performance criteria.

Another methodological challenge is to isolate the impacts of BID from those of all other actors. As I noted earlier, they work closely with others in delivering services and in their projects (e.g., the CCD's partnerships

*Accountability* 161

with the city government and others in the constructions of and operating public parks in Philadelphia). Because they are so intertwined with other actors, it is difficult to isolate the impacts of a BID management organization, as Jeremy Mitchell (2008, p. 95) recognizes.

A few researchers tried to isolate their effects using statistical models. In her study of the impacts of BIDs in Philadelphia, Hoyt (2005) found that existence of a BID made a difference in reducing thefts of cars and other property in its area. In their study in New York City, Ellen, Schwartz, and Voicu (2007) found that BIDs contributed to increases in commercial property values in their areas, but not in residential property values. In our study on the crime rates in Philadelphia, my colleagues and I found that BIDs had positive effects on some urban crime (graffiti, illegal dumping, and disorderly conduct) in Philadelphia, but their effects waned after their first five years of existence (Han, Morçöl, Hummer, & Peterson, 2017). The key issue in these studies is that the researchers tried to isolate the impacts of the *existence of a BID* in a defined area. One may *infer* from these findings the level of performance of BID management organizations, but these studies are *not direct measurements* of performance. They do not tell us anything about the specific acts of BIDs and their interactions with other actors, so that we could assess their performance for accountability purposes.

Then, is there a better way to understand the accountability of BID management organizations as actors in metropolitan governance? I stressed earlier in this chapter that accountability in governance networks should be conceptualized multidimensionally. There are no multidimensional empirical studies on BID management organization accountability that I am aware of. There is only one comprehensive study on the accountability provisions in the BID-enabling laws, which I conducted with my colleague (Morçöl & Karagoz, 2020).

These laws spell out how BID management organizations should be held accountable in principle, but they do not tell us what actually happens. One can infer that because laws are supposed to be followed and therefore, they should reflect reality, but as I noted earlier, BID management organizations may (and do) gain de facto authorities (not granted in laws) and their actions do not necessarily match their complex interdependencies and interactions with other actors. Still, it is useful to understand what the laws say.

Before I elaborate on the findings of Morçöl and Karagoz (2020) study, I should note that BIDs are "enabled" by general BID laws. Local governments can establish BIDs under these laws. BID-enabling laws have been enacted in all states of the United States, Washington, DC, and Puerto Rico. Similarly, Canadian provinces and the *länder* (states) of the Federal Republic of Germany passed their own laws (Hoyt, 2008; Morçöl, Vollmer & Mallinson, 2021). In the United Kingdom, England and Scotland have their separate BID-enabling laws (Blackwell, 2008).[10]

162  *Implications of the Complex Governance Networks Conceptualization*

In our analyses of the BID-enabling laws in the United States, my coauthor and I applied the framework I presented in Table 10.1 earlier in this chapter. Our goal was to identify the mechanisms of controllability (administrative/bureaucratic and political), transparency, responsibility, liability, and responsiveness provided in the laws for the three stages of the lifecycle of BIDs (creation, operation, and termination). Our general finding is that the state enabling laws implicitly recognize the complexity of the BID accountability issue by providing various and overlapping mechanisms for the three different forms of BIDs (subunit, public authority, and nonprofit).

The laws provide mechanisms of bureaucratic and political forms of control, transparency, and liability, but there is heavy emphasis on the bureaucratic and political forms of control and less on the transparency and liability mechanisms, particularly in the creation and termination of BIDs. A noteworthy finding is that laws that were passed in more recent decades emphasized political control mechanisms (e.g., voting by property owners), more so than bureaucratic/administrative mechanisms (e.g., appointment and removal of BID board members by local governments). This development reflects the evolution of the laws from hierarchical relations between local governments and BIDs (the subunit form of BID management) to more autonomous BID management organizations (public authorities and nonprofits). These political accountability mechanisms do not solve the problem of who, or what entity, will be accountable to whom. As I noted earlier in this chapter, there are controversies over to whom BID management organizations should be held accountable (property owners, residents, or larger publics).

Most laws authorize only property owners to vote in BID creation decisions and/or board member elections. Public hearings are the primary transparency mechanism provided in the laws. Normally, BID management organizations, like any other legal entity, can be held legally liable through courts. Some laws recognize legal liability specifically, but only in a manner to limit owners' rights to go courts against the creation or the specific assessment of their properties. The laws do not include provisions for the responsiveness of BID management organizations to property owners or others, which should be expected because responsiveness cannot be mandated by law. It is still important to highlight this issue because, as other studies show, informal mechanisms like responsiveness are important for BIDs (Meek & Hubler 2008; Morçöl & Patrick 2006; Morçöl & Zimmermann 2008b; Wolf 2008).

## Summary

Accountability is a very important issue in the public administration practice and scholarship and more broadly in democracy. It may be relatively easy to establish accountability mechanisms in hierarchical organizations,

*Accountability* 163

but in governance networks it is a challenge. This chapter was about those challenges.

After a brief overview of the conceptualizations of accountability in the general literature, I summarized the multidimensional conceptualizations of accountability in the public administration literature. The authors who contributed to the public administration literature acknowledge that accountability should be thought of on multiple dimensions. These multi-dimensional conceptualizations are particularly pertinent to complexity of governance networks. The authors of the literature on governance networks also recognize the multiple dimensions in their studies.

As important as these conceptualizations are, most of them do not acknowledge the emergent nature of accountability in complex systems, which governance networks are. Only one author acknowledged this emergent nature of accountability and applied in a case study (O'Connell, 2005, 2006).

In the last section of this chapter, I illustrated the challenges of the complexity of the accountability in metropolitan governance. After a brief overview of the implications of the well-known urban and local governance theories for accountability, I discussed the accountability issues in the case of business improvement districts, increasingly important actors in metropolitan governance. These studies on business improvement districts indicate that accountability should be conceptualized on multiple dimensions for them.

The conceptual discussions and illustrations in this chapter show that accountability is a complex phenomenon. The multidimensional frameworks of accountability mechanisms developed in the literature are important advances, but more conceptual refinements (e.g., how the concept of emergence can help us understand accountability better) and more empirical studies are needed on this topic in the future.

## Notes

1 *Meriam Webster*, Accountability. www.merriam-webster.com/dictionary/acc ountability
2 The *Analects* of Confucius, as translated by James Legge (1971/1893).
3 Federal Register, National Commission on the BP Deepwater Horizon Oil Spill and Offshore Drilling. www.federalregister.gov/documents/2010/05/26/2010-12805/national-commission-on-the-bp-deepwater-horizon-oil-spill-and-offsh ore-drilling
4 Wikipedia article, Deepwater Horizon Oil Spill. https://en.wikipedia.org/wiki/ Deepwater_Horizon_oil_spill#Deepwater_Horizon_drilling_rig
   *The New York Times*, Deepwater Horizon's Final Hours. www.nytimes.com/ 2010/12/26/us/26spill.html?_r=1&nl=todaysheadlines&emc=a2
5 Columbia Accident Investigation Board Report. http://s3.amazonaws.com/aka mai.netstorage/anon.nasa-global/CAIB/CAIB_lowres_full.pdf
6 Wikipedia, Space Shuttle *Columbia* Disaster. https://en.wikipedia.org/wiki/ Space_Shuttle_Columbia_disaster

164  *Implications of the Complex Governance Networks Conceptualization*

7 Wikipedia lists more than 30 examples of various forms of consolidation in the US metropolitan areas. https://en.wikipedia.org/wiki/Consolidated_city-cou nty#List_of_consolidated_city-counties.

8 Hoyt (2008) states that the first BID was the Bloor-Jane-Runnymede Improvement Area, which was created with a city ordinance passed in Toronto, Canada, in 1969 (pp. 118–119). The research my colleague and conducted suggests that there were earlier examples of BID laws in the United States: Nevada's General Improvement Districts Act of 1959, California's Parking and Business Improvement Area Act of 1965, and Pennsylvania's Business Improvements District Act of 1967 (Morçöl & Gautsch, 2013).

9 See the information about the histories of the parks and their operations at www.centercityphila.org/parks.

10 The Business Improvement Districts (England) Regulations 2004. www.legislat ion.gov.uk/uksi/2004/2443/contents/made

Business Improvement Districts (Scotland). www.gov.scot/policies/regenerat ion/business-improvement-districts-bids/

# 11 Democracy[1]

## Co-authored by Göktuğ Morçöl, Saahir Shafi, and Aravind Menon

Are complex governance networks compatible with democracy? Do they diminish or enhance it? To answer these questions, we should consider broader questions. What is democracy? Is it a common set of arrangements and practices applicable around the world and in different periods in history? Alternatively, are there different types of democracy that existed in different parts of the world at different times? These questions should be considered in the context of the state of democracy in the early 21st century and the history of democratic practices in human societies.

The term "democracy" was first used in ancient Athens (5th century BC), and some scholars consider the self-governing community of ancient Athens as the first proper example of democracy in human history (e.g., Miller, 2018, p. 13). But there is archaeological evidence that democratic practices existed in earlier human societies such as the communal assembly halls in the Sumerian city of Uruk in Mesopotamia (circa 3300 BC) and local assemblies of decision-making in Bali (circa 2000 BC) (Graeber & Wengrow, 2021, pp. 302–306, 320).

This chapter is not about the details of the historical evolution of democratic practices in detail, but we will make some references to historical examples, to understand better the context of the governance networks and democracy in the early 21st century. Obviously, democracy is a broad topic that has been covered in range of disciplines of study. Our primary focus in this chapter is the public administration literature.

There is an increasing concern that liberal democracies have been challenged by populist and/or neo-fascist movements and leaders around the world in the early 21st century (e.g., Albright & Woodward, 2018; Levitsky & Ziblatt, 2018; Stanley, 2018). After four years of the challenges the Trump administration posed to the liberal democratic institutions in the United States, some commentators hailed Joe Biden's victory in the presidential election of 2020 as an opportunity not only to restore these institutions, but also to strengthen them.

Quirk and Lizundia's (2020) Brookings Institution blog post is a good example of this hopeful thinking. The reader will see in this chapter that the issues he raises are directly relevant to our questions about the nature

DOI: 10.4324/9781003053392-14

166 *Implications of the Complex Governance Networks Conceptualization*

and types of democracy and their compatibility with complex governance networks. The authors argue that the core element of Biden's "democracy agenda" should be to strengthen "citizen-centered governance," in which "institutions and processes are open and transparent, informed by citizens' views, and address peoples' needs" (para. 4). Citizen-centered governance should create an enabling environment for "responsive, responsible, and accountable government"; it should allow for "greater democratic participation, decentralized public management, and the provision of citizen-friendly official information" (para 4).

We can make two observations on this recent literature on democracy. First, a mere listing of the concepts Quirk and Lizundia (2020) use in their argument (institutions, transparency in information dissemination, respective roles of governments and citizens, accountability, and decentralized organizational forms in public service delivery) shows that democracy can take on multiple forms on multiple dimensions. Second, the common reference frame in Albright and Woodward's (2018), Levitsky and Ziblatt's (2018), and Stanley's (2018) warnings about the dangers for democracy, as well as in Quirk and Lizundia's argument, is "liberal democracy." It is important to note this, because, as some scholars point out, liberal democracy is not the only possible type of democracy; it has also "deliberative/discursive" and "practice-based" types (e.g., Meijer, 2012). These two observations frame the discussions in this chapter.

## Conceptual Clarifications

Before we proceed, some conceptual clarifications are necessary. First, we will apply Max Weber's (2010) method of "ideal typification" as the conceptual tool in our analyses of the three types of democracy. Ideal types are purposeful abstractions, mental constructs, used to identify the salient aspects of a phenomenon under study and analyze them conceptually. We discussed the epistemological underpinnings of such abstractions and their usefulness as conceptual analytical tools elsewhere (Morçöl, Shafi, & Menon, 2022).

Second, we define democracy in terms of *participation* in the governing of common affairs and solving social problems, not in terms of *social equality* or *equity*. We will define three types of democracy based on three types of participation later in the chapter. It is important to make a conceptual distinction between participation and equality/equity here because some in the public administration literature associate the two closely together, as we discuss later in the chapter.

Democracy should be defined solely as participation, and it should be conceptually separated from social equality/equity, because the two do not necessarily coexist. Archaeological evidence shows that participation and equality/equity took on multiple forms in history and in some cases, they coexisted in a variety of configurations, but in others they did not (Graeber & Wengrow, 2021, pp. 76, 126, 302–306, 319–320). Individual actors

*Democracy*   167

participated in the processes of governing their societies or producing collective goods and services in various forms. Equality and equity were defined differently in different societies, depending on what the societies valued. Some valued the equality in accumulated wealth. In other societies, equality was defined in terms of accessing educational resources, or equality in accessing gods (for example, the king and a peasant being equal in front of God after they die). There were also various forms and degrees of participation in history; these forms coexisted with different forms and degrees of equality (or equity) in different human societies. Graeber and Wengrow cite examples of these coexisting forms in different historical periods and societies, from the ancient Sumerian city of Uruk (3300 BC) to ancient Athens (5th century BC).

Third, participation is related to self-organization, a key concept of complexity theory (Chapter 4). In fact, self-organization can be defined as a deeper form of participation. We discuss self-organization and its implications for democracy and governance networks in the next section.

## Self-Organization, the State, and Democracy

Self-organization is a core concept of complexity theory; complex systems are self-organized in principle and there are degrees of self-organization in systems (Chapter 4). These systems do not require external interventions or guidance to organize themselves. Because democracy is about participation by people (or segments of people) in the governance of a society (or a smaller community), the ultimate form of participation is self-governance. Then the question is, can human societies be self-governing, like self-organizing complex systems? Alternatively, do they need to be governed by external actors/forces? The answers to these questions have important implications for democracy.

For centuries, philosophers and social scientists have asked whether people can organize/govern themselves to solve their collective problems, or an organization with the power of coercion (e.g., the state) is necessary to solve such problems. In Hardin's (1968) "tragedy of commons" conjecture, which has been referred to a few times in this book, herders pursue their self-interest and try to maximize the appropriation of the resources they use commonly (grass as the food source of their herds), which leads to the depletion of these resources. The implication of this conjecture is that an external and coercive force must step in to prevent the depletion of the resources.

There are two conceptual responses to Hardin's interpretation of the exploitation of common resources: Friedrich Hayek's philosophical argument and Elinor Ostrom's social scientific response. Hayek (1973) defines two types of social order: grown (spontaneous) social order and made (designed) social order. Grown orders are self-generating and endogenously determined systems. An example would be the herders in Hardin's metaphorical pasture regulating themselves so that the common resources

168 *Implications of the Complex Governance Networks Conceptualization*

would not be depleted. Made orders are created exogenously. They are products of deliberate actions of actors external to the system. An example would be a government entity setting up the rules of grazing and enforcing them by force if necessary.

Hayek (1973) argues that grown orders are superior to made orders, because the former are the products of the complex interactions of multiple minds and they have the ability to capture/match the complexity of their environments, whereas the latter are limited by the external entity's limited cognitive capacity and are therefore unable to capture the complexity (p. 39). In other words, the multiple minds of the grazers would work better in managing the pasture because they can collectively understand the complexity of their environment better than external actors and govern it accordingly. An external entity (e.g., the state) would not be as successful because it has limited cognitive capacity to understand the complexity of the situation in the pasture.

Hayek (1973) recognizes that grown and made orders are abstractions and they can coexist in practice. Although Hayek strongly favors limiting governments' power in community affairs, he concedes that some deliberate (and external) design is unavoidable. According to Hayek (2013), then the most beneficial role governments can play is to create the conditions for spontaneous orders to emerge (p. 38).

The idea that people can govern themselves, without external interference, and the outcome of self-governance can be better than deliberate design is at the core of many conceptualizations of democracy. Some scholars studied the possibility and conditions of self-governance empirically. Elinor Ostrom's life-long and empirically grounded work on the problem of self-governance, which has been referred to in the previous chapters of this book, is a primary example. Ostrom (1990, 2005) not only demonstrates with evidence that people can govern themselves, but she also identifies the conditions under which self-governance is most likely to be successful. Her and her colleagues' empirical studies demonstrate that individuals can self-organize to manage "common pool resources" (such as a pasture, managed forests, and shared fisheries) without the unintended consequences Hardin warned about (i.e., tragedy of the commons).

Ostrom (1990) also shows that there are different forms and degrees of self-organization. The success or failure of a particular self-organized group of actors in solving their collective action problem depends on several factors. If the resources are salient for the actors, they are available in reasonably small areas (accessible), they can be feasibly improved, and their patterns of flow can be predicted by the members of the community (actors), then it is more likely that these members can govern (organize) themselves. If the actors are autonomous (capable of making their own decisions), they have a common understanding of the issues, they trust each other, and they have previous organizational and leadership experiences, then the likelihood for a successful self-organization is higher.

What is common in the conceptualizations by Hayek and Ostrom is that the state (or government) is an external force that can make deliberate decisions and intervenes to regulate collective action problems. Then, what is the state? They do not answer the question directly, but they seem to subscribe to the commonly accepted notion that the state is a unified entity with monopolized authority to use force over a defined piece of territory and group of people.

This is quite an accurate reflection of reality, according to Fukuyama (2011, p. 15). The modern state, which emerged in different parts of China between the 8th and 3rd centuries BC and matured in the 3rd century BC (p. 19), can act as a unified entity. Military and civilian bureaucracies enable the state to do so. These bureaucracies collect taxes, administer laws, mandate uniform weights and measures, and create public infrastructures (roads, canals, irrigation systems) (p. 110).

Bevir (2010, 2014) makes a counter point. He argues that the notion of the state as a unified entity is more fictional than real. In fact,

> [the] state is never monolithic and it always negotiates with others. Policy always arises from interactions within networks of organizations and individuals. Patterns of rule always traverse the public, private and voluntary sectors. The boundaries between state and civil society are always blurred. Transnational and international flows always disrupt national borders. In short, state authority is constantly remade, negotiated, and contested in widely different ways within widely varying everyday practices.
>
> (2014, p. 36)

This notion is built on a myth that began in the Renaissance and the Reformation period and was formulated and solidified by Jean Bodin and Thomas Hobbes; it later became entrenched in political thinking and has been taken for granted (Bevir, 2014, p. 55). Jessop (2016) agrees with Bevir's argument in general but points to a different beginning of the notion: Max Weber's conceptualization of bureaucracy in the early 20th century (p. 25). Weber's conceptualization is the basis of our ideal-typical definitions of democracy in this chapter, beginning with the next section.

Graeber and Wengrow's (2021, pp. 362–370) account of the anthropological and archaeological findings support Bevir's (2014) arguments in general. They show that there was no uniform organization that we could call "the state" in human history. Instead, there were three forms of social domination used by rulers: control of violence over a territory (sovereignty), control of information (bureaucracy), and charisma. These three forms, Graeber and Wengrow contend, coexisted in various combinations. What we call modern states today are combinations of the first two of these forms (sovereignty and bureaucracy) primarily, but charisma plays some roles in their formations as well.

# 170  *Implications of the Complex Governance Networks Conceptualization*

Scott (2008) and Jessop (2016) offer somewhat different conceptualizations of the state, but they too recognize the multiplicity of its forms. In Scott's conceptualization, governments are institutions that are "comprised of regulative, normative and culture-cognitive elements that, together with associated activities and resources, provide stability and meaning to social life" (p. 48). Jessop defines the state as "a complex ensemble…of institutions, organizations, and interactions, involved in the exercise of political leadership and in the implementation of decisions that are, in principle, collectively binding on its political subjects" (p. 16).

It is important to make one more point here: Even if the state is a unified entity, it is not necessarily a benefactor in its relations with the rest of the society. As Graeber and Wengrow (2021) observes, and Fukuyama (2011) agrees, what we call the state today emerged from the forms of social domination rulers used to control groups of people. Fukuyama notes that the creation of the state was not motivated by the desire to serve the public; instead, it was a product of tribal chiefs' desires to establish their domination over others with military force and conquest (pp. 110–112). The emergence of the state was not in response to a need to regulate common resources for the benefit of the communities.

We made three points in this section: that self-organization/self-governance can take on multiple forms, depending on the conditions; that the notion that the state is a unified entity that acts to solve collective problems is problematic; and that the nature of the state as a benefactor of society, rather than a dominator, is also questionable. These three points together paint a complex picture of democracy as participation in solving collective problems and the respective roles of the state and individual actors (citizens) in doing so. To better understand this complexity, we propose ideal-typical simplifications in the next section. In the following sections, we will apply the simplified conceptualization to governance networks.

## Ideal Types of Democracy

In this section, we conceptualize three ideal types of democracy: liberal, deliberative/discursive, and practice-based types. These ideal types are distinct as abstractions, but in real life they coexist in various combinations. Governmental organizations can play different kinds of roles in each type. These conceptualizations will help prepare for the discussions on governance networks and democracy, which is the main topic of this chapter.

### *Liberal Democracy*

We extracted the following composite characterization ("ideal type") of liberal democracy from the definitions in the literature (Esmark, 2007; Farazmand, 2010; Fukuyama, 2011, 2014; Ishakhan & Slaughter, 2014; Klijn & Koppenjan, 2016; Klijn & Skelcher, 2007; Miller, 2018; Saward,

2006; Sørensen & Torfing, 2006). These authors conceptualize liberal democracy as an institutionalized form of participation in governance by a group of people who reside within, or are otherwise affiliated with, a defined geographical territory. These people are considered "citizens." They are enabled to choose their representatives freely and fairly. The state has monopolistic power over the territory and it can exercise coercion over the residents of the territory (sovereignty). These characteristics are together known as the "nation-state." It is a "territorially defined political community," in which residents "govern themselves either through direct citizen participation or through the election of representatives" (Sørensen & Torfing, 2009, p. 234). The state is accountable to citizens through elections and other mechanisms (e.g., institutions of justice) and it adheres to a set of laws (the rule of law).

Two key elements in the above conceptualizations are the *territorial definition* of and the *monopolistic power* attributed to the state. These are the two elements that confound the debates on the implications of complex governance networks, as we discuss later in the chapter. Governance networks challenge the territorial definition of liberal democracy because membership in a governance network is not defined territorially. The monopoly of a central state is at least challenged by the multicentered nature of these networks. (In two earlier chapters of this book, Chapters 1 and 3, there were similar discussions on the implications of governance networks for the nation-states.)

These two key elements were problematic even before the emergence of governance networks. The definitions of geographical territory and polity define the forms and limits of participation (the core of any definition of democracy), and they do not ensure equality. For example, historically, the US Constitution did not ensure any form of participation by slaves or women, let alone equality in participation. US history is an account of the expansion of political participation through military and legislative actions. The Civil War abolished slavery and allowed participation by former slaves. The Nineteenth Amendment of the US Constitution ensured the voting rights for women. The Civil Rights laws of the 1960s strengthened the legal rights for racial minorities to vote.

The principle of participation may be direct or representational and in liberal democracies, the latter is more common. These two forms of participation were considered and debated in the founding document of the United States. In Federalist No. 10, Madison made a distinction between "direct democracy" ("a society consisting of a small number of citizens, who assemble and administer the government in person") and "republic" ("a government in which the scheme of representation takes place").[2] In the end, the "Founders" opted for the representative form (republic).

Liberal democracies evolved over centuries, primarily in Western Europe, North America, and Oceania. After this long evolutionary process, liberal democracy has not become a universally accepted norm, which can be observed in the evaluations of the state of liberal democracy around

172 *Implications of the Complex Governance Networks Conceptualization*

the world.[3] These evaluations show that a majority of countries cannot be considered as "full liberal democracies" in the sense that they do not have all the elements of the ideal type of liberal democracy as defined above.

Then, could all societies eventually adopt liberal representative democracy, even though they may not have done so yet? Huntington (1996) argues that this is not a likely scenario because liberal democracy is a product of the Christian—particularly Catholic and Protestant—Western civilization. He argues that all the other civilizations—the Orthodox (Russian), Sinic (Chinese), Islamic, Latin American, Hindu, Buddhist, and Japanese civilizations—are products of very different evolutionary paths and they are not compatible with liberal democratic norms. The rejections or questioning of the norms of liberal democracy by a range of populist leaders (e.g., Erdoğan in Turkey, Duterte in the Philippines, and Bolsonaro in Brazil) confirm Huntington's conclusion. But these norms are questioned, or challenged, also by the leaders of some "Western" countries by Huntington's definition (e.g., Trump in the United States, which has a Protestant and Catholic majority, and Orban in Hungary, which is majority Catholic). Orban explicitly opposed the "liberal restraints on popular sovereignty and praised the strengths of 'illiberal state'" (Miller, 2018, p. 16).

Acemoglu and Robinson (2012) and Fukuyama (2011, 214) demonstrate that liberal democratic institutions are neither inevitable, nor do they belong to an exclusive group of nations; they are products of multiple historical contingencies coming together. In Fukuyama's historical narrative, what he calls the three liberal democratic institutions (the state, rule of law, and accountable government) emerged and evolved disparately in various parts of the world in different time periods. Fukuyama observes that the state emerged in the 3rd century BC in China. The rule of law was a product of the belief of human societies in laws of nature (or God's laws) that were above even the wishes of absolute rulers. The notion that governments should be held accountable was a later development: In some European societies, lower-level chiefs initiated the movements to restrain the powers of absolute rulers. A primary example is the Magna Carta ("Great Charter of Freedoms"), which was dictated by a group of rebel barons to the King of England in 1215.[4]

The three institutions came together only after the Industrial Revolution (the last half of the 18th century and the first half of the 19th century). Following the Industrial Revolution, new social classes were created. Some of them, particularly middle classes, which made up a large proportion of the society, favored democratic institutions, whereas others, particularly landowners, were opposed to them. The rule of law and democratic accountability were supported by different social classes, the middle class and working class respectively, and the size of these social classes comparative to opposed groups (i.e., landowners) were a major driver toward the establishment of democratic institutions.

*Democracy* 173

In Acemoglu and Robinson's (2012) account, liberal democratic institutions were contingent on historical developments (p. 118). They observe that small social and political differences between societies led to vastly different outcomes in institution building. For example, both China and Japan were under absolute rule in the 19th century, when they interacted with foreign powers and they both faced foreign interventions, but in China, authoritarian rule was perpetuated, while Japan evolved into a democratic society.

Even after a centuries-old evolution and consolidation, liberal democratic institutions can be challenged by autocratic (typically right-wing populist) leaders, as we noted earlier. There are also those who challenged liberal democracy theoretically. The first theoretical challenge is that democracy, in general (participation in governance or self-governance), and liberal representative democracy, in particular, are not natural to humans. The biological evolution favors authoritarian forms of governing societies, not democratic/participatory ones (Somit & Peterson, 1997). Graeber and Wengrow's (2021) account of the anthropological and archaeological evidence does not support this contention. The evidence shows that in early human societies there were many examples of nonhierarchical and more participatory societies and that there is no particular pattern in human history from authoritarianism to democracy or vice versa.

The second theoretical challenge is posed by those who argue that liberal democracy is not sufficiently democratic, because it ignores the power disparities among individuals and groups and the limitations in their information processing capabilities. Some people are more powerful than others, which distorts democratic participation and decision-making. For example, "billionaires can buy elections," which is supported by empirical evidence.[5] Individuals and groups who are more economically and/or politically powerful can control the flow of information in a society, which distorts people's knowledge and preferences. That is partly because some people are not educated enough to process the available information. (As an example, consider the "vaccine hesitancy" that was based on misinformation and disinformation spread by anti-vaccine activists during the COVID-19 pandemic.)[6]

Schattschneider's (1960) now classical conceptualization that people are only "semisovereign" in American democracy encapsulates these arguments. He points out that although (liberal) democracy in principle can help solve a society's problems through people's participation in governing, its institutional structures do not allow everyone to participate equally. The government's agenda in solving society's problems is limited, and how the agenda is set determines policy outcomes. Not everyone has an equal opportunity in accessing the mechanisms of the government in general, and agenda setting in particular. Only those with economic means and the knowledge of institutional procedures can be influential in setting the agendas.

# 174 *Implications of the Complex Governance Networks Conceptualization*

### *Deliberative/Discursive Democracy*

If liberal democracy is not sufficiently democratic, then leaders and/or people must strive toward building more participatory and equitable forms of democracy, some theorists argue. The most well-known examples are critical theorists like Jürgen Habermas. They offer an alternative conceptualization of democracy: deliberative/discursive democracy.

What distinguishes deliberative/discursive democracy from liberal democracy is the former's specific emphases on authentic communication and deliberation by citizens to enhance participation in decision-making. Deliberative/discursive democracy theorists try to strengthen this participation particularly through the inclusion of marginalized voices—those who are disadvantaged because of their social statuses (i.e., race, gender, and social class)—in an enhanced and authentic deliberation (e.g., Dryzek, 2002, 2007; Fischer, 2003, 2009; Torgerson, 2003).

Deliberative/discursive democracy theorists do not suggest that liberal democratic institutions are not important. Instead, they argue that they should be expanded (Warren, 1992). In this expanded form of democracy, the members of a community should participate directly (not only through liberal institutional structures) and genuinely in policy deliberations and decision-making (Bevir, 2013, pp. 174–175).

The foundations of the theory of deliberative/discursive democracy can be traced back to Habermas's (1985) notion of "communicative rationality": that interactions and deliberations should be free of domination, deception, strategizing, and self-deception. An authentic deliberation is possible when participants express their preferences free from coercion and deception (Dryzek, 2002, p. 1). Democratic ideals should include political equality and citizens' rights to fundamental political liberties—which are essential components of liberal democracy—and they should be strengthened through authentic communication and deliberation (Dryzek, 2007). Human societies should move from a conceptualization of democracy as a protective model, which is the model of liberal representative democracy, to a developmental model, which actively strengthens the methods of communication and deliberation (Macpherson, 1979). Education is an essential element of deliberative/discursive democracy: Citizens should become educated about issues, the democratic process, and how they can participate in this process (Hansen, 2007).

### *Practice-Based Democracy*

Both liberal representative democracy and deliberative/discursive democracy are state (government) centric (Pierre & Peters, 2005). In liberal democracy, the state is the primary actor, regulator, and enforcer of institutional rules. In deliberative/discursive democracy, people communicate authentically and deliberate to influence governmental actions. Practice-based democracy differs from both, in the sense that it is based on actual citizen engagement in the practice of solving collective problems, not only through voting or participating in debates on governmental actions (Meijer, 2012). In practice-based democracy, *co-creation of public goods* is the norm and *self-governance* is the ideal. In this model, "citizens are seen not only as voters but also as problem solvers and co-creators of public goods" (p. 306).

To clarify what Meijer (2012) means by "co-creation of public goods" and how practice-based democracy can be a different model, a summary of his tripartite conceptualization of participation will be helpful. He proposes three forms of participation: *political participation, policy participation*, and *social participation*. "Political participation is the classical form of participation which focuses on influencing agenda-setting and decision-making" (p. 306). This form of participation can be exercised most typically in liberal representative democracy, but also in deliberative democracy. Citizens may participate in public hearings to help set the agenda for government decision-makers or help them make choices among alternatives (e.g., in participatory transportation planning). To the extent that these hearings are based on authentic deliberation and devoid of coercion, political participation fits into the model of deliberative/discursive democracy.

*Policy participation* is different in the sense that it defines more direct involvement in policymaking and implementation. It "concerns citizen input in government policies either when they are invited by governments or on their own initiative" (p. 306). Examples are political protests and participatory planning practices. To the extent that participatory planning and public hearings are based on authentic deliberation and are devoid of coercion, policy participation fits into the ideal-typical definition of deliberative/discursive democracy.

*Social participation* is about individuals building public goods and generating public value together (307). It differs from the other two types of participation in that citizens are involved in the direct production and distribution of public value and goods, outside the realm of the institutions and activities of the state. In this model, "citizens are seen not only as voters but also as problem solvers and co-creators of public goods" (p. 306). They may co-produce goods and services with other private actors in the community and/or the state. Social participation is the basis of practice-based democracy. The primary difference between this form of participation and the other two is that citizens are involved in the direct production and distribution of public values and goods. As such, social participation is the basis of practice-based democracy.

Various forms and examples of social participation (practice-based democracy) can be found in human history. An early example is the building of communal temples by the people in the Sumerian city of Uruk in Mesopotamia (circa 3300 BC). They built the temples without any direction by a central authority or hierarchical social organization. The city did not even have a state, or a ruler, for about the first thousand years of its existence. After the emergence of rulers in the city, the rulers worked

## 176   *Implications of the Complex Governance Networks Conceptualization*

alongside the common people in constructing these structures (Greaber & Wengrow, 2021, p. 299). Other historical examples include Japanese villagers managing forests and mountain meadows in the Tokugawa period (1600 – 1867) (McKean, 1992, p. 253); the "citizen agency" in Alexis De Tocqueville's (2000) description of American democracy in the 19th century (Meijer, 2012); the 20th century examples of the self-governance of Alpine meadows in Switzerland (Netting, 1972, 1996); and the common governance of Huerta irrigation systems in the Philippines (E. Ostrom, 1990).

Meijer (2012) points out that new technologies, particularly information technology, lowered the transaction costs of social participation, which enables the creation of many more examples of co-production of public values in our times (p. 308). Meijer cites the examples of open-source systems on the Internet (Wikipedia, LINUX, and R) and the co-production of public safety in the United States and the Netherlands. To Meijer's examples, we can add online platforms that enable collaborative scientific innovation and problem-solving. One such example is "Fold.it," a platform that enables Internet users to design new ways to fold proteins, thereby contributing to solving scientific puzzles and inventing new drugs to cure viral infections such as SARS-CoV-2 virus, cancer, and Alzheimer's.

### *Configurations of the Three Ideal Types*

As we noted earlier, the three forms of democracy we described above are ideal types: purposeful abstractions, mental constructs, used to identify the salient aspects of a phenomenon under study and analyze them conceptually (Weber, 2010). In practice, these abstractions exist in various configurations. For example, governmental institutions of liberal democracy (e.g., police departments) and citizens co-produce public safety in the United States and the Netherlands (Meijer, 2012). Such configurations can also be seen in the Dutch water boards and business improvement districts (BIDs). In both examples, governmental and nongovernmental actors participate in the co-production of public services. Nongovernmental actors participate in decision-making through voting in the elections of representatives in governments (political participation), debating or deliberating on decisions that will be implemented by governments (policy participation), and actively producing values that are beneficial to themselves and others (social participation).

The Dutch water boards, which appeared in their initial form in the 13th century, still exist today (Lazaroms & Poos, 2004; van Buuren et al., 2019). They are organizations of farmers and commercial and residential landowners whose aim is to create safety against flooding and drainage. The boards manage water barriers, waterways, water levels, water quality, and sewage treatment systems in their districts. They finance their operations with the taxes they levy on the landowners and can penalize tax evaders.

The self-governance model of water boards has coexisted and co-evolved with the Dutch state, from the era of the Counts of Holland to

Democracy 177

the Kingdom of Netherlands. Their forms and relations developed with the Dutch state, as the state evolved into a liberal representative democracy (Water Boards Netherlands, n.d.). The first water boards were formed as self-organizing councils, which were later chartered by the counts of Holland in the 13th century. They were granted the right to make their own bylaws, collect taxes, and deliver services in their areas. The experience with the self-governing of water boards affected the decentralized governmental structure of the formation of the Dutch Republic in the 16th and 17th centuries. Over the centuries, water boards took on the power of enforcing their rules and adjudicating disputes in their areas. They work together with local governments. For example, local governments collect sewage from households, and industries and water boards transport and treat it. The central Dutch government pays for the construction and maintenance costs of water barriers and main waterways and water boards manage them.[7]

In Chapter 10, BIDs were defined and their accountability issues were discussed. They are similar to the Dutch water boards in the sense that both are self-taxing and self-governing entities that are enabled through state laws and local ordinances. BIDs emerged in the second half of the 20th century in North America and then spread to other countries, including Germany, England, Ireland, the Netherlands, and South Africa (Hoyt, 2008; Morçöl & Zimmermann, 2008a). Their historical roots can be found in the US history, particularly the special assessment districts of the colonial era and the public authorities of the 19th century (Briffault, 1999).

The forms and functions of BIDs have evolved over time (Morçöl & Gautsch, 2013). Earlier in their history, BIDs were directly managed by local governments: The governments collected the extra taxes and delivered supplementary services to designated areas. Later, autonomous management organizations were created to collect taxes and deliver supplementary services. Many of these management organizations are nonprofits, and some others are public authorities. BID management organizations collect additional taxes and manage the delivery of some public services to defined commercial and/or residential urban areas. They also participate in local planning and even build public spaces in collaboration with other actors. In doing so, they share the finances and/or planning for some public projects (e.g., highway construction planning in metro Atlanta) (Morçöl &Zimmerman, 2008b) and parks and plazas in Philadelphia (see Chapter 10).

Meijer (2012) notes that Internet-based technologies have enabled new configurations of the three forms of participation. The Internet in general, and social media in particular, create opportunities for people to produce information (social participation), rather than being passive consumers of information. These technologies enable them to discuss and deliberate with large groups of others (policy participation), and hence can contribute to deliberative democracy. Obviously, these technologies also create opportunities to spread misinformation and disinformation, and that way they

178 *Implications of the Complex Governance Networks Conceptualization*

can contribute to distorting what Habermas and others called authentic communication. These distortions obviously can affect the citizens of a liberal democracy in their voting behaviors.

## Democracy in the Public Administration and Governance Networks Literatures

Now that we have covered the broad conceptual issues related to democracy (self-organization and ideal types of democracy), we can turn our attention to more specific conceptualizations and debates on democracy in the public administration and governance networks literatures.

It is important to begin this section with a summary of the early thinking in American public administration and make some references to the European literature. Although public administration did not begin in the United States or Europe,[8] the area of study known as public administration today was formulated primarily in the United States in the early 20th century and these formulations had their historical roots and parallels in Europe.

### *Public Administration and Democracy*

Wilson (1887), one of the founders of public administration as an area of study in the United States, argued that even though public administration is a technical area of study and practice (i.e., delivery of public services by governments), democratic values should be part of its practice and theory. He specifically argued that although Americans should learn about the European theories and practices of bureaucratic/hierarchical public administration of the late 19th century, they should Americanize them and adapt them to the democratic principles of the American constitution. Underlying this argument was that the US Constitution had created a fragmented federal system, which was quite different from the hierarchical bureaucracies of European countries at the time. (Also, remember De Tocqueville's (2000) observation in the early 19th century that Americans co-created public goods in their communities, which was obviously a conceptual challenge to a bureaucratic and centralized form of service delivery.)

Unbeknownst to Wilson, Max Weber, a European sociologist who is best known among public administration scholars for his ideal-typical definition of bureaucracy (the basis of the conceptual analytical tool of ideal types we use in this chapter), was also concerned about the implications of bureaucratic administration for democracy in the late 19th and early 20th centuries. Weber (2010) defined bureaucracy as an orderly, delineated, rule-bound, and hierarchical form of social organization (p. 196).[9] Anybody with the knowledge and skills to fulfill the duties as defined by the higher-up in this hierarchical organization could be a bureaucrat. Once appointed to a specific position in the organization, the bureaucrat had to separate their official duties from their private activities. They could be coerced

*Democracy* 179

to fulfill their duties, and they would be protected for carrying out their duties. A bureaucrat had to dedicate their entire working life to their vocation. Weber thought that with these characteristics, bureaucracy was necessary for democracy.

We should note here that although Weber did not use the term, he was referring to the liberal democracies of his time. The term "liberal" was a recent addition to the lexicon of the social theorists in Europe then.[10] Weber associated democracy closely with nation-states, particularly the German state of his time (Mommsen, 1989, p. 25). This association is important, because one of the most essential elements of the ideal type of liberal democracy is the territorial definitions made by nation-states, as we noted earlier in this chapter.

According to Weber (2010), the bureaucratic state was necessary for democracy, but it also was in contradiction with democracy. Bureaucracy was necessary for (liberal) democracy because this form of social organization required precision in knowledge, specialization of tasks, and expertise to carry them as fast as possible, according to Weber (p. 215). The bureaucratic expertise was necessary for the modern state, which was, in turn, necessary for democracy. The bureaucratic state was necessary to sweep away the patrimonial and plutocratic privileges of feudal classes, so that democratic institutions could be built (p. 225).

Weber (2010) acknowledged that the bureaucratic state was also in contradiction with democracy. While bureaucracy required official (and legal) definitions and procedures, democracy required informal social processes (p. 225). The basis of democracy was participation in governance by the *demos*, an "inarticulate mass," which could not govern itself, but needed to be governed by others, most preferably by a rationally ordered bureaucracy (p. 225). Also, the democratic principle of "equal rights" was in contradiction with bureaucracy. In a democracy, no individual or group should be privileged, or protected, as bureaucrats were protected (for carrying out their official duties) by their long-term tenures. Bureaucrats also acquired authority through their positions in governmental organizations. These protections and acquired authority ended up creating a "privileged caste" of bureaucrats, which was against the principle of equal rights in a democracy (p. 240).

Public administration scholars continued to be concerned about democracy in the 20th century. They were aware of the tensions between bureaucratic organizations (particularly bureaucratic governments) and democracy. Their conceptualizations were similar to those of Weber's, even though some of them did not even mention Weber.[11] Vincent Ostrom (1974) argued that the (hierarchical) bureaucratic form of organization was not compatible with American democracy, and instead "polycentric" (less hierarchical or nonhierarchical) forms. Dwight Waldo (1980), another leading theorist of American public administration, also acknowledged that bureaucracy and democracy were incompatible. That was because the former required hierarchically ordered authority relations, formal procedures, and

# 180  *Implications of the Complex Governance Networks Conceptualization*

efficiency and the latter required humanistic management (i.e., human rights, representation, and responsiveness).

In the 1980s, the issue of social equality, or equity, became part of the conceptualizations of public administration. The authors of the New Public Administration movement argued that public bureaucracies could and should play a more equalizing role in society and hence contribute to democracy (Frederickson, 1980). Similar arguments were made by the authors of the Blacksburg Manifesto (Wamsley et al., 1990) and related works (Goodsell, 2015): that Public Administration as an institution could play a role in enhancing equity in society, partly because it was more representative of underprivileged social groups in society, which was necessary for the democratization of society.

### Governance Networks and Democracy

As public administration scholars began to recognize the roles of governance networks in public policymaking and service delivery in the 1990s (see Chapter 3), some considered the implications of governance processes and networks for democracy (Bevir 2010, 2014; Dryzek 2007; Klijn & Koppenjan 2016; Klijn & Skelcher 2007; Sørensen & Torfing 2009; Torfing et al. 2012). A question these scholars ask is whether governance networks enhance or diminish democracy. Although not all the authors clearly state it, the main reference point for these authors is liberal democracy. There are occasional references to the concepts of deliberative/discursive democracy in the literature, while practice-based democracy is not even considered. We argue that it is this last type of democracy that is most compatible with governance networks.

Klijn and Koppenjan's (2016) conceptual categorization of the literature on governance networks and democracy is a good reference frame to make sense of the issues and points made in the literature. They identify "four conjectures" of the governance networks—democracy relations in the literature: *incompatible, complementary, instrumental,* and *transitional conjectures.* The first three conjectures use liberal democracy as their common reference point; deliberative/discursive democracy is part of the discussions in the transitional conjecture.

Those who adopt the incompatible conjecture argue that governance networks are considered to be incompatible with (liberal) democracy because (1) the former leads to multilevel systems in which sovereignty is shared; (2) they challenge the idea of political representation; (3) they change the nature of public administration, from being neutral public servants to active participants in policy processes; and (4) they challenge the separation between political system and society. All of these are characteristics of the ideal type of liberal democracy.

The authors of the instrumental conjecture argue that governance networks actually enable some political actors to exert authority over others within networks and control the outcomes of decision-making.

Hence, governance networks become a tool in the hand of the powerful elites to suppress or manipulate others and hence they diminish (liberal representative) democracy.

In the complementary conjecture, governance networks are viewed as complementary to liberal democracy. These authors argue that as the complexity of social problems increases in today's world, governance networks (can) provide additional linkages of representative governments (liberal democratic institutions) to society. Torfing and his colleagues' (2012) argument is an example. They note that governance can strengthen liberal democracy by distributing influence more equally, providing an intermediate level between elected representatives and citizens, and increasing the level of variety in policies by blurring the distinction between the public and private spheres (pp. 188–190).

The transitional conjecture enhances the scope of the discussion and includes both liberal democracy and deliberative democracy. In this conjecture, governance networks expand the boundaries of liberal democracy. They represent a transition from centralized forms of governments to more decentralized modes of governance. The traditional form of centralized governance is less relevant, or not relevant at all, to the changing needs of society brought about by globalization, proliferation of information technology, and changes in social affiliations. The complexity of social problems does not allow simple hierarchical solutions and the institutions of representative democracy may even be obsolete.

The transitional conjecture opens the door to new forms of deliberative democracy. Ishakhan and Slaughter (2014) argue that governance processes are compatible with deliberative democracy because they disperse decision-making across society and involve a larger number of stakeholders in the process. However, they note, this dispersal does not ensure undistorted communication or uncoerced participation. According to Dryzek (2007), to the degree that governance networks contribute to the implementation of three democratic ideals of popular control, political equality, and fundamental political liberties, they can be considered democratic.

The literature on governance networks and democracy does not mention practice-based democracy, despite that it is most compatible form of democracy with governance networks. Governance networks are systems in which public goods can be co-created (Meijer, 2012, pp. 306–307). Individual and organizational actors are involved in the direct production and distribution of public values and goods (social participation). They do not do so under the hierarchical authority of the state, but sometimes they collaborate with governmental agencies.

### *Role of the State: Meta-governance*

What is the role of the state (or a governmental agency) in governance networks? Is it a coequal actor with many other private and non-profit actors? Or, does it have a special role? Some authors use the term

## 182  Implications of the Complex Governance Networks Conceptualization

"meta-governance" to define the special role of the state in governance processes. According to Torfing and his colleagues (2012), in today's world, the state still plays important roles in securing democracy and regulating markets and networks. They define these roles as meta-governance. The state regulates "self-regulating governance networks by shaping the conditions under which they operate. It involves the attempts of politicians, administrators, or other governance networks to construct, structure and influence the game-like interaction within particular governance networks" (Sørensen and Torfing, 2005, p. 202).

Two key elements can be discerned in this conceptualization of meta-governance: that governance networks self-regulate and that the state shapes the conditions for this self-regulation. This conceptualization is similar to Elinor Ostrom's (1990, 2005) institutional analysis and development (IAD) framework. In her framework, governmental agencies set the rules for "action arenas" in which actors act to solve their collective problems. An example of this would be a government setting the rules for grazing a pasture and then the grazers regulating themselves within those rules in Hardin's (1968) tragedy of commons conjecture, which was referred to a few times earlier in this book.

Jessop (2016) uses the term meta-governance somewhat differently. He first defines four modes of governance in societies: "exchange" (economic markets), command (the state), dialogue (networks), and solidarity (small groups). He argues that all four are prone to failure. Then an external intervention, regulation, is needed. That is what Jessop calls meta-governance, which takes on the forms of meta-exchange (redesigning markets), meta-command (organizational or constitutional change), meta-dialogue (reordering of networks), and meta-solidarity (developing new identities, forms of solidarity) (p. 170). He also suggests that this higher-order meta-governance (what he calls "second-order governance") may also fail. Then a third-order meta-governance is necessary. He calls this level "collibration," in which governments play major roles, but they cannot act as complete sovereigns; they are *primus inter pares* in a complex, heterogenous, and multilevel network of social relations" (p. 173).

Jessop's observation that the state is *primus inter pares* in a multilevel network of social relations is a full-circle back to Bevir's (2014) argument that the state is decentered in governance processes. It is an acknowledgment that governance networks challenge the territorial sovereignty of the state and the institutional design approach of liberal democracy.

### Summary

The overview of the conceptualizations of democracy in this chapter suggests that complex governance networks force us to rethink democracy, its forms, and the roles of governmental organizations in governance processes. This rethinking can begin with the ideal-typical categorization of liberal, deliberative/discursive, and practice-based democracy and the

*Democracy* 183

associated forms of participation (political, policy, and social participation) (Meijer, (2012). This tripartite categorization can help us make sense of the varieties in democratic practices in today's world, with an understanding that these abstract categories exist in various combinations in practice. Then the task of researchers will be to study the specific combinations empirically.

Liberal representative democracy is concerned with institution building and maintenance, deliberative democracy is concerned with deliberation, and practice-based democracy is concerned with actions. The first two are government-centered views, the state is either a medium of participation (representative institutions) or a tool to ensure participation in social and political life (public administration, laws, courts). Liberal democracy is mostly concerned with building and maintaining institutions within a defined territory that is under the control of the state. People can use these institutions as instruments to participate in governing their societies. Deliberative democracy theorists argue that liberal democratic institutions are not sufficient and stress that authentic communication and deliberation should be the bases of participation. Practice-based democracy points to the realms outside governmental institutions where people can participate in the solutions of their collective problems.

Complex governance networks challenge the state's monopoly over territory and the institutionalized framework of liberal representative democracy, because governance processes and networks cut across the jurisdictional boundaries in which the sovereign state of liberal democracies are supposed to operate. They "decenter" the state in governance processes, as Bevir (2014) puts it. Then are governance networks still reconcilable with liberal democracy? The answer is yes, but it should play a newly defined role. Sørensen and Torfing (2005) and Jessop (2016) call it the role of "meta-governance," which is similar to Elinor Ostrom's (1990, 2005) conceptualization that governmental organizations set the rules for actors to govern themselves.

Several studies show that centralized and hierarchical (bureaucratic) forms of organization and multicentered (or less hierarchical) network forms of organization existed, and coexisted, in various parts of the world in human history (Bevir, 2014; Graeber & Wengrow, 2021; Weber, 2010). If the theorists of network society are correct that our societies have become more multicentered in recent decades (Castells, 1996; Jessop, 2016), then we need to consider the implications of these developments not only for liberal democracies, but also more broadly for the forms of participation in governing societies in our times.

## Notes

1 A different version of this chapter was published as a journal article in *Perspectives on Public Management and Governance* (Morçöl, Shafi, & Menon, 2022).

184  *Implications of the Complex Governance Networks Conceptualization*

2  Democracy or Republic, *Encyclopedia Britannica*. www.britannica.com/topic/democracy/Democracy-or-republic

3  Examples of these evaluations and ratings are the "Democracy Index" of the Economist Intelligence Unit (www.eiu.com/n/campaigns/democracy-index-2020/), the annual "Freedom in the World" reports by the Freedom House (https://freedomhouse.org/reports/freedom-world/freedom-world-research-methodology), Varieties of Democracy (V-Dem) Institute's studies on democracy (https://v-dem.net/), and the evaluations of the state of liberal democracy in various countries around the world by the Stanford Center on Democracy, Development, and the Rule of Law (https://cddrl.fsi.stanford.edu/research).

4  Magna Carta (Wikipedia entry). https://en.wikipedia.org/wiki/Magna_Carta

5  West, D. M. (2015, January 27). Can Billionaires Buy Elections? www.brookings.edu/blog/fixgov/2015/01/27/can-billionaires-buy-elections/

Drutman, L. (2015, April 20). How Corporate Lobbyists Conquered American Democracy: Business Didn't Always Have So Much Power in Washington. www.theatlantic.com/business/archive/2015/04/how-corporate-lobbyists-conquered-american-democracy/390822/

Crenson, M. A., & Ginsberg, B. (2004). *Downsizing Democracy: How America Sidelined Its Citizens and Privatized Its Public*. Baltimore, MD: Johns Hopkins University Press.

6  Just 12 People Are Behind Most Vaccine Hoaxes on Social Media, Research Shows. www.npr.org/2021/05/13/996570855/disinformation-dozen-test-facebooks-twitters-ability-to-curb-vaccine-hoaxes

Guatemala: Anti-vaccine Villagers Attack and Hold Nurses with Covid Jabs. www.bbc.co.uk/news/world-latin-america-58801096

In Romania, Hard-Hit by Covid, Doctors Fight Vaccine Refusal. www.nytimes.com/2021/11/08/world/europe/romania-covid-vaccine-refusal.html

7  Rijnland District Water Control Board, Who Are We and What Do We Do. https://web.archive.org/web/20090506101617/http://www.rijnland.net/algemene_onderdelen/talenversies/en

8  Fukuyama (2011) traces the roots of bureaucracy, which is closely associated with public administration today, to China in the 8th century BC. Graeber and Wengrow's (2021) account of early human history suggests that one cannot pinpoint the roots of hierarchical bureaucratic organizations and "the state" to a particular society. Instead, they demonstrate, elements of such organizations and the state (as a form of institutionalized power relations) emerged in the practices of several neolithic, even paleolithic, human societies in different parts of the world.

9  Weber's book was published in German in 1910. It's translation to English was published in 1948 and reprinted in 2001 and 2010.

10  Miller (2018) notes that the common usage of the term "liberal" began in the 19th century in Europe and the early 20th century in the United States (p. 14).

11  Possibly, they were not aware of his works, which were not translated into English until the 1940s.

# Conclusions
## A Summary of the Book's Contents

This book is about making the case for a complex governance networks conceptualization. My arguments are that governance processes and networks should be studied in the broader contexts of governance process theories, network sciences, and the history of human societies and that the *complexity* of governance networks should be underscored.

The term "governance networks" and similar ones (e.g., "collaborative networks," "public management networks") have been used for decades in the public administration literature. Public policy scholars used similar terms, like "policy networks." As the systematic literature review in Chapter 1 shows, there is an exponential increase in the number of publications on the topics related to governance, networks, and complexity in the social sciences. This review also shows that researchers in different fields have different interests. The researchers in ecological/environmental studies, economics, and business/management have applied the concepts of complexity theory widely since the early 2000s. The researchers in public administration/public policy and political science/international relations have been interested in governance networks and policy networks mainly; only in the 2010s complexity theory concepts entered into the picture of the literature in these areas of study.

This time lag in the public administration/public policy and political science/international relations literature shows that there is a need to clarify the concepts of complexity theory (such as self-organization, nonlinearity, emergence, and coevolution) and demonstrate their applicability in these areas of study. I also argue that these concepts should be applied within a systematic conceptualization: the complex governance networks conceptualization.

To make the case for this conceptualization, I needed to clarify each of its components (governance, networks, and complexity) and summarize their developmental contexts. Part I is about these clarifications and summaries. The term governance has been used in different contexts (e.g., corporate governance, international governance, local governance) for some time now without a clear and common definition. The most common understanding in these usages is that there are multiple actors involved

DOI: 10.4324/9781003053392-15

186 *Conclusions*

in governance processes and that governance systems/networks are multi centered (Chapter 2). The structures of these networks have been studied using social network analyses, whose basic principles and very brief history are covered in Chapter 3. The concepts of complexity theory (systems, nonlinearity, self-organization, emergence, and coevolution) are clarified and their origins in the natural and information sciences are summarized in Chapter 4.

The complex governance networks conceptualization should be placed in a broad historical context. To frame the discussion, in Chapter 1, I ask the question: How do human societies try to solve their collective problems? In answering this question, I cited several historical examples throughout the book.

There is a running example in most chapters of the book: the COVID-19 pandemic. The pandemic is a vivid example of how human societies try to solve their collective problems globally and locally. (As of the writing of this book, it was ongoing.) There is so much to learn from this pandemic experience for collective problem solving in human societies. I am sure voluminous studies will be conducted on it in almost every scientific field in the coming decades. I used the examples from the pandemic experience to illustrate how a complex governance networks conceptualization will be useful to gain an understanding of the processes of solving (or dealing with) collective problems.

At the core of the complex governance networks conceptualization, there is the micro–macro problem. Two questions I asked in Chapter 1 frame this problem. How do individual (micro-level) behaviors lead to collective (macro) outcomes? In turn, how do collective (institutional and cultural) structures affect individual behaviors? I answered these questions in Part II. Chapter 5 is about making the case for the micro–macro problem as the core problem of complex governance networks. In Chapter 6, I discussed how micro units (individual actors, agents) can be conceptualized. Are they "rational" or "boundedly rational"? How do the cognitive biases identified by psychologists affect their decision-making and actions? How viable are complexity theorists' concepts of reactive agents versus cognitive agents in characterizing the heterogeneity of individual actors? In Chapter 7, the topics were how micro-level behaviors and interactions lead to the generation of macro-level patterns and structures (emergence of macro from micro) and the mechanisms of emergence identified by complexity and network researchers. Chapter 8 was about whether and how macro structures (e.g., cultural norms and social institutions) affect micro (individual) beliefs, attitudes, and behaviors.

The concepts of the complex governance networks conceptualization have been applied by researchers individually, or in some combinations, using a range of innovative and advanced methodologies: social network analyses, systems dynamics simulations, agent-based simulations, and qualitative comparative analyses. There are very few, but an increasing number, of such applications on the COVID-19 pandemic. I cited these applications

Conclusions 187

in the relevant chapters and sections of the book. These applications demonstrate that the concepts of complex governance networks are not mere abstractions. They are relevant and useful conceptual tools, and their applications can help us solve, or deal with, our various collective problems, from local trash collection, to the management of estuaries, and dealing with global pandemics.

These concepts of the conceptualization have implications for a range of problem areas that have occupied the minds of political science, public policy, and public administration theorists: effectives, accountability, and democracy. These topics are covered in Part III.

Chapter 9 is about two concepts: wicked problems and effectiveness. The two are related as antonyms. The term wicked problems have been used in the literature quite casually to mean that social problems cannot be defined, their characteristics cannot be known, and they cannot be solved—let alone be solved effectively. Complexity theorists counter these usages and implications of the concept: These problems are complex and their characteristic and dynamics may not be known in their entirety, but we can still analyze and better understand them. Consequently, we can increase the effectiveness of our collective problem solving. It is necessary to recognize the complexity of the effectives of governance networks, which can be measured on multiple dimensions.

Accountability has been an important concept for the scholars and practitioners of public administration and the citizen in democratic societies. It is the topic of Chapter 10. It may be relatively easy to establish linear and hierarchical accountability mechanisms in bureaucracies, but that is not case for governance networks. In these networks, accountability should be conceptualized and practiced on multiple dimensions. Complexity theory suggests that accountability should be considered as an emergent phenomenon in complex systems, like governance networks.

Democracy is the topic of Chapter 11. Governance networks force us to rethink democracy. Democratic practices have taken on various forms, which can be captured using the ideal typical categorizations of liberal, deliberative/discursive, and practice-based democracy. These forms have existed in multiple configurations.

## The Complex Governance Networks Conceptualization

Do all these conceptual clarifications and elaborations in the chapters of the book add up to a conceptualization or a framework? In Chapter 1, I made a differentiation between the two, following *Merriam Webster*'s definitions of the terms. A conceptualization is a conceptual picture of a segment of reality, which is composed of multiple concepts. "Complex governance networks" is a conceptualization, a conceptual picture of how human societies solve, or attempt to solve, their collective problems in the early 21st century. The picture is composed of the concepts of governance, networks, and complexity theory. What brings these concepts together is

188    *Conclusions*

the micro–macro problem. In other words, this problem is the skeleton of the conceptualization.

A framework is a more articulate (structured) version of a conceptualization. The best examples of frameworks in the policy studies literature are Elinor Ostrom's (2005, 2009) institutional analysis and development and social-ecological systems frameworks. These two are frameworks—more than conceptualizations—for three reasons. First, Elinor Ostrom built them on the basis of earlier theories that been debated and refined over time, like Vincent Ostrom's polycentrism. Second, her frameworks are elaborate pictures (models) of the structural relations among the variables (concepts) of the systems they represent, not general and abstract assemblages of concepts. Third, these frameworks have been tested in numerous empirical studies over several decades by Ostrom and other researchers, and she revised and refined them in during her lifetime.

Compared to Ostrom's institutional analysis and development and social-ecological systems frameworks, what I propose in this book is not yet a framework. It can become one, with further elaborations, refinements, and empirical testing in the future. It has solid theoretical bases, like the micro–macro problem of sociology (Coleman, 1986), networks theorists' works on the types and properties of networks (see Chapter 3), and complexity theorists' works on the properties of complex systems (see Chapter 4). Many of these theories have been tested empirically, as I cited in relevant chapters of the book. Now, it is a matter of articulating the concepts and empirical findings to refine the conceptualization I propose in future works.

## General Conclusions

Even without making conceptual refinements and empirical testing, some general conclusions can be drawn from what I propose in this book. (I discussed the specific implications of each of the concepts of the complex governance networks conceptualization in the relevant chapters and sections of the book.) The first general conclusion is about the way we think of our collective problems: We need to appreciate the complexity of the world we live in and do not think in simplistic dichotomous terms about our collective problems (e.g., governments versus markets). Second, we need to rethink our preconceived notions of disciplinary boundaries between political science, public policy, and public administration. Third, the conceptual discussions in this book are not mere abstractions; they have practical implications. I elaborate on these three conclusions in the following subsections.

### *A Non-Dichotomous, Configurational View of Governance Processes*

In a world as complex as ours, dichotomous conceptual templates, such as markets versus governments, do not have much explanatory power.

*Conclusions*  189

Thinking in simplistic dichotomies is likely to mislead us in solving our collective problems. Scholars from different theoretical backgrounds criticized such simplistic dichotomies and offered alternatives.

Elinor Ostrom, whose works I cited in multiple chapters of the book, rejects simplistic dichotomies, like markets versus governments, and offers a configurational way of thinking as an alternative. This point is particularly important to emphasize, because her theoretical background is in polycentrism and her conceptualizations of self-organization and self-governance may sound, on the surface, like that she favors one side of a dichotomy: that purely self-organization is always best and that all our collective problems can be solved in multicentered systems (e.g., economic markets). In fact, she argues specifically against this line of thinking and shows why it is not only wrong, but also dangerous.

> Continuing to presume that complex policy problems are simple problems that can be solved through the adoption of simple designs that are given general names, as private property, government ownership, or community organization, is a dangerous academic approach. Dichotomizing the institutional world into "the market" as contrasted to "the state" is so grossly inadequate and barren that it is surprising how the dichotomy survives as a basic way of organizing academic studies and policy advice. Oversimplification of our design options is dangerous since it hides more of the working parts needed to design effective, sustainable institutions than it reveals.... And, it reduces our awareness of the need to monitor outcomes and improve them over time through better processes of learning and adaption.
>
> (E. Ostrom, 2005, p. 256)

Ostrom (2005) also dispels the myths that free markets equal to self-governance and that self-governance (or self-organization) is necessarily egalitarian. She cites several studies that demonstrated that markets may be dominated by few powerful actors. (Think of the monopolies and oligopolies in technology markets and the power law distribution of the Internet, which is dominated by a few websites like Google, Facebook, and Microsoft (see Chapters 3, 4, and 7 of this book).) As Ostrom notes, there are also studies that demonstrated that local self-organization is not necessarily egalitarian, but it may be dominated by local elites (p. 220). She also notes that although in many cases centralized governmental systems may not be as effective as locally self-organized common-pool resource governance systems, there is no common rule that would suggest that one or the other is always better (p. 222).

In Ostrom's view, we should think of the diversity of institutional arrangements in which our public policy problems exist. More specifically, she argues that there can be various configurations of relationships among governmental, nonprofit, and private actors that will generate different

190  *Conclusions*

solutions to social problems and the best configuration in a given case depends on its context (E. Ostrom, 1990, pp. 8–15; 2009).

Complexity theorists Colander and Kupers (2014, pp. 4–9) make similar arguments as Ostrom's. They argue that complexity theory rejects the polar opposites of government versus markets, "central governmental planning" versus "market fundamentalism" (laissez faire). In their view, governmental interventions and markets are not in opposition, but they coexist in the complex and evolving economic systems. They emphasize that social systems, including economic systems, have endogenous control mechanisms, which limits the roles governments in regulating them. As a result of the complexity and dynamism of these systems, a governmental policy that may be viable at one point under certain circumstances may not be so under others.

Then how can a government play a productive role in an economic system? Colander and Kupers argue that policymakers should understand that governments cannot solve collective problems alone, but they can help change the "ecosystem" that would enable people to solve their collective problems. This ecosystem is constituted by institutions, and institutional solutions should encourage bottom-up policy solutions (p. 43). They point out that collective institutions are necessary to deal with collective problems, but "the state" is only one of these institutions. (Think of cultural norms, informal organizations, religious institutions, etc.) Governmental actors can help create a "shared space" institutions that allow people to organize together from the bottom up in alternative collective organizations that complement or even replace the state in their subareas (p. 165). All these propositions do not mean necessarily that Colander and Kupers propose "small government solutions" to all policy problems.

> There are strong arguments that a small government is preferable in a complex system, but a small government will evolve only is a self-regulating policy has been built into institutions through previous cooperation efforts.... [A] small government should get in the way more purposefully, with more clarity, with a sharper focus, and playing a crucial role. A self-regulating policy is not deregulation; it is purposeful and smart policy and smart policy that can evolve with what it engenders.
>
> (p. 181)

David Graeber and David Wengrow (2021), whose book I cited several times in this book, demonstrate that Ostrom's and Colander and Kuper's key insights about the late 20th and early 21st centuries are valid also for tens of thousands of years of human history. Simplistic dichotomies like the government versus the market, or the state versus the society, do not accurately reflect what happened in the complex history of human societies. "The state," which conjures up images of a monocentric and hierarchical society, has not had a common form or a common origin in

*Conclusions* 191

history. Human societies have never been monocentric. They were never under the complete control of "the state," or a sovereign under another name. The notion of complete self-organization (or self-governance) does not reflect the reality of any society in history either. There were a variety of the forms of participation in the governing of societies (forms and degrees of democracy versus authoritarianism), and thus participation in collective problem solving. These forms coexisted with various degrees and forms of social equality (versus social hierarchy), in a variety of configurations.

The complex governance networks conceptualization I propose in this book resonates well with Ostrom's, Colander and Kuper's, and Graeber and Wengrow's depictions of how human societies deal with their collective problems. This conceptualization also has implications for the way our academic fields of study are structured.

### Convergence of the Fields of Study?

When political leaders, or public administrators, face public (collective) problems, do they solve them in separate compartments like politics, decision-making (policy analysis), and administration/management? Or, are all these activities combined in real-life problem-solving processes? Any practitioner of public administration, or a volunteer in community organizing, would agree that it is the latter, not the former. While dealing with a management problem, these actors make decisions (and occasionally make policies, rules that will guide future decisions and managerial practices) and encounter politics (including international, national, and local politics, interwoven with organizational politics).

Then, one might ask, why do we have separate fields of study under the names of "political science," "policy studies/policy analysis," and "public administration"? Do they not represent different aspects of what we can call "governance processes"?

Kettl (2002) shows that the intellectual leaders of these three fields tried hard to build "boundaries" around their fields since the early 20th century (pp. 5–20). Political science was the field from which public administration and public policy studies emerged. The intellectual leaders of public administration and public policy studies tried to carve out niches for their own fields with specific efforts to separate "administration" from "politics" (e.g., Goodnow, 1900) and "analysis" from "management/administration" (Dror, 1967). These efforts to separate the fields were institutionalized through the creations of separate professional associations for these fields: the American Political Science Association (1903), the American Society for Public Administration (1939), and the Association for Public Policy Analysis and Management (1979). The institutional separations went parallel to the creations of distinct educational programs for the practitioners of each field: political science programs for political professionals, master of public administration (MPA) programs

192  *Conclusions*

for public administrators, and master of public policy (MPP) programs policy analysts (Almond, 1996, pp. 65–67; Kettl, 2002, pp. 5–20).

These institutional and educational program-based separations have not necessarily created distinct field of study, however. As Almond (1996) notes, political science had large overlaps with history, philosophy, sociology, and psychology in the 19th century, and even after its separation from them in the early 20th century, it continued its strong relations with these fields. After the institutional separations of the professional organizations of public administration and policy analysis in the 1930s and 1970s, these fields maintained their ties with the American Political Science Association (APSA). APSA has sections for public policy studies and public administration studies. Policy Studies Organization, which is another professional organization of public policy scholars/practitioners, is affiliated with APSA.

The ties between the fields can also be observed in their educational programs. The studies on the MPA and MPP programs have found overlaps between the curricula of these two types of programs (Averch et al., 1992; Koven et al., 2008; Morçöl et al., 2020). Originally the MPA and MPP programs were designed to teach management skills and analytical skills, respectively. These studies show that indeed these differences can be observed in the curricula of these two kinds of programs, but there also many similarities. For example, there is no noticeable difference in the analytical skills taught between the MPA and MPP programs, although the latter were designed to distinguish themselves with their emphasis on analytical skills.

Do these overlaps point to a convergence trend among these the fields, at least in their educational programs? That's is yet to be seen. But the boundaries the intellectual leaders of the fields tried to set up seem to be eroding. The studies by governance and governance network researchers I cited in this book and the complex governance networks conceptualization I propose can help the educational programs evolve into a more comprehensive approach. That, in turn, can help change the scholarship and practice, with broader implications. As Colander and Kupers (2014) put it, "Ultimately, education is the way society replicates thinking, and the best way to change a system is to change it[s] replicator dynamics…" (p. 259).

### *Self-Organization and Adaptive Governance*

Two practical implications can be drawn from the complex governance networks conceptualization. First, policymakers (political decisionmakers), professional analysts and planners, and managers/administrators should have an appreciation of the complexity of governance processes. Linear, hierarchical, and strictly rule-bound policy planning and implementation practices are not likely to be effective. They should understand that systems they are dealing with are self-organizing (at varying degrees), systemic processes are nonlinear, and the outcomes of their interactions

*Conclusions*   193

with other actors in these systems are emergent (not preordained). Second, this appreciation of complexity should be supplemented with better planning and management approaches.

Complexity researchers have given some thought to these implications conceptually and offered empirical and practical guidance for practice. These researchers recognize the complexity of the systems in which policymakers, analysts, planners, and administrators/managers (including the self-organizing nature of such systems) and the need for these actors to take dynamic and adaptive approaches in system design and management. I cite four of these applications to illustrate the range of ideas and areas of applications.

Koehler (2003) applies the concepts of "heterochrony" and "time-ecology" in his proposal to facilitate local and regional economic development. He observes that economic development involves heterochronous actions by multiple actors in a given time ecology. What he means by this is that economic development happens within complex systems that are composed of actors whose interests, capacities, or timing preferences are not aligned (not synchronous). (Think about the different interests, capacities, and timing preferences of governmental agencies, private businesses, and nonprofits that play roles in local economic development.) This heterochrony creates some uncertainty in predicting the actions of these actors. The uncertainty can be reduced, however, by understanding the time-ecology of each actor (how their past relationships with other actors and coevolution with them have brought them to this point in time). Then, do we have tools to develop this understanding? Koehler's answer is yes: We can use agent-based simulations and systems-dynamic simulations (Chapters 4 and 5 of this book) for this purpose.

Koehler's approach is conceptually sophisticated and methodologically sound, but it is quite demanding. It requires that an organization or an individual actor should have the analytical capabilities to run the simulations and draw practical conclusions from them, which may not be practical in all cases. Others offer less analytical and more descriptive solutions.

Portugali (2000) proposes an "parallel-distributed planning" approach for urban areas. He argues that urban planning cannot be done by panners alone, no matter how sophisticated their theories and methods are. Instead, private and public actors should engage in planning activities from which planning parameters can emerge. In Portugali's view, professional planners should set general planning principles and leave other actors do their own interpretations and planning. Then the roles of professional planners would be to provide information to the public and enabling them to use user-friendly tools, geographic information systems (GIS) applications, in their planning. When there is a disagreement among these actors, a planning court can resolve the disagreements.

His planning approach is based on the understanding that cities are self-organizing, open, and complex systems. Portugali draws parallels between self-organizational planning and the parallel-distributed system

194    *Conclusions*

of the human mind. The subsystems in the mind "plan" for themselves and their actions are coordinated spontaneously. Likewise, in a parallel-distributed planning of a city, all agents and agencies would plan by themselves. Each agent (individuals, families, planning agencies, etc.) would be a self-organizing system, but there would be interplays among them. Each plan by an individual actor participates in a process in which various configurations of plans would compete and cooperate until one of them wins and new systemic order parameters emerge. These new parameters would shape the future activities of agents and reproduced in future actions.

Buijs and his colleagues (2018) propose a complexity theory-based approach to flood risk management and illustrate it in their case studies in five countries. They first recognize that the well-known characteristics of complex systems (multiplicity of actors and factors, their interconnectivity, nonlinear feedback loops) create knowledge gaps about the parameters of these socioecological systems and uncertainties in predicting the systems' behaviors. They offer a typology of approaches to the planning for and the management of flood risks, based on how much is known about the actors in the systems and system parameters. These types from "path-dependent planning" (actors and system parameters are known), to "collaborative planning" (system parameters are known, but actors are not), "adaptive planning" (actors are known, but not the system's parameters), and "co-evolutionary planning" (neither the actors nor the system's parameters are known). Given that there are many uncertainties in identifying the actors and parameters of flood risk management systems, they propose, either adaptive planning or co-evolutionary planning will be necessary.

Van Meerkerk and his colleagues (2013) focus on a particular problem in the water management systems in the Netherlands: how water managers use their judgments to demarcate the boundaries of the complex social-ecological systems in which they operate. The managers make boundary judgments to estimate who the actors are; what the values, interests, and priorities are important for these actors; and what the institutional structures that affect the system (laws, regulations, and organizational structures) are. In their case studies in the Netherlands, the authors observe that the managers who made "tight" boundary judgments (those who excluded many relevant actors and factors in their boundary demarcations) were not effective. They reach the conclusion that to be effective, managers need "boundary spanning" skills (i.e., the skills to manage the interfaces between their organizations and their environments).

### So What?

The COVID-19 pandemic, one of the biggest collective problems human societies have faced in history, has not ended yet as of the writing of this book. It is likely to transition into a phase when the SARS-CoV-2 virus will no longer disrupt the economies and other functions of societies, as

## Conclusions 195

it has done in the last couple of years. There will be other pandemics and even bigger global problems, like the ongoing climate crisis, in the future. Meanwhile, we will continue to have local collective problems—like trash collection, crime, and paving the streets. Humans devised methods to deal with their collective problems, from local forms of cooperation to national and international bureaucracies. These methods worked, in various combinations, depending on their historical and geographic circumstances.

The argument in this book is that to better understand our collective problems in the early 21st century and deal with them more successfully, we need a complex governance networks conceptualization. Many good scholars have already developed the concepts that constitute this conceptualization. They showed that multiple interdependent actors take parts in governance processes in which humans solve their collective processes; that the patterns and structures in their relations can be discerned and studied as networks; and that these patterns are self-organizational, nonlinear, and dynamic and the structures are emergent. In other words, these networks are complex systems. The conceptualization I propose in this book brings together these conceptual tools and many analytical tools that have been developed in the last few decades. It is only an early effort to be refined in future works.

# References

Acemoglu, D. (2002, June 5). The post-COVID state. www.project-syndicate.org/onpoint/four-possible-trajectories-after-covid19-daron-acemoglu-2020-06?utm_source=Project%20Syndicate%20Newsletter&utm_campaign=139bcd43ce-op_newsletter_2020_06_05&utm_medium=email&utm_term=0_73bad5b7d8-139bcd43ce-105541825&mc_cid=139bcd43ce&mc_eid=019d42168c.

Acemoglu, D., & Robinson, J. A. (2012). *Why nations fail: The origins of power, prosperity, and poverty*. Largo, MD: Crown Books.

Agranoff, R. (2007). *Managing within networks: Adding value to public organizations*. Washington, DC: Georgetown University Press.

Albright, M., & Woodward, B. (2018). *Fascism: A warning*. New York: Harper.

Allen, P. M. (1982). Evolution, modeling, and design in a complex world. *Environment and Planning B*, 9, 95–11.

Allen, P. M., & Sanglier, M. (1981). Urban evolution, self-organization, and decision making. *Environment and Planning A*, 13, 167–183.

Allen, P. M., Engelen, G., & Sanglier, M. (1986). Towards a general dynamic model of the spatial evolution of urban systems. In B. Hutchinson, & M. Batty (Eds.), *Advances in urban system modeling* (pp. 199–220). Amsterdam: Elsevier Science Publishers.

Allen, P. M., Sanglier, M., Engelen, G., & Boon, F. (1985). Towards a new synthesis in the modeling of evolving complex systems. *Environment and Planning B*, 12, 65–84.

Almond, G., (1996). Political science: The history of the discipline. In R. E. Goodin & H- D. Klingeman (Eds.), *A handbook of political science* (pp. 50–96). Oxford: Oxford University Press.

Anderson, P. (1972). More is different. *Science*, 177, 393–396.

Anderson, P. (1999). Complexity theory and organization science, *Organization Science*, 10, 216–232.

Andresani, G., & Ferlie, E. Studying governance within the British public sector and without – Theoretical and methodological issues. *Public Management Review*, 8(3), 415–431.

Ansell, C., & Gash, A. (2008). Collaborative governance in theory and practice. *Journal of Public Administration Research and Theory*, 18(4), 543–571.

Arrow, K. J. (1951). *Social choice and individual values*. New York: Wiley.

Averch, H., Dluhy, M. and Elmore, R. F. (1992) Teaching public administration, public management, and policy analysis: convergence or divergence in the master's core. *Journal of Policy Analysis and Management*, 11(3), 541.

## References 197

Axelrod, R. (1997). *The complexity of cooperation: Agent-based models of competition and collaboration*. Princeton, NJ: Princeton University Press.

Barabasi, A. (2002). *Linked: The new science of networks*. Cambridge, MA: Perseus Publishing.

Barabási, A., & Albert, R. (1999). Emergence of scaling in random networks. *Science*, 286, 509–512.

Bar-Yam, Y. (2002). Complexity rising: From human beings to human civilization, a complexity profile, in *Encyclopedia of Life Support Systems* (EOLSS), developed under the Auspices of the UNESCO. Oxford: EOLSS Publishers.

Batty, M. (2007). *Cities and complexity: Understanding cities with cellular automata, agent-based models, and fractals*. Cambridge, MA: MIT Press.

Baumgartner, F. R., & Jones B. D. (2002). Positive and negative feedback in politics. In F. R. Baumgartner & B. D. Jones (Eds.), *Policy dynamics* (pp. 3–27). Chicago, IL: University of Chicago Press.

Baumgartner, F. R., Jones B. D., & Mortensen, P. B. (2018). Punctuated equilibrium theory: Explaining stability and change in public policymaking. In C. M. Weible and P. A. Sabatier (Eds.), *Theories of the policy process* (pp. 55–102). New York: Westview Press.

Becker, C. J., Grossman, S. A., Dos Santos, B., Management, R. U. I. of B. D., & Association, I. D. (2011). *Business Improvement Districts: Census and National Survey*. Washington, DC: International Downtown Association.

Bednar, J., & Page, S. (2007). The emergence of cultural behavior within multiple games. *Rationality and Society*, 19(1), 65–97.

Behn, R. D. (2001). *Rethinking democratic accountability*. Washington, DC: Brookings Institution Press.

Benner, T., Reinicke, W., & Witte, J. (2004). Multisectoral networks in global governance: towards a pluralistic system of accountability. *Government and Opposition*, 39(2), 191–210. doi:10.1111/j.1477-7053.2004.00120.x

Benton, T. (1977). *Philosophical foundations of three sociologies*. London: Routledge & Kegan Paul.

Berardo, R., & Scholz, J. (2010). Self-organizing policy networks: Risk, partner selection, and cooperation in estuaries. *American Journal of Political Science*, 54(3), 632–649.

Bevir, M. (2010). *Democratic governance*. Princeton, NJ: Princeton University Press.

Bevir, M. (2013). A theory of governance. Retrieved from https://escholarship.org/uc/item/2qs2w3rb

Bevir, M. (2014). Decentering governance. In B. Ishakhan & S. Slaughter (Eds.), *Democracy and crisis: Democratising governance in the twenty-first century* (pp. 25–43). New York: Palgrave Macmillan.

Bevir, M., & Richards, D. (2009). Decentering policy networks: A theoretical agenda. *Public Administration*, 87(1), 3–14

Bhaskar, R. (1975). *A realist theory of science*. Leeds: Leeds Books.

Bianconi, G., & Barabási, A.- L. (2001). Competition and multiscaling in evolving networks. *Europhysics Letters*, 54(4), 436–442.

Blackwell, M. (2008). Business improvement districts in England: The UK government's proposals, enactment, and guidance. In G. Morçöl, L. Hoyt, J. W., Meek, & U. Zimmermann (Eds.), *Business improvement districts: Research, theories, and controversies* (pp. 451–472). Boca Raton, FL: CRC Press.

Borgatti, S. P., Everett, M. G., and Johnson, J. C. (2018). *Analyzing social networks* (2nd ed.). Los Angeles, CA: Sage Publications.

## 198 References

Bovens, M., Schillemans, T., & Goodin, R. E. (2014). Public accountability. In M. Bovens, T. Schillemans, and R. E. Goodin (Eds.), *The Oxford handbook of public accountability* (pp. 1–21). Oxford: Oxford University Press.

Bresser, H. T. A., & O'Toole, L. J. (1998). The selection of policy instruments: A network-based perspective. *Journal of Public Policy*, 18(3), 213–239.

Briffault, R. (1999). A government for our time? Business improvement districts and urban governance. *Columbia Law Review*, 99(2), 365–477. https://doi.org/10.2307/1123583

Bubar, K. M., Reinholt, K., Kissler, S. M., Lipsitch, M., Cobey, S., Grad, Y. H., & Larremore, D. B. (2021). Model-informed COVID-19 vaccine prioritization strategies by age and serostatus. *Science*, 371, 916–921. https://doi.org/10.1126/science

Buijs, J. M., Boelensb, L., Bormannc, H., Restemeyerd, B., Terpstraa, T., Van der Voorna, T. (2018) Adaptive planning for flood resilient areas: Dealing with complexity in decision-making about multilayered flood risk management. Association of European Schools of Planning (AESOP) Conference Paper. Gothenburg, Sweden. https://d1wqtxts1xzle7.cloudfront.net/58155951/20180424PaperAesopFRAMES-with-cover-page-v2.pdf?Expires=1642796628&Signature=ArHdLgcKc5HWgczxVCE-p0dUKhgYSoySo7Ctf2~4UBQckwzS0b8aMk-5EB2cwkBA3Ml9k-9HK7btxmNOg5HdGqOqwA32aZpyALnc2zSyZG4XQC3Yw2BpUeocBYjNpPamLh3cppY0J5IPduuZyNFPFeVnddta6QwQNd6G5Jbof4sgR9rdsjw617o57ffw7JHvgV4nuE9k7-9OhSmz5vO6hH4fGNzeElXVpEEBZ-VJRFkYq2A-Hf00KCQZqlsRxjtTec2vUz09sV4iq2BNZrmakUMbEmk8gJ2QuwOpb5w0ZXnFKGgql00I7k973Ae9bnBZpujwhn7x1-lf0bmODp0Ymw__&Key-Pair-Id=APKAJLOHF5GGSLRBV4ZA

Cantner, U., & Graf, H. (2006). The network of innovators in Jena: An application of social network analysis. *Research Policy*, 35(4), 463–480.

Capra, F. (1996). *The web of life: A new scientific understanding of living systems.* New York: Anchor Books.

Carrozza, C. (2015). Democratizing expertise and environmental governance: Different approaches to the politics of science and their relevance for policy analysis. *Journal of Environmental Policy & Planning*, 17(1), 108–126. http://dx.doi.org/10.1080/1523908X.2014.914894

Castells, M. (2000). *The rise of the network society.* Oxford: Blackwell.

Castelvono, W., & Sorrention, M. (2018). Engaging with complexity in a public programme implementation, *Public Management Review*, 20(7), 1013–1031.

Catlaw, T. J. (2009). Governance and networks at the limits of representation. *The American Review of Public Administration*, 39(5), 478–498. https://doi.org/10.1177/0275074008323975

Cave, D., Bubola, E. & Sang-Hun C. (2021). Long slide looms for world population, with sweeping ramifications. *New York Times*, May 24, 2021. https://nyti.ms/3fdlaIZ

Centola, D. (2020). *How behavior spreads: The science of complex contagions.* Princeton, NJ: Princeton University Press.

Cheremukhin, A., Golosov, M., Guriev, S., & Tsyvinski, A. (2015). The economy of People's Republic of China from 1953. National Bureau of Economic Research Working Papers, No. 21397. www.nber.org/papers/w21397

Cochran, C. L., & Malone, E. F. (1995). *Public policy: Perspectives and choices.* New York: McGraw-Hill.

## References   199

Cohen, M. D., Riolo, R. L., & Axelrod, R. (2001). The role of social structure in the maintenance of cooperative regimes. *Rationality & Society*, 13, 5–32.

Colander, D., & Kupers, R. (2014). *Complexity and the art of public policy: Solving society's problems from the bottom up.* Princeton, NJ: Princeton University Press.

Coleman, J. S. (1986). Social theory, social research, and a theory of action. *The American Journal of Sociology*, 91(6), 1309–1335.

Coleman, J. S. (1992). Introducing social structure into economic analysis. In M. Zey (Ed.), *Decision making: Alternatives to rational choice models* (pp. 265–272). Thousand Oaks, CA: Sage.

Comfort, L. (1994). Self-Organization in Complex Systems. *Journal of Public Administration Research and Theory: J-Part*, 4(3), 393–410. Retrieved June 9, 2021, from http://www.jstor.org/stable/1181895

Comfort, L. K. (1999). Nonlinear dynamics in disaster response: The Northridge, California, earthquake, January 17, 1994. In E. Elliott & L. D. Kiel (eds.), *Nonlinear dynamics, complexity, and public policy* (pp. 139–152). Commack, NY: Nova Science Publishers.

Comfort, L. K. (1999). *Shared risk: Complex systems in seismic response.* Bingley: Emerald Publishing.

Compston, H. (2009). *Policy networks and policy change.* New York: Palgrave Macmillan.

Cook, B. J. (2014a). *Bureaucracy & self-government: Reconsidering the role of public administration in American politics* (2nd ed.). Baltimore, MD: Johns Hopkins University Press.

Cook, B. J. (2014b). Regime leadership for public servants. In D. F. Morgan & B. J. Cook (Eds.) *New public governance: A regime-centered perspective* (pp. 197–208). Armonk, NY: M. E. Sharpe.

Crowley, K., & Head, B. W. (2017). The enduring challenge of 'wicked problems': revisiting Rittel and Webber. *Policy Sciences*, 50, 539–547. https://doi.org/10.1007/s11077-017-9302-4

Dasgupta, R. (2018, April 18). The demise of the nation state. *Guardian* www.theguardian.com/news/2018/apr/05/demise-of-the-nation-state-rana-dasgupta?CMP=share_btn_link

del Rio, C., Omer, S. B., & Malani, P. N. (2021). Winter of omicron—The evolving COVID-19 pandemic. *Journal of American Medical Association.* Published online December 22, 2021. Doi:10.1001/jama.2021.24315.

Dent, Eric B. (1999). Complexity science: A worldview shift. *Emergence: Complexity & Organization*, 1, 5–19.

De Tocqueville, A. (2000). *Democracy in America.* New York: Bantam.

Dreyfus, S. E. (1984). Beyond rationality. In M. Grover, M. Thompson, & A. P. Wierzbicki (Eds.), *Plural rationality and interactive decision processes* (pp. 55–64). Berlin: Springer-Verlag.

Dror, Y. (1967). Policy analysts: a new professional role in government service. *Public Administration Review*, 27(3), pp. 197–203.

Dror, Y. (1967) Policy analysts: a new professional role in government service. *Public Administration Review*, 27(3), pp. 197–203.

Dryzek, J. S. (2002). *Deliberative democracy and beyond: Liberals, critics, contestations.* Oxford: Oxford University Press on Demand.

Dryzek, J. S. (2007). Networks and democratic ideals: Equality, freedom, and communication. In E. Sørensen & J. Torfing (Eds.), *Theories of democratic network governance* (pp. 262–273). London: Palgrave Macmillan.

## 200  References

Dubnick, M. J. (2003). Accountability and ethics: Reconsidering the relationships. *International Journal of Organization Theory and Behavior*, 6(3), 405–441.

Dubnick, M. J. (2011). Move over Daniel we need some "accountability space." *Administration & Society*, 43(6), 704–716.

Dubnick, M. J., & Frederickson, H. G. (2014). Introduction: The promises of accountability research. In M. J. Dubnick & H. G. Frederickson (eds.). *Accountable governance: Problems and promises* (pp. xiii–xxxii). Armonk, NY: M. E. Sharpe.

Dye, T. R. (2013). *Understanding public policy* (14th ed.). Boston, MA: Pearson.

Edwards, W., & Tversky, A. (Eds.) (1967). *Decision making: Selected readings.* Middlesex: Penguin Books.

Ehrlich, P. R. & Raven, P. H. (1964). Butterflies and plants: A study in coevolution. *Evolution*, 18, 586–608.

Ellen, I. G., Schwartz, A. E., & Voicu, I. (2007). The Impact of Business Improvement Districts on Property Values: Evidence from New York City [with Comments]. Brookings–Wharton Papers on Urban Affairs, 1–39.

Emerson, K., & Nabatchi, T. (2015). *Collaborative governance regimes.* Washington, DC: Georgetown University Press.

Emerson, K., Nabatchi, T., & Balogh, S. (2012). An integrative framework for collaborative governance. *Journal of Public Administration Research and Theory: J-Part*, 22(1), 1–29. www.jstor.org/stable/41342607

Engelen, G. (1988). The theory of self-organization and modeling complex urban systems. *European Journal of Operational Research*, 37, 42–57.

Eppel, E. (2012). What Does It Take To Make Surprises Less Surprising? The contribution of complexity theory to anticipation in public management, *Public Management Review*, 14(7), 881–902.

Epstein, J. M. (2006). *Generative social science: Studies in agent-based computational modeling.* Princeton, NJ: Princeton University Press.

Epstein, J. M., & Axtell, R. (1996). *Growing artificial societies; Social science from the bottom up.* Washington, DC: Brookings Institution Press.

Esmark, A. (2007). Democratic accountability and network governance—problems and potentials. In *Theories of democratic network governance* (pp. 274–296). London: Palgrave Macmillan.

Falconer, K. (2014). *Fractal geometry: Mathematical foundations and applications* (3rd ed.). Chichester: Wiley.

Falleth, E. I., Hanssen, G. S., & Saglie, I. L. (2010). Challenges to democracy in market-oriented urban planning in Norway. *European Planning Studies*, 18(5), 737–753.

Farazmand, A. (2010). Bureaucracy and democracy: a theoretical analysis. *Public Organization Review*, 10(3), 245–258.

Feiock, R. C. (2009). Metropolitan governance and institutional collective action. *Urban Affairs Review*, 44(3), 356–377. https://doi.org/10.1177/1078087408324000

Feiock, R. C. (2013). The institutional collective action framework. *Policy Studies Journal*, 41(3), 397–425.

Feiock, R. C., Steinacker, A., & Park, H. J. (2009). Institutional collective action and economic development joint ventures. *Public Administration Review*, 69, 256–270. https://doi.org/10.1111/j.1540-6210.2008.01972.x

Ferlie, E., Fitzgerald, L, McGivern, G., Dopson, S., & Bennett, C. (2011). Public policy networks and 'wicked problems': A nascent solution? *Public Administration*, 89(2), 307–324.

## References 201

Finer, H. (1936). Better government personnel. *Political Science Quarterly*, 51(4), 569–599.

Finer, H. (1941). Administrative responsibility in democratic government. *Public Administration Review*, 1(4), 335–350. Doi:10.2307/972907

Fischer, F. (1990). *Technocracy and the politics of expertise*. Newbury Park, CA: Sage.

Fischer, F. (2003). *Reframing public policy: Discursive politics and deliberative practices*. Oxford: Oxford University Press.

Fischer, F. (2009). *Democracy & expertise: Reorienting policy inquiry*. Oxford: Oxford University Press.

Florida, R. (2020, July 2). The Forces That Will Reshape American Cities. https://www.bloomberg.com/news/features/2020-07-02/how-coronavirus-will-reshape-u-s-cities

Forester, J. (1993). *Critical theory, public policy, and planning practice: Toward a critical pragmatism*. Albany, NY: State University of New York Press.

Forrester, J. W. (1969). *Urban dynamics*. Cambridge, MA: MIT Press.

Forrester, J. W. (1961). *Industrial dynamics*. Waltham, MA: Pegasus Communications.

Forrester, J. W. (1971). *World dynamics*. Waltham, MA: Pegasus Communications.

Foster, K. A. (1999). *The political economy of special-purpose government*. Washington, DC: Georgetown University Press.

Frederickson, H. G. (1980). *New public administration*. Tuscaloosa: The University of Alabama Press.

Frederickson, H. G. (2002, April). Public administration in the era of blurred boundaries. *PA Times*, 11.

Friedland, R., & Robertson, A. F. (Eds.). (1990). *Beyond the marketplace: Rethinking economy and society*. New York: Aldine de Gruyter.

Friedrich, C. J. (1940). Public policy and the nature of administrative responsibility. In Harvard University Graduate School of Public Administration (Ed.), Public policy (pp. 3–24). Cambridge, MA: Harvard University Press.

Fuchs, C. (2002). Some implications of Anthony Giddens' works for a theory of social self-organization. *Emergence: Complexity and Organization*, 4(3), 7–35.

Fukuyama, F. (2011). *The origins of political order*. New York: Farrar, Straus, and Giroux.

Fukuyama, F. (2014). *Political order and political decay: From the industrial revolution to the globalization of democracy*. New York: Farrar, Straus, and Giroux.

Gerrits, L. (2008). The gentle art of coevolution: A complexity theory perspective on decision making over estuaries in Germany, Belgium and the Netherlands (PhD Dissertation, Erasmus University Rotterdam). Retrieved from http://publishing.eur.nl/ir/repub/asset/11152.

Gerrits, L. (2010). Public decision making as coevolution. *Emergence: Complexity & Organization*, 12(1), 19–28.

Gerrits, L. (2012). *Punching clouds: An introduction to the complexity of public decision-making*. Litchfield Park, AZ: Emergent Publications.

Gerrits, Lasse, Marks, Peter, & van Buuren, Arwin. (2009). Coevolution: A constant in nonlinearity. In G. Teisman, Arwin van Buuren, & Lasse Gerrits (Eds.), *Managing complex governance systems: Dynamics, self-organization and coevolution in public investments* (pp. 134–153). London: Routledge.

Geyer, R., & Rihani, S. (2010). *Complexity and public policy: A new approach to 21st century politics, policy and society*. London: Routledge.

## 202    References

Giddens, A (1984). *The constitution of society: Outline of the theory of structuration*, Berkeley, CA: University of California at Berkeley.

Gilbert, N. (2020). *Agent-based models* (2nd ed.). Los Angeles, CA: Sage.

Gillis, J. (2010, December 21). "A Scientist, His Work and a Climate Reckoning." *New York Times*. (www.nytimes.com/2010/12/22/science/earth/22carbon.html?nl=todaysheadlines&adxnnl=1&emc=a2&pagewanted=2&adxnnlx=1293037216-ExNkZYkOns9bBCabuMwWkg; accessed on December 22, 2010).

Gleick, J. (1987). *Chaos: Making a new science*. New York: Penguin Books.

Goldsmith, S., & Eggers, W. D. (2004). *Governing by network: The new shape of the public sector*. Washington, DC: Brookings Institution Press.

Goodnow, F. (1900). *Politics and administration*. New York: Russell and Russell.

Goodsell, C. T. (2015). *The new case for bureaucracy*. Los Angeles, CA: Sage.

Goodsell, C. T. (2016). Publicness. *Administration & Society, 49*(4), 471–490.

Goodsell, C. T. (2022). *Outlandish perspectives on public administration*. Newcastle upon Tyne, UK: Cambridge Scholars Publishing.

Gore, A. (1993). Report of the National Performance Review: Creating a government that works better and costs less. Washington, DC: US Government Publications.

Graeber, D., & Wengrow, D. (2021). *The dawn of everything: A new history of humanity*. New York: Farrar, Strauss, and Giroux.

Grafstein, R. (1993). In defense of the rationality assumption. Paper presented at the Annual meeting of the American Political Science Association, Washington, DC; September.

Guastello, S. J. (1995). *Chaos, catastrophe, and human affairs: Applications of nonlinear dynamics to work, organizations, and social evolution*. Mahwah, NJ, Lawrence Erlbaum Associates.

Habermas, J. (1985). *Theory of communicative action*, Vol 1: *Reason and the rationalization of society*. Boston, MA: Becon Press.

Hahn, T. (2011). Self-organized governance networks for ecosystem management: who is accountable? *Ecology and Society*, 16(2). https://doi.org/10.5751/ES-04043-160218

Hamilton, D. K. (2014). *Governing metropolitan areas: Growth and change in a networked age* (2nd ed.). New York: Routledge.

Han, S., Morçöl, G., Hummer, D., & Peterson, S. A. (2017). The effects of business improvement districts in reducing nuisance crimes: Evidence from Philadelphia. *Journal of Urban Affairs*, 39(5), 658–674. https://doi.org/10.1080/07352166.2016.1262691

Hansen, A. D. (2007). Governance networks and participation. In E. Sorensen & J. Torfing (Eds.), *Theories of democratic network governance* (pp. 247–261). London: Palgrave Macmillan.

Hardin, G. (1968). The tragedy of the commons. *Science*, 1243–1248.

Harper, K. (2021a) *Plagues upon the earth: Disease and the course of human history*. Princeton, NJ: Princeton University Press.

Harper, K. (2021b). Ancient Rome has an urgent warning for us. *New York Times*. https://nyti.ms/2LS7nvv

Hartnett, G. S., Vardavas, R., Baker, L., Chaykowsky, M., Gibson, C. B., Girosi, F., Kennedy, D. P., & Osoba, O. A. (2020). Deep Generative Modeling in Network Science with Applications to Public Policy Research. RAND Corp. https://doi.org/10.7249/WRA843-1

*References* 203

Haus, M., & Heinelt, H. (2005). How to achieve governability at the local level? In M, Haus, H. Heinelt, & M. Stewart (eds.), *Urban governance and democracy: Leadership and community involvement* (pp. 12–39). New York: Routledge.

Hayek, F. A. (1973). *Rules and order*. Vol. 1 of *Law, legislation, and liberty*. Chicago, IL: University of Chicago Press.

Hayek, F. A. (2013). *The constitution of liberty: The definitive edition*. London: Routledge.

Head, B. W. (2019.) Forty years of wicked problems literature: Forging closer links to policy studies, *Policy and Society*, 38(2), 180–197. DOI: 10.1080/14494035.2018.1488797

Head, B. W., & Alford, J. (2015). Wicked problems: Implications for public policy and management. *Administration & Society*, 47(6), 711–739. DOI: 10.1177/0095399713481601.

Heinelt, H. (2010). *Governing modern societies: Towards participatory governance*. New York: Routledge.

Helbing, Dirk, Kühnert, Christian, Lämmer, Stefan, Johansson, Anders, Gelsen, Björn, Ammoser, Hendrik, West, Geoffrey B. (2009). Power laws in urban supply networks, social systems, and dense pedestrian crowds. In D. Lane, Sander van der Leeuw, Denise Pumain, Geoffrey West (Eds.), *Complexity perspectives in innovation and change* (pp. 433–450). New York: Springer.

Hendriks, B (2010) City-wide governance networks in Nairobi: Towards contributions to political rights, influence, and service delivery for poor and middle-class citizens? *Habitat International*, 34(1), 59–77. DOI10.1016/j.habitatint.2009.07.001

Hogarth, R. M., & Reder, M. W. (Eds.) (1986). *Rational choice: The contrast between economics and psychology*. Chicago, IL: The University of Chicago Press.

Holland, J. H. (1995). *Hidden order: How adaptation builds complexity*. New York: Basic Books.

Holland, J. H (1998). *Emergence: From chaos to order*. New York: Basic Books.

Honderich, T. (1995). Enlightenment. In T. Honderich (Ed.), *The Oxford companion to philosophy* (pp. 236–237). Oxford: Oxford University Press.

Hoyt, L. M. (2005). Do business improvement district organizations make a difference? Crime in and around commercial areas in Philadelphia. *Journal of Planning Education and Research*, 25(2), 185–199. https://doi.org/10.1177/0739456X05279276

Huntington, S. P. (1996). *The clash of civilizations and the remaking of the world order*. New York: Simon & Schuster.

Ilachinski, A. (2001). *Cellular automata: A discrete universe*. Singapore: World Scientific.

Isett, K., Mergel, I., LeRoux, K., Mischen, P., & Rethemeyer, R. (2011). Networks in public administration scholarship: Understanding where we are and where we need to go. *Journal of Public Administration Research and Theory*, 21, I157–I173. Retrieved February 8, 2021, from http://www.jstor.org/stable/40961926

Ishakhan, B., & Slaughter, S. (2014). Introduction. In B. Ishakhan and S. Slaughter (Eds.), *Democracy and crisis: Democratizing governance in the twenty-first century* (pp. 1–22. London: Palgrave.

Islam, F. (2021, December 10). How the West invited China to eat its lunch. www.bbc.co.uk/news/business-59610019

Jenkins-Smith, H. C., Nohrstedt, D., Weible, C. M., & Ingold, K. (2018). The advocacy collation framework: An overview of the research program. In Weible,

204 *References*

C. M., & Sabatier, P. A. (Eds.,), *Theories of the policy process* (pp. 135–172). New York: Westview Press.

Jessop, B. (1990). *State theory: Putting the capitalist state in its place.* State College, PA: The Pennsylvania State University Press.

Jessop, B. (2001). Institutional re(turns) and the strategic—Relational approach. *Environment and Planning A*, 33, 1213–1235.

Jessop, B. (2004). Critical semiotic analysis and cultural political economy. *Critical Discourse Studies*, 1(2), 159–174.

Jessop, B. (2008). *State power: A strategic-relational approach.* Cambridge: Polity Press.

Jessop, B. (2016). *The state: Past, present, future.* Cambridge: Polity Press.

Johnston, E. W., Nan, N., Zhong, W., & Hicks, D. (2008). Between implementation and outcomes, growth matters: Validating an agent-based modeling approach for understanding collaboration process management. *The Innovation Journal: The Public Sector Innovation Journal*, 13(3), 1–31.

Kahneman, D. (2011). *Thinking fast and slow.* New York: Farrar, Straus, and Giroux.

Kapucu, N. & Demiroz, F. (2011). Measuring performance for collaborative public management using network analysis methods and tools. *Public Performance and Management Review*, 34(4), 551–581.

Kapucu, N., & Hu, Q. (2020). *Network governance: Concepts, theories, and applications.* New York: Routledge.

Kauffman, S (1993). *The origins of order: Self-organization and selection in evolution.* New York: Oxford.

Kauffman, S (1995). *At home in the universe: The search for laws of self-organization and complexity.* New York: Oxford.

Keat, R, & Urry, J. (1975). *Social theory as science.* London: Routledge & Kegan Paul.

Kearns, K. P. (2011). Accountability in the nonprofit sector: Abandoning the one-size-fits-all approach. In *Accountable governance: Problems and promises*, New York: M. E. Sharpe.

Keast, R., & Mandell, M. P. (2013). Network performance: A complex interplay of form and action. *International Review of Public Administration*, 18(2), 27–45.

Kettl, D. F. (1988a). Government by proxy and the public service. *International Review of Administrative Sciences*, 54(4), 501–515. https://doi.org/10.1177/002 085238805400401

Kettl, D. F. (1988b). *Government by proxy: (Mis?)managing federal programs.* Washington, DC: CQ Press.

Kettl, D. F. (2002). *The transformation of governance: Public administration for twenty-first century America.* Baltimore, MD: The Johns Hopkins University Press.

Kettl, D. F. (2015). *The transformation of governance: Public administration for twenty-first century* (updated edition). Baltimore, MD: The Johns Hopkins University Press.

Kickert, W. J. M., Klijn, E., -H, & Koppenjan, J. F. (1997). Introduction: A management perspective on policy networks. In J. M. Kickert, E.-H Klijn, & J. F. Koppenjan (Eds.), *Managing complex networks: Strategies for the public sector* (pp. 1–13). Thousand Oaks, CA: Sage.

Kiel, L. D. (1992). The nonlinear paradigm: Advancing paradigmatic process in the policy sciences. *Systems Research*, 9(2), 27–42.

## References    205

Kiel, L. D. (1994). *Managing chaos and complexity in government: A new paradigm for managing change, innovation, and organizational renewal.* San Francisco, CA: Jossey-Bass.

Kim, Y., & Zhang, J. (2016). Digital government and wicked problems. *Government Information Quarterly*, 33, 769–776.

Klijn, E. -H. (1997). Policy networks: An overview. In J. M. Kickert, E.-H Klijn, & J. F. Koppenjan (Eds.), *Managing complex networks: Strategies for the public sector* (pp. 14–34). Thousand Oaks, CA: Sage.

Klijn, E. -H. (2001). Rules as institutional context for decision making in networks: The approach to postwar housing district in two cities. *Administration & Society*, 33(2), 133–164.

Klijn, E. H., & Koppenjan, J. (2016). *Governance networks in the public sector.* New York: Routledge.

Klijn, E. H., & Skelcher, C. (2007). Democracy and governance networks: Compatible or not? *Public Administration*, 85(3), 587–608.

Knodt, Eva M. (1995). Foreword. In Niklas Luhmann (Ed.), *Social systems.* Stanford, CA: Stanford University Press.

Knoke, D., and Yang, S. (2008). *Social network analysis.* Thousand Oaks, CA: Sage Publications.

Koehler, G. (2003). Time, complex systems, and public policy: A theoretical foundation for adaptive policy making. *Nonlinear Dynamics, Psychology, and Life Sciences*, 7(1), 99–114.

Koliba, C., Meek, J. W., & Zia, A. (2011). *Governance networks in public administration and policy.* Boca Raton, FL: CRC Press.

Koliba, C. J., Meek, J. W., Zia, A., & Mills, R. W. (2019). *Governance networks in public administration and public policy* (2nd ed.). New York: Routledge.

König, D. (1936/1990). *Theory of finite and infinite graphs.* Boston, MA: Birkhäuser. doi:10.1007/978-1-4684-8971-2. ISBN 978-1-4684-8971-2.

Kooiman, J. (1993). Social-political governance: Introduction. In J. Kooiman (Ed.), *Modern governance: New government–society interactions* (pp. 1–6). London: Sage.

Koppell, J. G. S. (2003). *The politics of quasi-government: Hybrid organizations and the dynamics of bureaucratic control.* New York: Cambridge University Press.

Koppell, J. G. (2005). Pathologies of accountability: ICANN and the Challenge of "multiple accountabilities disorder." *Public Administration Review*, 65(1), 94–108. https://doi.org/10.1111/j.1540-6210.2005.00434.x

Koppenjan, J. & E.-H. Klijn (2004). *Managing uncertainties in networks: a network approach to problem solving and decision making.* London: Routledge.

Kosko, B. (1993). *Fuzzy logic: The revolutionary computer technology that is changing our world.* New York: Touchstone.

Koven, S. G., Goetzke, F. and Brennan, M. (2008) Profiling public affairs programs: the view from the top. *Administration and Society*, 40(7), pp. 691–710.

Kwuimy, C. A. K., Nazari, F., Jiao, X., Rohani, P., & Nataraj, C. 2020. Nonlinear dynamic analysis of an epidemiological model for COVID-19 including public behavior and government action. *Nonlinear Dynamics*, 101, 1545–1559. https://doi.org/10.1007/s11071-020-05815-z

Landau, M. (1969). Redundancy, rationality, and the problem of duplication and overlap. *Public Administration Review* (July/August), 346–358.

Lasswell, H. D. (1951). The policy orientation. In D. Lerner, & H. Lasswell (Eds.), *The policy sciences: Recent development in scope and method* (pp. 1–17). Stanford, CA: Stanford University Press.

## 206   References

Latora, V., Nicosia, V., & Russo, G. (2017). *Complex networks: Principles, methods and applications.* Cambridge: Cambridge University Press.

Lazaroms, R. & Poos, D. (2004). The Dutch water board model. *Journal of Water Law,* 15(3–4), 137–140.

Legge, J. (1971). *Confucian analects: The great learning, and The doctrine of the mean.* New York: Dover Publications [originally published in 1893].

Lehto, K., & Salmien, A. (2012). Accountable to whom? Exploring the challenge of multiple accountabilities in Finnish public administration. *Halduskultuur,* 13) (2), 147–162.

Lejano, R. (2018). *Frameworks for policy analysis: Merging text and context.* New York: Routledge.

Leonard, R. D. (2001). Evolutionary archeology. In Ian Hodder (Ed.), *Archeological theory today* (pp. 65–97). Cambridge: Polity Press.

Levitsky, S., & Ziblatt, D. (2018). *How democracies die.* New York: Crown.

Lichbach, M. A. (2003). *Is rational choice theory all of social science?* Ann Arbor, MI: University of Michigan Press.

Long, N. E. (1949). Power and administration. *Public Administration Review,* 9(4), 257–264.

Luhmann, N. (1995). *Social systems.* Stanford, CA: Stanford University Press.

MacDonald, P. K. (2003). Useful fiction or miracle maker: The competing epistemological foundations of rational choice theory. *American Political Science Review,* 97(4), 551–565.

Macpherson, C. B. (1979). The life and times of liberal democracy. *Science and Society,* 43(2), 234–236.

Mann, M. (2021). *The new climate war: The fight to take back our planet.* New York: Public Affairs.

Mardsen, P. V., & Friedkin, N. E. (1993). Network studies of social influence. *Sociological Methods & Research,* 22, 127–151.

Marion, R. (1999). *The edge of organization: Chaos and complexity theories of formal social systems.* Thousand Oaks, CA: Sage.

Marsh, D., & Rhodes, R. A. W. (1992). Introduction. In D. Mash & R. A. W. Rhodes (eds.), *Policy networks in British government.* Oxford: Clarendon Press.

Matrajt, L., Eaton, J., Leung, T., & Brown, E. R. 2020. Vaccine optimization for COVID-19: Who to vaccinate first? *Science Advances,* 7, eabf1374. https://doi.org/10.1126/sciadv.abf1374

Maturana, H. R, & Varela, F. J. (1980). *Autopoiesis and cognition: The realization of the living.* Dordrecht, Holland: D. Reidel.

McGinnis, M. D. (ed.) (1999). Introduction. In M. D. McGinnis (Ed.), *Polycentricity and local public economies: Readings from the workshop in political theory and policy analysis* (pp. 1–27). Ann Arbor, MI: The University of Michigan Press.

McKean, M. A. (1992). Success on the commons: a comparative examination of institutions for common property resource management. *Journal of Theoretical Politics,* 4(3), 247–281.

Meadows, Donella H. (2008). *Thinking in systems: A primer.* Westchester Junction, VT: Chelsea Green Publishing.

Meek, J. W., & Hubler, P. (2008). Business improvement districts in the Los Angeles metropolitan area: implications for local governance. In G. Morçöl, L. Hoyt, J. Meek, & U. Zimmermann (Eds.). *Business improvement districts: Research, theory, and controversies* (pp. 197–220). Boca Raton, FL: CRC Press.

*References* 207

Meek, J.W, & Marshall, K. S. (2018). Cultivating resiliency through system shock: the Southern California metropolitan water management system as a complex adaptive system, *Public Management Review*, 20(7), 1088–1104.

Meier, K. J., & O'Toole, L. J. (2006). *Bureaucracy in a democratic state.* Baltimore, MD: Johns Hopkins University.

Meijer, A. J. (2012). The do it yourself state. *Information Polity*, 17, 303–314.

Meloche, J. P., & Vaillancourt, F. (2015). Designing proper fiscal arrangements for sub-local decentralization in Montreal. *Journal of Urban Affairs*, 37(5), 530–547.

Mettler, S., & SoRelle, M. (2018). Policy feedback theory. In C. M. Weible and P. A Sabatier (Eds.), *Theories of the policy process* (pp. 103–134). New York: Westview Press.

Miller, J. (2018). *Can democracy work? A short history of a radical idea, from Ancient Athens to our world.* New York: Farrar, Straus, and Giroux.

Miller, J. H. & S. E. Page (2007). *Complex adaptive systems: an introduction to computational models of social life.* Princeton, NJ: Princeton University Press.

Mitchell, J. (2008). *Business improvement districts and the shape of American cities.* Albany, NY: State University of New York Press.

Mitchell, M. (2009). *Complexity: A guided tour.* Oxford: Oxford University Press.

Mitchell, S. (2009). *Unsimple truths: Science, complexity, and policy.* Chicago, IL: The University of Chicago Press.

Mommsen, W. J. (1989). *The political and social theory of Max Weber: Collected essays.* Chicago, IL: The University of Chicago Press.

Morçöl, G. (2002). *A new mind for policy analysis: Toward a post-Newtonian and postpositivist epistemology and methodology.* Westport, CT: Praeger.

Morçöl, G. (2010). Center City District: A case of comprehensive downtown district. *Drexel Law Review*, 3(1), 271–286.

Morçöl, G. (2012a). *A complexity theory for public policy.* London: Routledge.

Morçöl, G. (2012b). The micro–macro problem as the core problem of complexity theory of policy processes. In L. Gerrits, P. Marks, & F. Boons (Eds.), *COMPACT 1: Public administration in complexity* (pp. 307–322). Litchfield Park, AZ: Emergent Publications.

Morçöl, G. (2014). Self-organization in collective action: Elinor Ostrom's contributions and complexity theory. *Complexity, Governance & Networks*, 1(2), 9–22.

Morçöl, G. (2016, March). "Publicness" as an emergent property of complex governance systems. Paper presented the 77th National Conference of the American Society for Public Administration, Seattle, WA.

Morçöl, G., & Gautsch, D. (2013). Institutionalization of business improvement districts: A longitudinal study of the state laws in the United States. *Public Administration Quarterly*, 37(2), 238–277.

Morçöl, G., & Karagoz, T. (2020). Accountability of business improvement district in urban governance networks: An investigation of state enabling laws. *Urban Affairs Review*, 56(3), 888–918. https://doi.org/10.1177/1078087418793532

Morçöl, G., & Patrick, P. A. (2006). Business improvement districts in Pennsylvania: Implications for democratic metropolitan governance. *International Journal of Public Administration*, 29(1–3), 137–171. http://dx.doi.org/10.1080/01900690500409013

Morçöl, G., Shafi, S., & Menon, A. (2022). Governance networks, bureaucracy, and democracy. *Perspectives on Public Management and Governance,* 5(2), 84–96. https://doi.org/10.1093/ppmgov/gvab034.

## 208  References

Morçöl, G., Tantardini, M., Williams, A., & Slagle, D. R. (2020). Master of Public Administration and Master of Public Policy degrees: Differences and similarities in the curricula and course contents. *Teaching Public Administration*, 38(3), 313–332. https://doi.org/10.1177/0144739420915758

Morçöl, G., Vollmer, A., & Mallinson, D. J. (2021). Business improvement district enabling laws in the United States and germany: A comparative analysis of policy learning. *Urban Affairs Review*. https://doi.org/10.1177/1078087421 1025551

Morçöl, G., & Wolf, J. F. (2010). Understanding business improvement districts: A new governance framework. *Public Administration Review*, 70(6), 906–913. https://doi.org/10.1111/j.1540-6210.2010.02222.x

Morçöl, G., Yoo, E., Azim, F., & Menon, Aravind. (2021). The collaborative governance networks literature: A comprehensive and systematic review. In J. Meek (Ed.), *Handbook on collaborative public management* (pp. 36–49). Cheltenham: Edward Elgar.

Morçöl, G., & Zimmermann, U. (2008a). Metropolitan governance and business improvement districts. In G. Morçöl, L. Hoyt, J. Meek, & U. Zimmermann (Eds.). *Business improvement districts: Research, theory, and controversies* (pp. 27–50). Boca Raton, FL: CRC Press.

Morçöl, G., & Zimmermann, U. (2008b). Community improvement districts in metropolitan Atlanta. In G. Morçöl, L. Hoyt, J. Meek, & U. Zimmermann (Eds.), *Business improvement districts: Research, theory, and controversies* (pp. 349–372). Boca Raton, FL: CRC Press.

Muir, J. & Mullins, D. (2015). The Governance of mandated partnerships: the case of social housing procurement. *Housing Studies*, 30(6), 967–986.

Murrell, J. B. (2007). *Differential persistence of variation in prehistoric milling tools from the Middle Rio Puerco Valley, New Mexico*. Oxford: Archaeopress.

Musso, J. A., & Weare, C. (2015). From participatory reform to social capital: Micro-motives and the macro-structure of civil society networks. *Public Administration Review*, 75(1), 150–164).

Nabatchi, T. (2012). Putting the "public" back in public values research. *Public Administration Review*, 77(5), 699–708.

Nadler, S. (1993). *Causation in early modern philosophy: Cartesianism, occasionalism, and preestablished harmony*. State College, PA: Penn State University Press.

Netting, R. M. (1972). Of men and meadows: Strategies of Alpine land use. *Anthropological Quarterly*, 45(3), 132–144.

Netting R. M. (1996) What Alpine peasants have in common: Observations on communal tenure in a Swiss village. In D. G. Bates & S. H. Lees (Eds.), *Case studies in human ecology* (pp. 219–230). Boston, MA: Springer.

Newell, A., & Simon, H. A. (1972). *Human problem solving*. Englewood Cliffs, NJ: Prentice Hall.

Newman, M, Barabási, A-L, & Watts, D. (2006). Introduction, in Newman, M, Barabási, A-L, & Watts, D. (Eds.), *The structure and dynamics of networks* (pp. 1–8). Princeton, NJ: Princeton University Press.

Newman, M., Barabasi, A.-L., & Watts, D. (2006). A brief history of the study of networks. In M. Newman, A. L. Barabasi, & D. Watts, (Eds.), *The structure and dynamics of networks*. Princeton, NJ: Princeton University Press.

Nicolis, G., & Prigogine, I. (1989). *Exploring complexity: An introduction*. New York: W. H. Freeman & Co.

## References 209

Nye jr., J. S. (2002). Information technology and democratic governance. In E. C. Kamarck & J. S. Nye (eds.), *Governance.com: Democracy in the information age* (pp. 1–16). Washington, DC: Brookings Institution Press.

Ogibayashi, S. (2021). Can agent-based modeling enable scientific policy making based on an understanding of causal mechanisms? *Journal on Policy and Complex Systems*, 7(1), 33–39.

O'Connell, L. (2005). Program accountability as an emergent property: The role of stakeholders in a program's field. *Public Administration Review*, 65(1), 85–93.

O'Connell, L. (2006). Emergent accountability in state–local relations: Some lessons from solid waste policy in Kentucky. *Administration & Society*, 38(4), 500–513. https://doi.org/10.1177/0095399706290635

O'Toole, L. (1997). Treating networks seriously: Practical and research-based agendas in public administration. *Public Administration Review*, 57(1), 45–52.

O'Brien, M. J., & Lyman, R. L. (2002). *Applying evolutionary archeology: A systematic approach*. New York: Kluwer.

Olson, Jr. M. (1965). *The logic of collective action: Public goods and the theory of groups*. Cambridge, MA: Harvard University Press.

Ostrom, E. (1990). *Governing the commons: The evolution of institutions for collective action*. Cambridge: Cambridge University Press.

Ostrom, E. (1999). Institutional rational choice: An assessment of the institutional analysis and development framework. In P. A. Sabatier (Ed.), *Theories of the policy process* (pp. 35–72). Boulder, CO: Westview.

Ostrom, E. (2005). *Understanding institutional diversity*. Princeton, NJ: Princeton University Press.

Ostrom, E. (2009). A general framework for analyzing sustainability of social-ecological systems. *Science*, 325(5939), 419–422.

Ostrom, E., & Parks, R. B. (1999). Neither gargantuan nor the land of Lilliputs: Conjectures on mixed systems of metropolitan organization. In M. D. McGinnis (Ed.), *Polycentricity and local public economies: readings from the workshop in political theory and policy analysis* (pp. 284–305). Ann Arbor, MI: The University of Michigan Press.

Ostrom, V. (1974). *The intellectual crisis in American public administration* (Rev. ed.). Tuscaloosa: The University of Alabama Press.

Ostrom, V. (1999a). Polycentricity (Part 1). In M. D. McGinnis (Ed.), *Polycentricity and local public economies: readings from the workshop in political theory and policy analysis* (pp. 52–74). Ann Arbor, MI: The University of Michigan Press. (Reprinted from the original paper presented at the annual meeting of American Political Science Association in 1972).

Ostrom, V. (1999b). Polycentricity (part 2), in M. D. McGinnis (Ed.), *Polycentricity and local public economies: Readings from the Workshop in Political Theory and Policy Analysis* (pp. 119–138). Ann Arbor, MI: The University of Michigan Press. (Reprinted from the original paper presented at the annual meeting of American Political Science Association in 1972).

Ostrom, V., Tiebout, C. M., Warren, R. (1961). The organization of government in metropolitan areas: A theoretical inquiry. *American Political Science Review*, 55(4), 831–842.

Pagliusi, S., Jarrett, S., Hayman, B., Kreysa, U., Prasad, S. D., Reers, M., Hong Thai, P., Wu, K., Zhang, Y. T., Baek, Y. O., Kumar, A., Evtushenko, A., Jadhav, S., Meng, W., Dat, D. T., Huang, W., & Desai, S. (2020). Emerging manufacturers

## 210  *References*

engagements in the COVID −19 vaccine research, development and supply. *Vaccine*, 38(34), 5418–5423. https://doi.org/10.1016/j.vaccine.2020.06.022

Parsons, T. (1937). *The structure of social action: A study in social theory with special reference to a group of recent European writers* (1st Ed.). New York: McGraw-Hill.

Pearl, J. (2009). *Causality: Models, reasoning and inference* (2nd ed.). Cambridge: Cambridge University Press.

Perow, C. (1984). *Normal accidents: Living with high-risk technologies.* New York: Basic Books.

Perrow, C. (1986). *Complex organizations: A critical essay* (3rd ed.). New York: McGraw Hill.

Peters, B. G. (2017). What is so wicked about wicked problems? A conceptual analysis and a research program. *Policy and Society*, 36(3), 385–396. https://doi.org/10.1080/14494035.2017.1361633

Peters. G. B., & Pierre, J. (1998). Governance without government? Rethinking public administration. *Journal of Public Administration Research and Theory*, 8 (2), 223–243.

Pierre, J. & Peters, G. B. (2005). *Governing complex societies: Trajectories and scenarios.* Basingstoke: Palgrave McMillan.

Portugali, J. (2000). *Self-organization and the city.* Berlin: Springer-Verlag.

Price, D. (1965). The scientific foundations of science policy. *Nature*, 206, 233–238.

Prigogine, I. (1997). *The end of certainty: Time, chaos, and the new laws of nature.* New York: The Free Press.

Prigogine, I., & Stengers, I. (1984). *Order out of chaos: Man's new dialogue with nature.* New York: Bantam Books.

Provan, K. G., & Kenis, P. (2008). Modes of network governance: Structure, management, and effectiveness. *Journal of Public Administration Research and Theory*, 18, 229–252.

Provan, K. G., & Milward, H. B. (1995). A preliminary theory of interorganizational network effectiveness: A comparative study of four community mental health systems. *Administrative Science Quarterly*, 40(1), 1–33. https://doi.org/10.2307/2393698

Provan, K. G., & Milward, H. B. (2001). Do networks really work? A framework for evaluating public sector organizational networks. *Public Administration Review*, 61(4), 414–431.

Provan, K. G., Fish, A., & Sydow, J. (2007). Interorganizational networks at the network level: A review of the empirical literature on whole networks. *Journal of Management*, 33(3), 479– 516.

Quirk, P., & Lizundia, E. (2020, December 16). Strengthening citizen-centered governance should be a core element of the Biden administration's democracy agenda. www.brookings.edu/blog/order-from-chaos/2020/12/16/strengthening-citizen-centered-governance-should-be-a-core-element-of-the-biden-administrations-democracy-agenda/

Raab, J., Mannak, R., & Cambré, B. (2015). Combining structure, governance, and context: A configurational approach to network effectiveness. *Journal of Public Administration Research and Theory*, 25(2), 479–511.

Radin, B. A. (2013). *Beyond Machiavelli: Policy analysis reaches midlife* (2nd ed.). Washington, DC: Georgetown University Press.

Radin, B. A., & Romzek, B. S. (1996). Accountability expectations in an intergovernmental arena: The national rural development partnership. *Publius*, 26(2), 59–81.

References   211

Rhodes, M. L., Murphy, J., Muir, J., & Murray, J. A. (2011). *Public management and complexity theory: Richer decision-making in public services*. London: Routledge.

Rhodes, R. A. W. (1997). *Understanding governance: Policy networks, governance, reflexivity and accountability*. Maidenhead: Open University Press.

Rivlin, A. M. (1971). *Systematic thinking for social action*. Washington, DC: Brookings Institution.

Rittel, H., & Webber, M. (1973). Dilemmas in a general theory of planning. *Policy Sciences*, 4(2), 155–169.

Romzek, B. S., & Dubnick, M. J. (1987). Accountability in the public sector: Lessons from the challenger tragedy. *Public Administration Review*, 47(3), 227–238. https://doi.org/10.2307/975901

Romzek, B. S., Ingraham, P. W. (2000). Cross pressures of accountability: Initiative, command, and failure in the Ron Brown Plane crash. *Public Administration Review*, 60(3), 240–253.

Romzek, B. S, & Johnston, J. M. (2005). State social services contracting: Exploring the determinants of effective contract accountability. *Public Administration Review*, 65(4), 436–449.

Romzek, B. S., LeRoux, K., & Blackmar, J. M. (2012). A preliminary theory of informal accountability among network organizational actors. *Public Administration Review*, 72(3), 442–453.

Romzek, B., LeRoux, K., Johnston, J., Kempf, R., & Piatak, J. (2014). Informal accountability in multisector service delivery collaborations. *Journal of Public Administration Research and Theory: J-Part*, 24(4), 813–842. Retrieved July 15, 2021, from http://www.jstor.org/stable/24484873

Rosenkopf, L., & Padula, G. (2008). Investigating the Microstructure of network evolution: Alliance formation in the mobile communications industry. *Organization Science*, 19(5), 669–806.

Rosser, J. B. (2000). Aspects of dialectics and non-linear dynamics. *Cambridge Journal of Economics*, 24, 311–324.

Rossi, P. H., Lipsey, M. W., & Freeman, H. E.(2004). *Evaluation: A systematic approach* (7th ed.). Thousand Oaks, CA: Sage.

Rungkitwattanakul, D., Yabusaki, A., Singh, D., Lawson, P., Nwaogwugwu, U., Iheagwara, O. S., & Mere, C. (2021). COVID-19 vaccine hesitancy among African American hemodialysis patients: A single-center experience. Hemodialysis international. International Symposium on Home Hemodialysis, 10.1111/hdi.12922. Advance online publication. https://doi.org/10.1111/hdi.12922

Sabatier, P. A. (2007). The need for better theories. In P. Sabatier (Ed.), *Theories of the policy process* (pp. 3–17). Cambridge, MA: Westview Press.

Sabatier, P. A., & Jenkins-Smith, H. (1993). *Policy change and learning: An advocacy coalition approach*. Boulder, CO: Westview Press.

Salamon, L. M. (2002). The new governance and the tools of public action: An introduction. In L. M. Salamon (Ed.), *The tools of government: A guide to new governance* (pp. 1–47). Oxford: Oxford University Press.

Saltztein, A. L. (2003). *Governing America's urban areas*. Belmont, CA: Thomson Wadsworth.

Salzano, M. (2008). Economic policy hints from heterogeneous agent-based simulations. In K. Richardson, L. Dennard, and G. Morçöl (eds), *Complexity and policy analysis: Tools and methods for designing robust policies in a complex world* (pp. 167–196). Goodyear, AZ: ISCE Publishing.

## 212  References

Saward, M. (2006). Democracy and citizenship: Expanding domains. In J. S. Dryzek, B. Honig, & A. Phillips (Eds.), *The Oxford handbook of political theory.* Oxford: Oxford University Press.

Sawyer, R. K. (2005). *Social emergence: Societies as complex systems.* Cambridge: Cambridge University Press.

Scheinert, S., Koliba, C., Hurley, S., Coleman, S., & Zia, A. (2015). The shape of watershed governance: Locating the boundaries of multiplex networks. *Complexity, Governance & Networks*, 2, 65–82. DOI: 10.7564/15-CGN25

Schelling, T. C (2006). *Micromotives and macrobehavior.* New York: W. W. Norton.

Scholz, J., Berardo, R., & Kile, B. (2008). Do networks solve collective action problems? credibility, search, and collaboration. *The Journal of Politics*, 70(2), 393–406. doi:10.1017/s0022381608080389

Schoder, D., Putzke, J., Metaxas, P. T., Gloor, P. A., & Fischbach, K. (2014) Information systems for "wicked problems." *Business Information Systems Engineering*, 6, 3–10. https://doi.org/10.1007/s12599-013-0303-3

Scott, W. R. (2008). *Institutions and organizations: Ideas and interests.* Los Angeles, CA: Sage.

Shafritz, J. M., & Hyde, A. C. (2017). *Classics of public administration* (8th ed.). Boston, MA: Cengage Learning.

Sharma, M., Batra, K., & Batra, R. (2021). A Theory-based analysis of COVID-19 vaccine hesitancy among African Americans in the United States: A recent evidence. *Healthcare*, 9(10), 1273. MDPI AG. Retrieved from http://dx.doi.org/10.3390/healthcare9101273

Siciliano, M., Carr., J. B., & Hugg, V. G. (2020). Analyzing the effectiveness of networks for addressing public problems: Evidence from a longitudinal study. *Public Administration Review*, 81(5), 895–910.

Simon, A. A. (2007). *Public policy: Preferences and outcomes.* New York: Pearson/Longman.

Simon, H. A. (1947). *Administrative behavior.* New York: Macmillan.

Simon, H. A. (1952). "Development of theory of public administration": Replies and comments. *American Political Science Review*, 46, 494–496.

Simon, H. A. (1979). Rational decision making and business organizations. *The American Economic Review*, 69(4), 493–513.

Simon, H. A. (1986). Rationality in psychology and economics. In R. M. Hogarth & M. W. Reder (Eds.), *Rational choice: The contrast between economics and psychology* (pp. 25–40). Chicago, IL: The University of Chicago Press.

Simon, H. A., & associates. (1992). Decision making and problem solving. In M. Zey (Ed.), *Decision making: Alternatives to rational choice models* (pp. 32–53). Newbury Park, CA: Sage. ISBN: 0803947518, pp. 32–53.

Sirianni, C. (2007). Neighborhood planning as collaborative democratic design: The case of Seattle. *Journal of the American Planning Association*, 73(4), 373–387. http://dx.doi.org/10.1080/01944360708978519

Smith, A. (1902). *The wealth of nations.* Princeton, NJ: Princeton University Press.

Snellen, I. (2002). Conciliation of rationalities: The essence of public administration. *Administrative Theory & Praxis*, 24(2), 323–346.

Somit, A., & Peterson, S. A. (1997). *Darwinism, dominance, and democracy: The biological bases of authoritarianism.* Westport, CT: Praeger.

Sorensen, E. (2006). Metagovernance: The changing role of politicians in processes of democratic governance. *American Review of Public Administration*, 36(1), 98–114.

## References    213

Sørensen, E., & J. Torfing. (2005). The democratic anchorage of governance networks. *Scandinavian Political Studies*, 28(3), 195–218.

Sørensen, E., & Torfing, J. (2006). Introduction governance network research: Towards a second generation. In E. Sørensen & J. Torfing (Eds.), *Theories of democratic network governance* (pp. 1–21). London: Palgrave Macmillan.

Sørensen, E., & Torfing, J. (2009). Making governance networks effective and democratic through metagovernance. *Public Administration*, 87(2), 234–258.

Souilmi, Y., Lauterbur, M. E., Tobler, R., Huber, C. D., Johar, A. S., Moradi, S. V., Johnston, W. A., Krogan, N. J., Alexandrov, K., & Enard, D. (2021). An ancient viral epidemic involving host coronavirus interacting genes more than 20,000 years ago in East Asia. *Current Biology*, 31(16), 3504–3514.e9. https://doi.org/10.1016/j.cub.2021.05.067

Stanley, J. (2018). *How fascism works: the politics of us and them*. New York: Random House.

Schattschneider, E. E. (1960). *The semisovereign people: A realist's view of democracy in America*. New York: Holt, Rinehart and Winston.

Stephens, G. R., & Wikstrom, N. (2000). *Metropolitan government and governance: Theoretical perspectives, empirical analysis, and the future*. New York: Oxford University Press.

Stewart, J. & Ayres, R. (2001). Systems theory and policy practice: An exploration. *Policy Sciences*, 34(1), 79–94.

Stone, C. N. (1989). *Regime politics: Governing Atlanta, 1946–1988*. Lawrence, KS: The University of Kansas Press.

Stone, D. (1997). *Policy paradox: The art of political decision making*. New York: W. W. Norton & Company.

Sylvester, J. (1878). On an application of the new atomic theory to the graphical representation of the invariants and covariants of binary quantics, with three appendices. *American Journal of Mathematics*, 1(1), 64–104. doi:10.2307/2369436

Taylor, F. W. (1947). *Scientific management*. New York: Harper & Row.

Taylor, M. C. (2001). *The moment of complexity: Emerging network culture*. Chicago, IL: The University of Chicago Press.

Teisman, G. R., van Buuren, A., & Gerrits, L. (Eds.). (2009). *Managing complex governance systems: Dynamics, self-organization and coevolution in public investments*. London: Routledge.

Thomson, M. A., Perry, J. L., Miller, T. K. (2009). Conceptualizing and measuring collaboration. *Journal of Public Administration Research and Theory*, 19(1), 23–56.

Tiebout, C. M. (1956). A pure theory of local public expenditure. *Journal of Political Economy*, 64, 416–424.

Torfing, J., Peters, G. B., Pierre, J., & Sørensen, E. (2012). *Interactive governance: Advancing the paradigm*. Oxford: Oxford University Press.

Torgerson, D. (2003). Democracy through policy discourse. In T. M. Hajer & H. Wagenaar (Eds.), *Deliberative policy analysis: Understanding governance in network society* (pp. 139–171). Cambridge: Cambridge University Press.

True, James L., Jones, Bryan D., & Baumgartner, Frank R. (2007). Punctuated equilibrium theory: Explaining stability ad change in public policymaking. In Paul A. Sabatier (Ed.), *Theories of the policy process* (2nd ed., pp. 155–188). Cambridge, MA: Westview Press.

## 214 *References*

Tullock, G. (1979). Public choice in practice. In C. S. Russell (Ed.), *Collective decision making: Applications from public choice theory* (pp. 27–45). Baltimore, MD: The Johns Hopkins University Press.

Tversky, A., & Kahneman, D. (1986). Rational choice and the framing of decisions. In R. M. Hogarth & M. W. Reder (Eds.), *Rational choice: The contrast between economics and psychology* (pp. 67–94). Chicago, IL: The University of Chicago Press.

Van Buuren, A., Gerrits, L., & Marks, P. (2009). Public policy-making and the management of coevolution. In G. Teisman, Arwin van Buuren, and Lasse Gerrits (Eds.), *Managing complex governance systems: Dynamics, self-organization and coevolution in public investments* (pp. 154–171). London: Routledge.

Van Bueren, E. M., Klijn, E- H., & Koppenjan, J. Fm. (2003). Dealing with wicked problems in networks: Analyzing an environmental debate from a network perspective. *Journal of Public Administration Research and Theory*, 13(2), 193–212.

Van Meerkerk, I. van, Buuren, M. W. van & Edelenbos, J. (2013). Water managers' boundary judgments and adaptive water governance. An analysis of the Dutch Haringvliet sluices case. *Water Resources Management*, 27 (7): 2179–2194.

Vardavas, R., de Lima, P. N., Davis, P. K., Parker, A. M., & Baker, L. M. (2021). Modeling infectious behavior: The need to account for behavioral adaptations in COVID-19 Models. *Journal on Policy and Complex Systems*, 7(1), 21–32.

Van Buuren, A., Van Meerkerk, I., & Tortajada, C. (2019). Understanding emergent participation practices in water governance. *International Journal of Water Resources Development*, 367–382. https://doi.org/10.1080/07900 627.2019.1585764

Ventriss, C. (2003). Rethinking rationality. *Administrative Theory & Praxis*, 25(1), 131–136.

Von Bertalanffy, L. (1968). *General system theory: Foundations, development, applications.* New York: George Braziller.

Waldo, D. (1948). *The administrative state: A study of the political theory of American public administration.* New York: Ronald Press.

Waldo, D. (1952). Development of theory of democratic administration. *The American Political Science Review*, 46, 81–103.

Waldo, D. (1980). *The enterprise of public administration.* Novato, CA: Chandler & Sharp Publishers.

Waldrop, M. (1992). *Complexity: The emerging science at the edge of chaos.* New York: Touchstone.

Wamsley, G. L., Bacher, R. N., Goodsell, C. T., Kronenberg, P. S., Rohr, J. A., Stivers, C. M., & Wolf, J. F. (1990). *Refounding public administration.* Newbury Park, CA: Sage.

Warren, M. (1992). Democratic theory and self-transformation. *The American Political Science Review*, 86(1), 8–23.

Wasserman, S., & Faust, K. (1994). *Social network analysis: Methods and applications.* Cambridge: Cambridge University Press.

Water Boards (Netherlands). Wikipedia entry. https://en.wikipedia.org/wiki/Water _board_(Netherlands)

Watts, D. J., & Strogatz, S. H. (1998). Collective dynamics of "small-world" networks. *Nature*, 393(6684), 440–442. http://dx.doi.org.ezaccess.libraries.psu. edu/10.1038/30918

Weber, M. (2010). *From Max Weber: Essays in sociology*. (translated and edited by H. H. Gerth and C. Wright Mills). London: Routledge. (e-book version: ProQuest eBook central https://ebookcentral.proquest.com)

Weber, M. (2011). *Methodology of the social sciences* (reprint of the 1949 original translation by Edward A. Shils & Henry A. Finch). New Brunswick, NJ: Transaction Publishers.

Webber, M. M. (1983). The myth of rationality: Development planning reconsidered. *Environment and Planning B: Planning and Design*, 10(1), 89–99.

White, L. D. (1939). *Introduction to the study of public administration* (rev. ed.). New York: Macmillan.

Wilks, S., & Wright, M. (1987). Conclusion: Comparing government-industry relations—states, sectors, and networks. In S. Wilks & M. Wright (eds.), *Comparative government–industry relations*. Oxford: Clarendon Press.

Wilson, W. (1887). The study of administration. *Political Science Quarterly*, 2(2), 197–222. https://doi.org/10.2307/2139277.

Wilson, W. (1941). The study of administration. *Political Science Quarterly*, 56(4), 481–506.

Wolf, J. F. (2008). Business improvement districts' approaches to working with local governments. In G. Morçöl, L. Hoyt, J. Meek, & U. Zimmermann (Eds.), *Business improvement districts: Research, theory, and controversies* (pp. 269–288). Boca Raton, FL: CRC Press

Yerasimos, S. (1974). *Az gelişmişlik sürecinde Türkiye* [Turkey in the process of underdevelopment]. İstanbul: Gözlem Yayınları

Yin, H. (2017). Network structure and governance performance: What makes a difference. *Public Administration Review*, 78(2), 195–205.

Zaheer, A. & Soda, G. (2009). Network evolution: The origins of structural holes. *Administrative Science Quarterly*, 54, 1–31.

Zhang, X., Wang, J., & Xu, L. (2019). Between autonomy and supervision: The interpretation of community supervisory committee reform in Hangzhou, China. *Cities*, 88, 91. http://dx.doi.org/10.1016/j.cities.2019.01.007

Zia, A. (2013). *Post-Kyoto climate governance: Confronting the politics of scale, ideology and knowledge*. London: Rutledge.

Zia, A., Kauffman, S., Koliba, C., Beckage, B., Vattay, G., & Bomblies, A. (2014). From the habit of control to institutional enablement: Re-envisioning the governance of social-ecological systems from the perspective of complexity sciences. *Complexity, Governance & Networks*, 1(1), 79–88.

Zia, A., Norton, B. G., Noonan, D. S., Rodgers, M. O., & DeHart-D., L. (2006). A quasi-experimental evaluation of high-emitter non-compliance and its impact on vehicular tailpipe emissions in Atlanta, 1997–2001. *Transportation Research Part D*, 11, 77–96.

Zia, A., Widener, M., Metcalf, S., & Koliba, C. (2017). Modeling voting decisions in governance networks for agents with heterogeneous mental models and alternate network structures. *Proceedings of the Social Science Society of the Americas*, 1–7. https://doi.org/10.1145/3145574.3145592

# Index

*Note*: Figures are indicated by *italics*. Tables are indicated by **bold**. Endnotes are indicated by the page number followed by 'n' and the endnote number e.g., 20n1 refers to endnote 1 on page 20.

accountability 139–40, 162–3, 187; and absolute rulers 142; and BIDs 159–62; and complex systems 150–4; conceptualizations/models of 140–3; and governance networks 148–50, **149**; and metropolitan governance 154–7, *156*; multidimensional conceptualizations/models of 143–7, **145–6**

accountability mechanisms 140–50, **145**, **149**, 154–6, 163; and BID management organizations 160, 161, 162

Acemoglu, Daron 62, 172, 173

actors 127; and accountability 139–40, 152, 153–4; and citizens of practice-based democracy 175; and complex systems 49–51, 65; and constraints 119; and equality/equity 166–7; and goals 135; and governance 22; and governance networks 34–5; and individual actions and collective consequences 79–80; individuals and states 23–4; and the micro-macro problem 76–9; and networks and systems 115–16, 120–1; nongovernmental 22; and public policymaking 2–3, 22; and rationality 85–90; and the rationality problem 94–6; and selfishness/self-seeking 54–5; and self-organization 51, 53, 168; and the state 1; and systemness 46–8; *see also* agents; multiactor processes

advocacy coalitions 46, 83; and bounded rationality 90; and the micro-macro problem 121

Africa 26

African Americans: and civil rights 114; and vaccine hesitancy 64–5, 95, 129

agency and the state 17–18

agency-structure problem 80

agenda setting 173

agent-based modeling (ABM) 96, 107–9, 193; and downward causation 115; and structuration theory 118

agent-based simulations (ABS) 81

agents: and complex systems 94–8; and downward causation 115; and parallel-distributive urban planning 194; and the rationality assumption 91–2; *see also* actors; cognitive agents; reactive agents

aggregation and complex systems 96, 99–101, 104, 109

Agranoff, Robert 4, 34, 37

airlines/airports and preferential attachment 106

Albert, Reka 33, 67, 68, 105

Albright, Madeleine 166

American democracy 171, 173, 176

American government and public administration 19–20; and BIDs 158–9, 160–2; and bureaucracy 179–80; and COVID-19 vaccine rollout 25–7, 63–4, 119–20; and democracy 178; and effectiveness 137; and global warming 60; and governance networks 33; social policies and policy feedback theory 114

American Political Science Association (APSA) 191, 192

*Analects* (Confucius) 141

Anderson, Paul 52, 102
Ansell, Chris 21, 136
anthropology 169, 173
anti-discrimination laws 112
anti-vaxxers 39; *see also* vaccine
  hesitancy
Antonine Plague 13, 61, 129
ants and cognitive capacity 96–7
Aristotle 51–2, 85
Arrow, Kenneth J. 79, 88
Arts and Humanities Citation Index
  (AHCI) 5
Astra-Zeneca 63
Athens 165
Atlanta 106, 177
Australia 136, 159
authoritarianism 173
autopoiesis theory 113
Axelrod, Robert 83, 100–1
Axtell, Robert 99

Barabási, Albert-László 30, 33, 48;
  and preferential attachment 67, 68,
  105, 106
Bar-Yam, Yaneer 95–6, 108
Batty, Michael 45
Baumgartner, Frank R. 50–1, 90
Bayesian statistical models 88
behavioral contagion 115–16
Behn, Robert D. 144
Belgium 59
Berardo, Ramiro 35–6, 107, 137
Bertalanffy, Ludwig von 43–5, 46,
  56–7
betweenness centrality 36
Bevir, Mark 3, 4, 169, 182
Biden, Joseph R. 165, 166
biological examples of emergent
  properties 102
BioNTech 26, 63
Bodin, Jean 169
bounded rationality 86, 88–9, 90–1,
  92–3; and structuration theory
  118
Brazil 172
bridging 137
Briffault, Richard 160
Britain 18, 100, 161
British Petroleum (BP) and Deepwater
  Horizon oil spill 150–1
Brookings Institution 109, 165
bureaucracy 133, 169, 178–80; and
  accountability 141–2, 144, 187
business improvement districts (BIDs)
  157–62, 177

Campbell, Donald 112
Canada 156; and BIDs 158–9, 161,
  164n8
Capra, Frithjof 43, 57
Castells, Manuel 3
Catholic Church as emergent social
  structure 101
Catlaw, Thomas 11
causality and accountability 140
causation 44, 96, 98; *see also* downward
  causation
Center for Countering Digital Hate 66
centerless society 35
Centers for Disease Control (CDC) 68
centrality 36
centralization 44, 47
chaos theory 43, 45, 58
China 141, 169, 172, 173
Chinese bureaucracy 141
Christianity and liberal democracy 172
cities 155, 156, 158–61, 194; *see also*
  urban areas and systems theory
citizen-centered governance 166
citizenship definition and individuals 114
City Center District (CCD)
  Philadelphia 159–60
clean energy governance networks 137
Cleveland, Harlan 19
climate crisis 60, 77, 131, 195
Clinton, Bill 33
co-creation of public goods 175
coevolution and complexity theory 43,
  57–60, 69; and COVID-19 pandemic
  60–2
cognitive agents 91–2, 93, 96, 186; and
  structuration theory 116–17, 118
cognitive capacity 78–9, 85, 90; and
  complex systems 96–7
cognitive maps and complexity theory
  94, 96–8
cognitive psychology 86, 88, 92–3; and
  structuration theory 118
Colander, David 48, 190, 192
Coleman, James S. 79–81, 99
collaborative governance 8; definitions
  of 21–2; literature on 11–12
collaborative regional governance
  conceptualizations 156
collective choices 99
collective outcomes and individual
  actors 23–4
collective problem-solving 17, 186, 188,
  191, 194–5; and economics 190;
  and effectiveness 132–8; and the
  micro-macro problem 76–9; and

## 218  *Index*

multiple actors 22, 27, 75; and practice-based democracy 174–5; and self-governance 167; and self-organization 55–6
collibration 182
Collins, Dr. Francis 129
Columbia space shuttle 151
Comfort, Louise 4, 45
common pool resources (CPR) 55–6; *see also* "tragedy of the commons"
commons *see* "tragedy of the commons"
communicative rationality and deliberative democracy 174
complementary economies and coevolution 58
complex adaptive systems theory 43, 48, 52; *see also* complexity theory
complex collaborative systems and American government 20, 25–7
complex collective behaviors and individual understanding 95–6
complexes of elements in systems theory 44, 46, 56–7
complexity theory 41–5, 68–9; and coevolution 57–60; and complex systems 188; and COVID-19 pandemic 60–8; and emergence 56–7; and flood risk management 194; and individual actors 97–9; and irreducibility 102–4; literature on 4, **7**, 8–12, *10*; and macro to micro effects 114, 121; and methodological tools 76; and micro to macro processes 100–1; and networks and systems 48, 185; and nonlinearity 50–1; and public policymaking 3, 189–90, 192–3; and the rationality problem 91, 93–6; and self-organization 51–6, 167; and structuration theory 116–21; and wicked problems 125, 127, 128–9, 131, 138, 187; *see also* complex adaptive systems theory
complex systems 43–5, 48–9; and accountability 150–4; and agents 86, 91; and downward causation 112–13; and feedback loops 50–1; and macro properties 95–6; and vaccine manufacture and rollout 27, 63, 65–8; *see also* systemness
conceptualizations of complex governance networks 187–8
configurational approach to studying network effectiveness 136–7

Confucius 141
Congress (US) 60
controllability and accountability 144, **149**
co-production 175–6
coronavirus 13, 25, 60–1
COVID-19 pandemic xii, 3, 12–13, 38–9, 186, 194–5; and coevolution 60–2; and individual actors' knowledge 95; and libertarian values 46; and multiple actors 25–7; and nonlinearity 65–7; and self-organization 67–8; and systems modeling 108–9; and vaccines 63–5; and virus mutation 97; and wicked problems 129–30; *see also* delta variant coronavirus; omicron variant coronavirus; SARS-CoV-2
Cret Park Philadelphia 159
crime prevention networks 136–7
crime rates and BIDs 161

Darwinian evolution 104
Dasgupta, Rana 2
decentering and policymaking/governance 22, 182–3
decision-making processes in individuals 86, 87–90; and bounded rationality 90–1
Deepwater Horizon oil spill 150–1
degree centralities and social network analysis 35–6
deity and accountability 142
deliberative/discursive democracy 174, 183
Delta Airlines 106
delta variant coronavirus 13, 60, 62, 65–6, **66**, 97, 105
democracy 165, 166, 187; and bureaucracy 179–80; defining conceptualizations of 166; and governance networks 180–1, 182–3; ideal types of 170–8; *see also* deliberative/discursive democracy; liberal democracy; practice-based democracy
democracy agenda (Biden) 166
democratic anchorage and accountability 148–50
democratic political systems 22
demographics 82
De Tocqueville, Alexis 176, 178
dichotomous conceptual templates 188–9
differential persistence and emergence 104–5

## Index 219

Dilworth Park Philadelphia 159–60
disaster response networks 137
distanciation and social structures 119
downward causation 112–13, 117–18, 122
duality of structure 117–18
Dubnick, Melvin J. 144, **145–6**, 147
Dunn, William Newlin xv
Durkheim, Émile 117
Duterte, Rodrigo 172
Dye, Thomas R. 41
dynamics in systems 41, 45, 52–3, 88, 121, 138, 187, 190, 192; and wicked problems 130, 131; *see also* systems dynamics modeling (SDM)

economics 82, 190, 193
education 64, 95; and deliberative democracy 174; and masters programs in public administration/ policy 191–2
effectiveness and public problems 125, 132–4, 187; and governance networks 134–8
Egypt 61
Ehrlich, Paul 57
electronic technology revolution 19
emergence and complexity theory 43, 44, 56–7, 96, 99–101, 109; mechanisms of 104–6; and the micro-macro problem 99; and structuration theory 117, 120
emergent accountability 153, 157
emergentist philosophy and science 102–3
Emerson, Kirk 4, 12, 21–2
England 161, 172, 177
Enlightenment philosophy 85, 95
Epstein, Joshua M. 91, 96, 99, 102–3; and downward causation 115; and structuration theory 117, 118
equality/equity and democracy 166–7, 173; and bureaucracy 179, 180
ethical rules 141
Euler, Leonard 30, 32
European Union (EU) 2, 19
evolutionary biology 44, 51, 52, 57–8; and authoritarianism 173; and COVID-19 pandemic 61–2; and differential persistence 104–5

Facebook 29, 66, 105
Farazmand, Ali 170
Fauci, Dr. Anthony 67
FedEx 25, 26, 65

feedback loops in complex systems 50–1, 52, 53; and coevolution 59
Feiock, Richard C. 56
Finer, Herman 143
Fischer, Frank 87–8
fitness landscapes 57–8
flood risk management 194
Florida, Richard 62
Food and Drug Administration (FDA) (US) 63
Forester, John 87–8
Forrester, Jay W. 45, 51, 53
Foster, Kathryn 158
Fox News 39, 65, 68
fractal geometry models 45
frameworks, conceptual i, xii–xiii, 82–3, 150, 163; *see also* advocacy coalitions; institutional analysis and development (IAD) framework; intergovernmental relations framework; multidimensional accountability framework; social-ecological systems framework
France 18
Frederickson, H. George 19–20, 144, **145–6**, 147
free markets 189, 190
Friedrich, C. J. 143
Fukuyama, Francis 142, 169, 170, 172
fuzzy logic 118–19

game theory 88–9
geographic information systems (GIS) and urban planning 193
Georgia 155
Germany 59, 137–8, 161
Gerrits, Lasse 4, 47–8, 59
Geyer, Robert 45
Giddens, Anthony 46–7, 65, 116–21, 122
globalization 19, 35
global warming 60, 77, 131, 195
goals: and accountability 152–3; and decision-making 88–9; and effectiveness 133; and networks and systems 135–6; and systemness 47–8, 59–60
Goodnow, Frank J. 24, 191
Goodsell, Charles T. 18
Google 105
Google Scholar 126
Gore, Albert 134
governance 17–27
governmental decision-making and bounded rationality 90

## 220  *Index*

government by proxy 20–1
governments and private organizations 20, 22
Graeber, David 24, 167, 169, 173, 190
graph theory 30–1, 32
Gulf of Mexico 150

Habermas, Jürgen 174, 178
Hamilton, David K. 155, 157
Hardin, Garret 23, 54, 77–8, 167–8, 182
Hayek, Friedrich 78–9, 167–8, 169
Heinelt, Hubert 22, 144, **145–6**, 147
heterochrony and time-ecology in economic development 193
hierarchies in complex systems 24, 49
hierarchy and accountability 141–3, 144, 155, 162
history and human society 133, 167, 172–3, 184n8, 190–1; and democracy 165; and pandemics 12, 61, 129
Hobbes, Thomas 169
Holland, John H. 100, 101, 103–4
Homans, George 79
homophily 39
Hungary 172
Huntington, Samuel P. 172

ideal types and democracy 166
individual actions and collective consequences 79–80, 85, 113; and actors' knowledge 94–7; and the "invisible hand" 98
Industrial Revolution and democracy 172
influencers and COVID-19 pandemic 66–7
informal accountability framework 150
information systems and wicked problems 130–1
infrastructure 29
Ingraham, P. W. 147
Instagram 66
institutional analysis and development (IAD) framework xiii, 25, 42, 53–4, 56, 83, 188; and meta-governance 182; and the micro-macro problem 121; and the rationality assumption 86
instrumental empiricism and the rationality assumption 89
interdependency relations and actors 47, 49, 81

intergovernmental relations framework 155
integrative frameworks 135
Internet 58, 176, 177; and preferential attachment 105–6
Internet of Things (IoT) 29–30
"invisible hand," individuals and collective outcomes 98, 100
Iowa 137
Iraq 2
Ireland 177
irreducibility and systems 44, 57, 101, 102–4, 109
Israeli vaccination take-up study 39

Japan 173, 176
Jena 137–8
Jenkins-Smith, Hank 83
Jessop, Bob 3, 34, 170; and the agency-structure problem 80; on governance 22; on meta-governance 182
judgement/judges and accountability 140, 147

Kahneman, Daniel 86, 88, 118
Kaliningrad 30
Kant, Immanuel 52
Kapucu, Naim 4, 37, 135, 137
Katrina (hurricane) 137
Kauffman, Stuart 52, 57–8, 102; and emergentism 103; and "NK model" 59
Kentucky 153–4
Kenya 156
Kettl, Donald F. 4, 18, 19, 134, 191; and accountability 148; and complexity 41; and definition of governance networks 34; and government by proxy 20–1
Kiel, L. Douglas 4, 45
kinship relations and social integration 47
Klijn, Erik Hans 4, 34, 35; and accountability 152; and democracy 180; and policy network theories 48; and structuration theory 121
knowledge and the consequences of actions 94–5
Koehler, Gus 193
Koliba, Christopher J. 4, 34, 83, 144, 148
König, Dénes 32
Königsberg bridge problem 30–1, *31*
Kooiman, Jan 2, 19
Koppel, Jonathan G. S. 144, 147

## Index 221

Koppenjan, Joop F. M. 4, 34, 35, 152, 180
Korea 63
Kosko, Bart 118–19
Kristianstads Vattenrike Biosphere Reserve 152
Kupers, Roland 48, 190, 192

Lacks, Henrietta 64
language and downward causation 114–15, 118–19
Laplace, Pierre Simon 77–8, 84n3
Laplace's demon 77, 84n3
Levitsky, Steven 166
liberal democracy 166, 170–3, 183; and accountability 142–3, 150; and the four conjectures 180–1; and populism 165
LinkedIn 29
LINUX 176
literature review 4–12
logical positivism 85
Luhmann, Niklas 35, 113, 115

macro-level behaviors 95–6
macro-level networks empirical studies 36–7
macro to micro processes 112, 186; and autopoiesis theory 113; and policy feedback theory 114; and structuration theory 116–21
Madison, James 171
Magna Carta 172
Mann, Michael E. 131, 132
masters programs in public administration/policy 191–2
mathematics and network science 30–3
Meadows, Donella H. 50, 52
Meek, Jack W. 4, 34
Meier, Kenneth J. 34
Meijer, Albert J. 175, 176, 177
Merriam-Webster xii–xiii, 139, 187
Merton, Robert 79
meso-level theories of governance networks 83
Mesopotamia 165, 175–6
meta-governance 150, 183; and the state 181–2
metropolitan governance xiii; and accountability 154–7, 156, 163; and BIDs 157–62; see also cities; urban areas and systems theory
micro and macro level governance networks 35, 36

micro-macro-micro processes and structuration theory 120
micro-macro problem 3, 75, 94, 99, 186, 188; and agents 85, 87, 92–3; background and development of 79–81; and collective problem-solving 76–9; and downward causation 112; and emergence 57; and multiple levels 83; and policy process theories 82–3; and social systems 81–2; see also macro to micro processes; micro to macro processes
micro to macro processes 96–101; and accountability 152; and differential persistence 104–5; modeling of 107–9; and the mystery gap 103; and preferential attachment 105–6
Middle East 2, 61
Mitchell, Jeremy 160, 161
Mitchell, Sandra 113
Moderna 25–6
Moreno, Jacob 32
Morgan, Lloyd 102
mRNA vaccines 25–6, 63
multiactor processes 41–2, 185–6, 195; and accountability 139; and BIDs 160–1; and effectiveness 134–5; and flood risk management 194; and wicked problems 127, 131–2
multi-centered networks 148, 157, 171, 183, 189
multi-centered policymaking processes 19, 22, 75, 155–6
multi-centered societies 3, 19
multidimensional accountability framework **145–6**, 148, 154, 155, 157, 162
multidisciplinarity 188

Nabatchi, Tina 4, 12, 21–2, 114
National Aeronautics and Space Administration (NASA) 151
National Institutes of Health (NIH) (US) 25–6
National Performance Review report (Gore) 134
nation-state, the 2–3, 171, 179
natural systems and teleology 59
negative sanctions and individual actors 119
Netherlands 59, 137, 194; Dutch water boards 176–7
network function framework 37
network mapping 31–2, 32

222 *Index*

networks 29–40, 185, 188, 195; and accountability 150–3; and effectiveness 135–7; governing by 21; and self-organization 53–6; and structuration theory 121; and systems 48–9; and wicked problems 127, 130; *see also* preferential attachment in networks; scale-free networks; social network analyses (SNA)
network science 30, 32–3; micro and macro level research 35–8; and universal structures 40
network structures 136
Newman, Mark 30
New Public Management movement 143
New York City 161
New Zealand 11, 159
NK model 59
nodes and connections in social network analysis 35–6
nodes and hubs in preferential attachment 67, 106
nonlinearity in complex systems 43, 50–1; and COVID-19 pandemic 65–7, 108; and mechanisms of emergence 104
Northern Ireland 156

O'Connell, Lenahan 152, 153–4, 157
Olson, Mancur 24
omicron variant coronavirus 13, 60, 62, 66, 97, 105
Orbán, Viktor 172
Ostrom, Elinor xi, 2, 4, 18, 189; and bounded rationality 90–1; and complexity 42; and downward causation 113–14, 121; and polycentrism 25, 132; and self-organization 53–6, 67–8, 69, 78, 167, 168–9; *see also* institutional analysis and development (IAD) framework
Ostrom, Vincent xi, 2, 18, 23, 98, 113; and bureaucracy 179; and polycentrism 24–5
O'Toole, Laurence J. 34, 48–9
Ottoman Empire 2

Page, Scott E. 92, 101
pandemics 12–13, 61, 129
parallel-distributive planning 193–4
Parsons, Talcott 79
participation and democracy 166, 183; and liberal democracy 171, 173;

and self-organization 167; tripartite conceptualization of 175
Pennsylvania 151
performance management 134, 160
Perrow, Charles 151–2
Peters, Guy 4, 17, 18–19
Pfizer 26, 63
Philadelphia 155, 159–61
Philippines 176
*Philosophical Essay on Probabilities, A* (Laplace) 84n3
philosophy: and collective problem-solving 77–8; and emergentism 102–3; and the rationality problem 85; and self-organization 51–2, 167–9
Pierre, Jon 4, 17, 18–19
Plato 77, 85
policy action systems 47–8
policy analysis 20, 22, 130
policy analysis methodologies and wicked problems 127–8
policy feedback theory 113; and downward causation 121
policy networks 34
policy process theories: and bounded rationality 90–1; and the micro-macro problem 82–3
*Policy Sciences* (journal) 126
political accountability 142, 144, 148
political science 6, 8, 11, 143, 185, 191–2
politicians and bureaucrats 143
polycentrism 18, 23–5, 27, 132, 188; and accountability 155–6; and governance 75
population based models (PBMs) 108
power law distributions 33, 67–8, 105–6, 107; *see also* preferential attachment in networks; scale-free networks
practice-based democracy 174–6, 183
preferential attachment in networks 33, 105, 107; and COVID-19 pandemic 67, 68; *see also* power law distributions; scale-free networks
Price, Derek J. de Solla 111n14
Prigogine, Ilya 52, 81
program evaluation 134, 147
progressive segregation and progressive centralization 44
Provan, Keith 19, 34, 36, 136; and effectiveness 136; and typology 38
public administration xii, 191; and accountability 139, 163; and

American mismatch problem 19–20; and effectiveness 133–8; and governance 18–19; and governance networks 34, 185; and government by proxy 20–1; literature on 4–9, *5*, *6*, *7*, *10*; Wilsonian principles of 24
public choice theory 54
public management networks 34
*Public Management Review* 12
publicness xv
public policymaking xii, 2–3, 191, 192–3; and complexity 41–2, 189–90; and effectiveness 132–4; and networks and systems 48; state centered 22; and wicked problems 127, 130
public service delivery: and effectiveness 134; and polycentrism 23–4
Puerto Rico 158, 161
punctuated equilibrium theory 42, 121; and bounded rationality 90; and feedback loops 50–1; and the micro-macro problem 82

QAnon 29

Radin, Beryl A. 22, 147
Raiffa, Howard 88
rational behavior by individuals 55; and collective outcomes 23–4; and the micro-macro problem 82
rational choice theory 100, 113
rationality assumption 86–90; and agents 92; and complexity theory 91
rationality problem 85–6, 94–6
reactive agents 91, 93, 96, 186
Reagan, Ronald 33
reducibility *see* irreducibility and systems
Renaissance and concept of the state 169
*Republic, The* (Plato) 77
responsibility, liability and accountability 144, **145–6, 149**
responsiveness and accountability 144–7, **146, 149**
Rhodes, Mary Lee 4
Rhodes, R. A. W. 4, 21, 34, 37
Rittel, Horst W. J. 125–6, 127–8, 130–2, 138
Rivlin, Alice M. 134
RNA 58, 60
R-naught transmission 66

Roman legions 141
Romzek, Barbara S. 147, 150

Sabatier, Paul A. 83
Salamon, Lester 4, 19, 134; and public governance 20
Samsung 106
SARS-CoV-2 13, 25, 60, 62; and differential persistence 105; and transmissibility 65–6, **66**; variant mutations 97; and wicked problems 129
Sawyer, R. Keith 43, 101; and emergentism 103; and social causation 112–13, 115; and structuration theory 117, 118, 120
scale-free networks 33, 111n14; and power law 105–6; and preferential attachment 106
Schattschneider, Elmer E. 173
Schelling, Thomas C. 81–2, 96–7, 98; and language 114–15
Science Citation Index (SCI) 5
scientific realism and the rationality assumption 89
Scotland 161
self-governance 8, 167–8, 189; literature on *7*, 11; and practice-based democracy 175
selfishness 23–4, 54, 77
self-organization 8, 41, 51–6, 170, 189, 192–3; and complexity theory 42, 43; and COVID-19 pandemic 67–8; and emergence 57; literature on *7*, 10–11; and meta-governance 182; and parallel-distributive urban planning 194; and participation 167
self-referentiality 59–60
self-regulation 182, 190
Simon, Herbert A. 41–2, 85–6; and bounded rationality 88–9, 90, 92–3, 118; and micro to macro processes 100; and Waldo debate 133–4
small government solutions and policy problems 190
small-world networks 33
Smith, Adam 98, 100, 113
social causation 112–13, 117–18, 122
social classes and the Industrial Revolution 172
social-ecological systems framework 25, 42, 188, 194
social evolution and viruses 61–2
social integration 46–7

## Index

social media 177; and behavioral contagion 115–16; and COVID-19 pandemic 68; and misinformation 129; as networks 29–30; and vaccine hesitancy 39, 65, 66–7

social network analyses (SNA) 31–3, 41, 75, 81, 186; and degree centralities 35–6; and downward causation 115; and effectiveness 137–8; and preferential attachment 107; and relations among actors 47

social orders, spontaneous and externally designed 78, 167–8

social participation 175–6

social phenomena and psychology 103

Social Science Citation Index (SSCI) 5, **7**, 8

social structures and individuals 117–21

social systems 45–8, 65; and autopoiesis theory 113; and the micro-macro problem 81–2

social theory and the micro-macro problem 79

societal transformations 1

society and individuals 100

sociograms 32

sociology and the micro-macro problem 79–81

socio-technical systems 12, 151

Sørensen, Eva 4, 34, 135, 148–50

South Africa 159, 177

South Korea 108

sovereignty 35, 172, 173, 180, 182; and nation-states 2, 169, 171, 183, 191; and rule of law 142

stakeholders: and democracy 181; and wicked problems 127, 130, 134

Stanley, J. 166

state-centered 21

states 1–3, 169–70; as agents 17–18; and individual actors 23–4; and liberal democracy 172; and meta-governance 181–2; and small government 190; see also nation-state, the

statistical decision theory 88

Strogatz, Steven 33

structural constraints 119

structuration theory 116–21, 122

*Structure of Social Action, The* (Parsons) 79

subjective expected utility in decision-making 88–90

Switzerland 176

Syria 2

system integration 46–7

systemness 46–8

systems: and COVID-19 vaccines 63–5; and networks 48–9; and self-organization 51–3

systems dynamics modeling (SDM) 96, 107–8, 193

systems theories 43–5

taxation 23

Taylor, Frederick 133

technologies: and coevolution 58; and social participation 176, 177–8

Teisman, Geert 45, 76, 92

teleology 52; and emergentism 102–3; and natural systems 59

territorial sovereignty principle and states 2, 171

Thatcher, Margaret 100, 110n7

thermodynamics and systems theories 52, 81–2

Three Mile Island nuclear disaster 151–2

Tiebout, Charles 23

Torfing, Jacob 4, 34, 135, 148–50, 181, 182

TRACE ABM 109

"tragedy of the commons" 23–4, 54, 77–8, 167, 182; *see also* common pool resources (CPR)

transparency and accountability 144, **145, 149**

Treaty of Westphalia 2

Trump, Donald 1, 39; and liberal democracy 165; and vaccine hesitancy 64

Tullock, Gordon 54

Turkey 172

Tuskegee Syphilis Study 64

Tversky, Amos 86, 88, 118

Twitter 29, 66

two-mode networks 9–10, *10*, *32*

typologies in macro-level networks research 36–8

United Kingdom (UK) 161

United Nations (UN) 19

United States *see* American democracy; American government and pubic administration

urban and regional studies 156–7, *156*

urban areas and systems theory 45, 53

*Index* 225

urban planning 193–4
urban regime theories 155
Uruk 165, 167, 175–6

vaccine hesitancy 39, 46, 64–5; and
behavioral contagion 116; and
individual actors' knowledge 95; and
social/system integration 47; and
structuration theory 119–20
vaccines: manufacture and distribution
13, 25–7, 63–5; and wicked problems
129
variant mutations *see* delta variant
coronavirus; omicron variant
coronavirus
virtue and ethical behavior 141
viruses 58–9, 61, 69; and cognitive
capacity, purpose and mutation 97;
*see also* delta variant coronavirus;
omicron variant coronavirus;
SARS-CoV-2

Waldo, Dwight 133–4, 179
Waldrop, M. Mitchell 102
Wamsley, Gary L. 180
Warren, Robert 23
Washington, DC 158, 161
Washington State 26
Wasserman, Stanley 31, 32, 47
Watts, Duncan 30, 33

Webber, Melvin M. 125–6, 127–8,
130–2, 138
Weber, Max 34, 133, 141, 166, 169,
178–9
Web of Science (WoS) 4–6, *5*, *6*, 9; and
accountability *156*; and complexity
theory 43, 76; and governance 18;
and wicked problems *126*
Wengrow, David 24, 167, 169, 173,
190
White, Leonard D. 133
wicked problems 3, 125, 187;
conceptualizations of 127–9; and
COVID-19 pandemic 129–30;
literature on 126–7, *126*, 130–2
Wikipedia 84, 111n14, 176
Wilson, Woodrow and public
administration 21, 24, 178
women's rights 114
Woodward, Bill 166
World Bank 19
World Health Organization
(WHO) 63
World Wide Web 33, 67

Yahoo 105
YouTube 105

Zia, Asim 4, 34
Ziblatt, Daniel 166

# Taylor & Francis eBooks

www.taylorfrancis.com

A single destination for eBooks from Taylor & Francis with increased functionality and an improved user experience to meet the needs of our customers.

90,000+ eBooks of award-winning academic content in Humanities, Social Science, Science, Technology, Engineering, and Medical written by a global network of editors and authors.

## TAYLOR & FRANCIS EBOOKS OFFERS:

- A streamlined experience for our library customers
- A single point of discovery for all of our eBook content
- Improved search and discovery of content at both book and chapter level

## REQUEST A FREE TRIAL
support@taylorfrancis.com